# CONSIDERING STUDENTS, TEACHERS AND WRITING ASSESSMENT: VOLUME 2, EMERGING THEORETICAL AND PEDAGOGICAL PRACTICES

# PERSPECTIVES ON WRITING

Series Editors: Rich Rice and J. Michael Rifenburg
Consulting Editor: Susan H. McLeod
Associate Editors: Jonathan M. Marine, Johanna Phelps, and Qingyang Sun

The Perspectives on Writing series addresses writing studies in a broad sense. Consistent with the wide ranging approaches characteristic of teaching and scholarship in writing across the curriculum, the series presents works that take divergent perspectives on working as a writer, teaching writing, administering writing programs, and studying writing in its various forms.

The WAC Clearinghouse and University Press of Colorado are collaborating so that these books will be widely available through free digital distribution and low-cost print editions. The publishers and the series editors are committed to the principle that knowledge should freely circulate and have embraced the use of technology to support open access to scholarly work.

**Recent Books in the Series**

Amy Cicchino and Troy Hicks (Eds.), *Better Practices: Exploring the Teaching of Writing in Online and Hybrid Spaces* (2024)

Genesea M. Carter and Aurora Matzke (Eds.), *Systems Shift: Creating and Navigating Change in Rhetoric and Composition Administration* (2023)

Michael J. Michaud, *A Writer Reforms (the Teaching of) Writing: Donald Murray and the Writing Process Movement, 1963–1987* (2023)

Michelle LaFrance and Melissa Nicolas ((Eds.), *Institutional Ethnography as Writing Studies Practice* (2023)

Phoebe Jackson and Christopher Weaver (Eds.), *Rethinking Peer Review: Critical Reflections on a Pedagogical Practice* (2023)

Megan J. Kelly, Heather M. Falconer, Caleb L. González, and Jill Dahlman (Eds.), *Adapting the Past to Reimagine Possible Futures: Celebrating and Critiquing WAC at 50* (2023)

William J. Macauley, Jr. et al. (Eds.), *Threshold Conscripts: Rhetoric and Composition Teaching Assistantships* (2023)

Jennifer Grouling, *Adapting VALUEs: Tracing the Life of a Rubric through Institutional Ethnography* (2022)

Chris M. Anson and Pamela Flash (Eds.), *Writing-Enriched Curricula: Models of Faculty-Driven and Departmental Transformation* (2021)

Asao B. Inoue, *Above the Well: An Antiracist Argument From a Boy of Color* (2021)

Alexandria L. Lockett, Iris D. Ruiz, James Chase Sanchez, and Christopher Carter (Eds.), *Race, Rhetoric, and Research Methods* (2021)

# CONSIDERING STUDENTS, TEACHERS AND WRITING ASSESSMENT: VOLUME 2, EMERGING THEORETICAL AND PEDAGOGICAL PRACTICES

Edited by Diane Kelly-Riley, Ti Macklin, and Carl Whithaus

The WAC Clearinghouse
wac.colostate.edu
Fort Collins, Colorado

University Press of Colorado
upcolorado.com
Denver, Colorado

The WAC Clearinghouse, Fort Collins, Colorado 80523
University Press of Colorado, Denver, Colorado 80203
© 2024 by Diane Kelly-Riley, Ti Macklin, and Carl Whithaus. This work is licensed under a Creative Commons Attribution-NonCommercial-NoDerivatives 4.0 International license.
ISBN 978-1-64215-232-6 (PDF) 978-1-64215-233-3 (ePub) 978-1-64642-671-3 (pbk.)
DOI 10.37514/PER-B.2024.2326

Library of Congress Cataloging-in-Publication Data

Names: Kelly-Riley, Diane, editor. | Macklin, Tialitha M. (Tialitha Michelle), 1977– editor. | Whithaus, Carl, editor.
Title: Considering students, teachers, and writing assessment / edited by Diane Kelly-Riley, Ti Macklin, and Carl Whithaus.
Description: Fort Collins, Colorado : The WAC Clearinghouse ; Denver, Colorado : University Press of Colorado, 2024. | Series: Perspectives on writing | Includes bibliographical references. | Contents: v. 1. Technical and political contexts — v. 2. Emerging theoretical and pedagogical practices.
Identifiers: LCCN 2024013164 (print) | LCCN 2024013165 (ebook) | ISBN 9781646426195 (v. 1 ; paperback) | ISBN 9781646426713 (v. 2 ; paperback) | ISBN 9781642152166 (v. 1 ; adobe pdf) | ISBN 9781642152173 (v. 1 ; epub) | ISBN 9781642152326 (v. 2 ; adobe pdf) | ISBN 9781642152333 (v. 2 ; epub)
Subjects: LCSH: English language—Rhetoric—Study and teaching—Evaluation. | English language—Rhetoric—Study and teaching—Social aspects. | English language—Rhetoric—Study and teaching—Political aspects. | English language—Composition and exercises—Evaluation | English language—Composition and exercises—Social aspects. | English language—Composition and exercises—Political aspects. | LCGFT: Essays.
Classification: LCC PE1404 .C63374 2024 (print) | LCC PE1404 (ebook) | DDC 808/.042071073—dc23/eng/20240507
LC record available at https://lccn.loc.gov/2024013164
LC ebook record available at https://lccn.loc.gov/2024013165

Copyeditor: Andrea Bennett
Designer: Mike Palmquist
Cover Photo: Image by Rawpixel.com. Image ID 25357.
Series Editors: Rich Rice and J. Michael Rifenburg
Consulting Editor: Susan H. McLeod
Associate Editors: Jonathan M. Marine, Johanna Phelps, and Qingyang Sun

The WAC Clearinghouse supports teachers of writing across the disciplines. Hosted by Colorado State University, it brings together scholarly journals and book series as well as resources for teachers who use writing in their courses. This book is available in digital formats for free download at wac.colostate.edu.

Founded in 1965, the University Press of Colorado is a nonprofit cooperative publishing enterprise supported, in part, by Adams State University, Colorado State University, Fort Lewis College, Metropolitan State University of Denver, University of Alaska Fairbanks, University of Colorado, University of Denver, University of Northern Colorado, University of Wyoming, Utah State University, and Western Colorado University. For more information, visit upcolorado.com.

**Citation Information:** Kelly-Riley, Diane, Ti Macklin & Carl Whithaus (Eds.). (2024). *Considering Students, Teachers, and Writing Assessment: Volume 2, Emerging Theoretical and Pedagogical Practices*. The WAC Clearinghouse; University Press of Colorado. https://doi.org/10.37514/PER-B.2024.2326

**Land Acknowledgment.** The Colorado State University Land Acknowledgment can be found at landacknowledgment.colostate.edu.

# CONTENTS

Introduction to Volume 2, Emerging Theoretical and Pedagogical Practices . . . 3
   *Diane Kelly-Riley, Ti Macklin, and Carl Whithaus*

PART 4. THEORETICAL EVOLUTIONS: CONSIDERING FAIRNESS AND ASPIRING TO JUSTICE

Retrospective. A Reflective Analysis: Toward Fairness . . . . . . . . . . . . . . . . . . 13
   *Mya Poe*

Chapter 11. Moving Beyond Holistic Scoring through Validity Inquiry . . . . 29
   *Peggy O'Neill*

Chapter 12. Rhetorical Writing Assessment: The Practice and Theory
of Complementarity . . . . . . . . . . . . . . . . . . . . . . . . . . . . . . . . . . . . . . . . . . 51
   *Bob Broad and Michael Boyd*

Chapter 13. Articulating Sophistic Rhetoric as a Validity Heuristic
for Writing Assessment . . . . . . . . . . . . . . . . . . . . . . . . . . . . . . . . . . . . . . . . 67
   *Asao B. Inoue*

Chapter 14. Ethical Considerations and Writing Assessment . . . . . . . . . . . . 93
   *David Slomp*

PART 5. STUDENTS' AND TEACHERS' LIVED EXPERIENCES

Retrospective. Toward Fairness in Writing Assessment . . . . . . . . . . . . . . . . 107
   *Diane Kelly-Riley, Ti Macklin, and Carl Whithaus*

Chapter 15. Civil Rights and Writing Assessment: Using the Disparate
Impact Approach as a Fairness Methodology to Evaluate Social Impact . . . 117
   *Mya Poe and John Aloysius Cogan, Jr.*

Chapter 16. Let Them In: Increasing Access, Completion, and Equity
in English Placement Policies at a Two-Year College in California . . . . . . . 161
   *Leslie Henson and Katie Hern*

Chapter 17. Neurodivergence and Intersectionality in Labor-Based
Grading Contracts . . . . . . . . . . . . . . . . . . . . . . . . . . . . . . . . . . . . . . . . . . . 187
   *Kathleen Kryger and Griffin X. Zimmerman*

v

Contents

Chapter 18. Engaging in Resistant Genres as Antiracist Teacher Response...209
   *Shane Wood*

Coda .................................................237
   *Victor Villanueva*

Editors and Retrospective Contributors ........................... 241

# CONSIDERING STUDENTS, TEACHERS AND WRITING ASSESSMENT: VOLUME 2, EMERGING THEORETICAL AND PEDAGOGICAL PRACTICES

# INTRODUCTION TO VOLUME 2, EMERGING THEORETICAL AND PEDAGOGICAL PRACTICES

**Diane Kelly-Riley**
University of Idaho

**Ti Macklin**
Boise State University

**Carl Whithaus**
University of California, Davis

The two volumes of *Considering Students, Teachers and Writing Assessment* focus on the increasing importance of students' and teachers' lived experiences within the development and use of writing assessments. These two volumes examine key themes from scholarship published in *The Journal of Writing Assessment* *(JWA)* in the past twenty years. Together, the volumes reflect upon how writing assessment research has contributed to five major themes: (1) technical psychometric issues, particularly reliability and validity; (2) politics and public policies around large scale writing assessments; (3) the evolution of—and debates around—automated scoring of writing; (4) the major theoretical changes elevating fairness within educational measurement and writing assessment; and (5) the importance of considering the lived experiences of the humans involved in the assessment ecology. Each section is introduced by current scholars in writing assessment who reflect upon and frame the issues of the past and comment on the ways in which these issues may unfold in the future. Volume 1 explores dynamic issues connected to reliability and validity and how writing assessment contributed to the evolutions of these concepts, the shifting political context of writing assessment, and the rise of automated scoring of writing. This second volume focuses on the evolution of theoretical and pedagogical considerations in writing assessment scholarship and explores the broader history about the structures and lasting impacts of writing assessment yet to be explored.

Volume 2 of *Considering Students, Teachers and Writing Assessment* captures the interactions between the developments pushed forward by evolving technical, political, and societal contexts. We are poised at a moment in time where the theoretical developments within writing assessment—particularly the push towards fairness as a major category on par with reliability and validity—coincide with increasing awareness of racism and social inequities. The year 2020 was a watershed, a moment in writing assessment research that represents a shift towards more direct attention to these issues. This awareness has shone a light on scholars and research subjects that have been disregarded or uninvestigated. Awareness is not enough. For this change to have staying power, it must grow from the work that has been done in the field over the last twenty years, and it must also forge new paths. In this volume, *Emerging Theoretical and Pedagogical Practices* traces how writing assessment research and practices have changed as the lived experiences of students and teachers have become a more central concern to the field. The collection charts out the ways in which writing assessment scholarship published in *the Journal of Writing Assessment* accelerated the response to calls for more equitable and socially just educational practices. *Journal of Writing Assessment* scholarship also engaged with calls to increase the fairness of not only writing assessments but also the ways they are used. The increasing emphasis on anti-racist teaching practices in composition studies has seen the development of writing assessment tools such as contract grading become more widespread.

## ARRIVING AFTER HISTORY: FOSTERING SOCIAL JUSTICE AND FAIRNESS IN WRITING ASSESSMENT PRACTICES

Drawing on the research published in *the Journal of Writing Assessment* over the last twenty years, this volume explores how writing assessment scholars have incorporated students' and teachers' lived experiences into our understandings of how writing assessment systems work. These chapters challenge writing assessment experts to develop more equitable and socially just educational practices that work across a variety of educational contexts. The intersection of writing assessment, method, and the lived classroom setting has uniquely shaped the larger field of educational measurement and assessment. Most certainly, writing assessment has evolved from portfolio and programmatic assessment to more socially-situated methods: directed self-placement, contract grading, disciplinarily situated outcomes assessment measured through writing, antiracist writing assessments, and responses to the use of automated scoring of writing for large scale testing purposes. The emergence of these areas of writing assessment work points towards a productive new turn in writing assessment: one that considers writing assessment located in relationship to the lived experiences of students and teachers. Rather than seeing assessment primarily as measurement, we can see assessment as an evidentiary argument, situated in social contexts, centered on students' developing competencies in valued activities, and shaped by purposes and values—chief among them validity, fairness, and equity. The development of these situated writing assessment techniques suggests the potential for more socially attentive forms of educational measurement.

The last twenty years have seen a shift away from a myopic focus on reliability and validity as the gold standard in assessment studies towards the importance of developing broader approaches that document how validity, reliability, and fairness interact with one another. In addition, writing assessment researchers examine how these constructs actually work—or don't work—when put into practice in different secondary and post-secondary contexts. The role that post-secondary writing instructors played in this shift from focusing on reliability and validity to considering multiple, contextualized measures has often received only minor attention in the research literature. However, teachers in the fields of writing studies and composition studies have contributed to the development of writing assessment as a discipline, and they are increasingly helping to shape many aspects of today's large-scale, as well as classroom-based, writing assessment practices. This collection represents a pathway forward that combines writing assessment grounded in social contexts to promote productive societal change. *Emerging Theoretical and Pedagogical Practices* charts out the ways in which scholarship published in *the Journal of Writing Assessment* has assisted the field of writing assessment to further evolve in response to calls for more equitable and socially just educational practices.

## DEVELOPING FAIRNESS IN PSYCHOMETRICS

In 2014, the *Standards for Educational and Psychological Testing* issued another major revision which outlined the importance of considering the consequences of assessments on test takers. The *Standards* defined fairness as

> the validity of test score interpretations for intended use(s) for individuals from all relevant subgroups. A test is fair that minimizes the construct-irrelevant variance associated with individual characteristics and testing contexts that otherwise would compromise the validity of scores for some individuals. (AERA, APA & NCME, 2014, p. 219)

As such, fairness became an essential consideration in writing assessment. The rapidly changing demographic of the US population makes this consideration especially salient. In the last 20 years, college enrollment and degree attainment have skyrocketed, and the demographic profile of the students who attend postsecondary study mirrors the rapidly changing demographic of the rest of the United States. In 2016, the total enrollment in degree-granting postsecondary institutions was nearly twenty million students (Hussar & Bailey, 2019, p. 59). As composition classrooms attended more to the diverse instructional backgrounds and needs of students and faculty within them, new areas of research emerged. Such writing assessment scholarship continues to evolve to consider the relationship between students, faculty, and assessment processes and how fairness is upheld.

The change in theoretical perspectives resulted in writing assessment scholars considering the contexts in which writing was taught and assessed and the people who occupied them. The work done in response to accountability mandates resulting in large scale writing assessment programs gave rise to a national effort of several programs that commonly articulated of outcomes that could be adjusted to the local student population and their demographics. Behm and his coauthors (2013) document a decade of the ways in which this type of approach played out in first-year writing programs across the US using the WPA Outcomes Statement for First-Year Composition. This statement (CWPA, 2019) provided a coherent articulation about the "writing knowledge, practices, and attitudes that undergraduate students develop in first-year composition, which at most schools is a required general education course or sequence of courses." As such, institutions could work toward a common set of practices while attending to the unique demographic features of their student populations as well as their specific institutional mission. As a result, this angle opened the door to further examine the people involved in the writing assessment ecologies (Inoue, 2015) as well as the institutions and disciplinary situations in which writing is taught (Kelly-Riley and Elliot, 2021).

Scholarship in the *Journal of Writing Assessment* has chronicled this change in focus from technical and political issues to one that more squarely considers the people involved. The two sections in this volume look at the theoretical evolutions and the ways in which consideration of people and institutional type and mission change the writing assessment enterprise.

## PART FOUR. THEORETICAL EVOLUTIONS: TOWARDS FAIRNESS AND ASPIRING TO JUSTICE

Part Four of this second volume examines the theoretical shifts that underscore the importance of teacher expertise and experience in writing assessment. Evolutions in the concepts of validity and fairness meant that writing could be understood as a socially situated construct, rhetorical contexts were important, and the ways in which we communicated with each other must be considered. Mya Poe, Professor of English and Director of the Writing Program at Northeastern University, documents how the changes in these constructs in educational measurement have opened doors to considerations of fairness and the impacts of assessment on demographic groups. She details how this work on fairness and ethics in writing assessment addresses social justice issues in writing assessment. Further, she sketches out how fairness and antiracist writing assessment practices can lead to new developments in the field.

In 2003, Peggy O'Neill began this conversation in *JWA* in "Moving Beyond Holistic Scoring through Validity Inquiry" emphasizing fairness and bringing local assessment to the forefront of student writing assessment. In this piece, O'Neill responds to the work of William L. Smith from the University of Pittsburgh who experimented on local assessment through both teacher and student perspectives shifting from assigning a numerical value to a piece of student writing to an assessment process that considers students' abilities relative to the instructional classes available. The placement system piloted by Smith and his colleagues asked teachers to directly place students into courses offered by the institution. Thus, Smith established a framework that recognized and valued the expertise of classroom composition teachers. O'Neill connects Smith's work to the evolving educational measurement scholarship related to validity theory.

Next, Bob Broad and Michael Boyd further illustrate the importance of teacher expertise in writing assessment in "Rhetorical Writing Assessment: The Practice and Theory of Complementarity" (2005). They argue for the need to understand writing in all its complexities, including accounting for local, situated elements. For them, communal writing assessment practices engage teachers in longer and more deliberate action and allow for fuller consideration of student performance. They also note that portfolio-based assessment facilitated this complexity and is needed to facilitate the shift away from a reliance on psychometrics which, in their view, had run its course.

In "Articulating Sophistic Rhetoric as a Validity Heuristic for Writing Assessment," Asao B. Inoue (2007) traces validity's genealogy to concepts in ancient rhetoric. Writing assessment's evolution of validity can be traced through the philosophies of the ancient Greeks. Inoue observes "the sophists' positions on *nomos–physis* and Protagoras' human-measure doctrine ask us to reconsider continually our own relationships to the cultural hegemony we often say we resist as intellectuals, but clearly must work within as teachers, assessors, validity researchers, and citizens, which in turn asks us to find ways to open the academy's doors a little wider" (p. 48). Mapping the arguments of ancient Greek philosophers onto current day concepts of validity helps document the consequences of moving validity from an objective construct to one that is socially situated. That move results in the consideration of the effects of assessments on the test takers and the considerations under which these tests are taken.

In "Ethical Considerations and Writing Assessment," David Slomp (2016) explores the development of the constructs of reliability, validity, and fairness and notes that the exclusion of classroom teachers' expertise from their modern-day development means that these constructs do not attend to broader social consequences. Our work in assessment must also be guided by ethics. He notes, "[these three concepts] reflect a narrow epistemological, ontological and axiological standpoint; they focus narrowly on intended uses and interpretations of test scores; and they handle key technical issues such as validity, reliability, and fairness as siloed concepts." As part of a Special Issue on a Theory of Ethics in Writing Assessment, Slomp and his co-authors articulate a theory of ethics for writing assessment that ultimately better serves students because it "assists all stakeholders in the assessment process in more thoroughly addressing questions regarding the moral aspects of assessment use" (p. 102). These moves toward fairness in writing assessment theory and practice enhance the possibilities for increasing equity.

# PART FIVE. IMPLICATIONS OF THE LIVED EXPERIENCES OF STUDENTS AND TEACHERS IN WRITING ASSESSMENT

In the final section of the two-volume collection, *Considering Students, Teachers and Writing Assessment,* we extend the conversation about fairness by considering the lived experiences of students and teachers within writing assessment systems. The chapters in this part of the book examine how writing assessments impact students' and teachers' lives. In the chapter, "Toward Fairness in Writing Assessment," we trace how fairness has been developed as a category and how it has increasingly been tied to the impact on students' lives. This work has led researchers to ask forceful questions about the contexts around writing assessment. Asao Inoue's (2015) emphasis on approaching writing assessment as a whole ecology rather than the development of an isolated test and Anne Ruggles Gere et al.'s insistence that writing assessment engage in "communal justicing" (2021, p. 384) have helped drive the field towards studying writing assessments *in situ*. That is, rather than only asking questions about validity, reliability, and generalizability, writing assessment scholars have increasingly asked what do these writing assessments look like when seen from students' and teachers' perspectives. Disparate impact analysis has become an essential method for operationalizing these approaches. Perhaps, even more importantly, the field has more directly taken up questions about learning differences; mitigating the impacts of racism, sexism, ableism, and poverty; and examining how writing assessments function within educational and social systems.

Introduction

The first chapter in this closing section, Mya Poe and John Aloysius Cogan Jr.'s "Civil Rights and Writing Assessment," critiques racist assessment practices and points the way toward developing antiracist forms of writing assessment. Their work is grounded in the experiences of students and teachers both inside and outside of the classroom. Their work is about how a disparate impact approach could be utilized as a method for evaluating unintended, racialized differences in learning outcomes, particularly the ways in which these may result from educational policies or practices that appear "neutral." Poe and Cogan argue that disparate impact analysis remains an underutilized conceptual and methodological framework within writing assessment. Disparate impact analysis allows the inclusion of lived experiences when analyzing a writing assessment system in ways that have not always been considered.

Leslie Henson and Katie Hern's "Let Them In: Increasing Access, Completion, and Equity in English Placement Policies at a Two-Year College in California" builds on this work around disparate impact analysis. They document how refinements to writing placement systems can reduce gaps in course completion outcomes. Their work draws on a disparate impact analysis and continues to ask questions about how students' lives and time-to-degree are impacted by changes to a community college writing placement system. Their focus on writing assessment and placement at a California community college explores the real-world impacts of changes to writing assessment systems.

In "Neurodivergence and Intersectionality in Labor-Based Grading Contracts," Kathleen Kryger and Griffin X. Zimmerman also address issues within students' lives by exploring questions around accessibility. They examine how labor-based grading contracts might be designed to honor neurodivergence and intersectional student identities rather than inscribing ableist, status quo identities. Their chapter shows how student experiences and identities cannot be separated from a writing assessment. In fact, they demonstrate how an assessment defines value (i.e., what is good writing) as well as constructs or limits the complexity of student identities. Grading contracts, like the reflective cover essays for portfolios, produce writing processes that can be framed in numerous ways. Kryger and Zimmerman's chapter aims to keep open the possibilities of grading contracts rather than having them generate language that confines and normalizes both approaches to writing and, ultimately, the ways in which students may write and think about their identities.

Finally, Shane Wood's "Engaging in Resistant Genres as Antiracist Teacher Response" grounds his approach to antiracist teacher response by focusing on how teachers respond to students. Wood, like Kryger and Zimmerman, challenges teachers to consider how their response practices reinforce dominant linguistic and social norms. Wood's work critiques the ways in which teacher response can sustain White language supremacy and bring harm to students. As an intense location for student-teacher interaction, teacher response to student writing is not only a vital aspect of writing assessment, but also a socialized location that can either replicate or challenge existing social norms. Adding fairness as a vital category within writing assessment has pushed forward theoretical developments in the field. The way these are operationalized and impact students' lives remains an area for further research and engagement. The principle of fairness must be followed up with developing writing assessment practices that attend to students' and teachers' lived experiences and the impacts of writing assessment systems on students' lives.

To close the two-volume collection, Victor Villanueva reflects on ways in which writing assessment scholarship informs the entire field and is, thus, relevant to all. He articulates the importance of engaging in purposeful and intentional scholarship that places the complexity of students' and teachers' lives and identities at the center of our work. His coda reminds us that writing assessment scholarship has implications beyond the silos of research areas in writing studies. In writing assessment scholarship, there have been waves of conversations that overlap and inform directions that need to be pursued; he notes that there are many perspectives and voices that have not been the focus of or included in the past twenty years of scholarship in *the Journal of Writing Assessment*. Villanueva notes the importance of expanding the definitions of fairness beyond teachers' and students' experiences and challenges us to bring a wider array of scholars in to investigate and address these issues.

## REFERENCES

American Educational Research Association, American Psychological Association & NCME. (2014). *Standards for educational and psychological testing*. American Educational Research Association.

Behm, N., Glau, G. R., Holdstein, D. H., Roen, D. & White, E. M. (Eds.). (2013). *The WPA Outcomes Statement: A decade later*. Parlor Press.

CWPA. (2019). WPA Outcomes Statement for First-Year Composition. https://wpacouncil.org/aws/CWPA/pt/sd/news_article/243055/_PARENT/layout_details/false.

Hussar, W. J. & Bailey, T. M. (2019). *Projections of education statistics to 2027* (46th edition). U.S. Department of Education, National Center for Education Statistics, Institute of Education Sciences, Washington D.C.

Inoue, A. B. (2015). *Antiracist writing assessment ecologies: Teaching and assessing writing for a socially just future*. The WAC Clearinghouse; Parlor Press. https://doi.org/10.37514/PER-B.2015.0698.

Kelly-Riley, D. & Elliot, N. (Eds.). (2021). *Improving outcomes: Disciplinary writing, local assessment and the aim of fairness*. Modern Language Association.

# PART 4.
# THEORETICAL EVOLUTIONS: CONSIDERING FAIRNESS AND ASPIRING TO JUSTICE

RETROSPECTIVE.
# A REFLECTIVE ANALYSIS: TOWARD FAIRNESS

**Mya Poe**
Northeastern University

What would test fairness bring to individual students? In many ways, this question is behind issues of fairness as debated in many other assessment journals for the last several decades. During the first two decades of *The Journal of Writing Assessment's* history, however, the question of fairness and justice for individual students has been shaped by a deep disciplinary commitment to the lived realities of writing assessment and wrestling with whether measurement theory helps us understand those realities.

Beyond *JWA*, researchers from different disciplinary contexts have long debated origin stories, developments in evidence-gathering, and implications for stakeholders. On one hand, educational measurement scholars have deliberated the expansive connotations of the term fairness (Boyer, 2020; Dorans & Cook, 2016; Gipps & Stobart, 2010; AERA, APA & NCME, 2014). On the other hand, they have fiercely proscribed narrow administrations of fairness to test design and development, test administration, scoring, and score interpretation (Dorans & Cook, 2016). Fairness and bias reviews suggest that fairness is something that can be observed in textual analysis (ETS, 2014, 2016) or ferreted out in the analytic tools created by designers, ranging from general linear models developed by Cleary (1968) and in more advanced forms, in use today. Following the *Standards for Educational and Psychological Testing,* many measurement researchers conjoin fairness with validity:

> Fairness is a fundamental validity issue and requires attention throughout all stages of test development and use. . . . [F]airness and the assessment of individuals from specific subgroups of test takers, such as individuals with disabilities and individuals with diverse linguistic and cultural backgrounds . . . is an overriding, foundational concern, and that common principles apply in responding to test-taker characteristics that could interfere with the validity of test score interpretation. (AERA, APA & NCME, 2014, pp. 49–50)

What makes a test fair is, as Xi (2010) argues, "comparable validity for all *relevant* groups" (p. 147). Likewise, Zieky (2016) claims that "the fairness argument is an extension of the validity argument. The goal of the fairness argument is to present evidence that the test is fair for various groups within the test-taking population" (p. 96).

Researchers from the writing studies community, such as my colleagues Oliveri, Elliot, and I (2023) have argued that the *Standards* offer other affordances to increase fairness: (a) accessibility (unobstructed opportunity for diverse groups to have equal opportunity to take a test and demonstrate construct standing); (b) universal design (designing a test and its associated delivery environment to maximize usability by all test takers); and (c) opportunity to learn content that is culturally sustaining to their own communities (the degree to which test results need to be evaluated for maximum community impact). We believe that, "making good decisions about our writing assessment practices for all students means attending to the various ways that we understand the impact of assessment on our students" (Poe & Cogan, 2016, p. 605). At the end of the day, no test is culture free, and assessment is about its effects on diverse individuals and communities. As I have argued elsewhere (Poe & Cogan, 2016), the authors of the *Standards* left the larger challenge for fairness—i.e., the relationship of assessment to social consequences—relatively untouched.

In each of the articles in this section of *Considering Fairness and Aspiring to Justice*, the authors wrestle with what disciplinary theories and methods should we use to "form attitudes or induce actions in other human agents" (Burke, 1950, p. 41). But to move directly to the articles themselves does not seem exactly right. I read each of the chapters in this section of *Considering Fairness and Aspiring to Justice*—exciting work by Peggy O'Neill, Bob Broad and Michael Boyd, Asao B. Inoue, and David Slomp—with Brad, my brother, born in September of 1966, in mind. Yes, I want to address what the author's historical situatedness means for the way they conceive of fairness. And I want to address what kinds of social implications each author considers. But, first, I want to talk about Brad.

## FRAMING FAIRNESS

According to my mother, Brad was a colicky infant. He rarely cried and showed little emotion as a toddler but took much interest in mechanical objects and family pets. When he was older, he built elaborate train tables with lights and gates that were operated by electrical circuits he had soldered. He would later spend hours reading books backwards and forwards, often selecting massive books on technical subjects as well as *Mad* magazine. He was disorganized, his handwriting was a scrawl, and his sense of sci-fi fan humor was often described as "warped" by my parents.

In school, he made few friends and seemed disinterested in schoolwork. In kindergarten school, Brad was diagnosed with a moderate sensorimotor development delay. My mother who was a teacher tried to coax Brad along, encouraging and working with him on balance and coordination. She tried to help him show emotion, which would only result in outbursts of anger. Later, IQ test results were very high, yet Brad often earned average and below-average grades. My father, who had dropped out of high school at age 17 often reacted with rage, unable to understand why someone so "smart" could be so "lazy." No amount of yelling and badgering and humiliation motivated Brad. Brad simply fell silent, seemingly emotionally vacant.

Brad struggled through high school but was able to enroll in college. He couldn't get into the engineering program he wanted, so he became a business major. As an undergraduate business major, he commuted to college, splitting his time between a job at an auto parts store, helping my father on the farm, and squeezing in homework. He could not manage the long commute, the demands of my father and the job, and the demands of college. He graduated college with barely a C average yet got a probationary enrollment in an evening MBA program at the same college. In graduate school, Brad struggled, once again trying to manage a life split across worlds and avoiding the required group projects of an MBA program. Yet, there was one thing that graduate school brought Brad—the VAX machine, an early supercomputer the size of a small refrigerator. Brad spent hours at the computer bank.

To this day, no one in my family knows what he was coding because Brad hung himself in 1993 at the age of 26. Unlike many people who leave textual artifacts of their lives behind—notes, scribbles of random ideas, tickets, receipts, documentation—Brad's life was undocumented except for some banking documents, some school notebooks, car manuals, and a letter from the MBA program stating that Brad was going to be expelled for poor grades. I saved a notebook from his desk—a notebook from his MBA studies—and the two exams that were tucked inside. Pages of his notes from his college notebook are illegible. Some are half-written. Others are filled with technical terms and graphs with no meta-commentary about the content. Much of the notebook is empty. A paper from a management course on leadership showed a grade of 19 out of 20 points. A fall 1992 final exam from an accounting class in the MBA program showed that he received 107.5 out of 120 points (89.6%). One written question asked test-takers to select a regression model and provide specific reasons for the selection of that model for a fictional character named "Alf" (perhaps a nod to the *Mad Magazine* character). The professor noted some comments in red on

Brad's written response, including -3 points noted next to a postscript that Brad had written: "Alf went on to run the Dan Quayle Presidential campaign in '96, when Dan was decisively defeated by Alfred E. Newman."

I start with this story about my brother Brad because Brad's story illustrates how what we see through assessment is deeply shaped by historical context. Brad died before the "autism epidemic" (Nuwer, 2016), but it is likely that if my brother was born today, he would be diagnosed on the autism spectrum (Hannant, 2016; Hyman et al., 2020). In the 1960s and 1970s, assessment instruments like sensory and motor development tests were used to determine physical delays that might indicate cognitive delays. IQ tests were common in schools like the one Brad attended to track students. Classroom assessment technologies, especially in the disciplines, were still largely summative, and notions of "progress" through degree programs were still largely tied to course grades. These systems of assessment accumulated to provide a measurement-based narrative of a child.

Brad's story also reminds us of the social implications of assessment. In the 1960s and 1970, if such assessment technologies existed to "measure" autism, it is unlikely that Midwestern suburban lower-middleclass schools would have had such assessment technologies to understand children like Brad. What they did have were assessment instruments like motor development tests and intelligence tests that had been refined into codified instruments delivered through school volunteers and classroom teachers. Furthermore, my father was unable to reconcile tests that showed competing narratives of his child—one delayed and one gifted. For my father, tests carried enormous social prestige. They were scientific diagnostic instruments that told the truth about his child. For people like my high school drop-out father, whose father and mother had eighth and sixth grade educations respectively, the message of tests was absolute. Concepts like "intelligence" were highly valued because Appalachian whites work within a cultural context in which they are often regarded as exoticized isolates yet also portrayed as inbred, immoral, and stupid. For my father, to have his son be labeled "gifted" was scientific proof that he *personally* was not genetically inferior. For my father, there was a familial obligation to live up to the term "gifted." No test designer was in the room when my father humiliated and kicked my "gifted" brother for getting bad grades, claiming that poor grades and test scores were merely the result of being "lazy."

My understanding of educational measurement has opened doors to understanding my brother's life left in assessment artifacts. The assessment artifacts of Brad's life provide a consideration of fairness and the impacts of assessment on different humans. Here was a student for whom assessment provided a narrative about his purported inner potential and documented his outward failings and blamed him for those failings. Here is a student who ultimately graduated from college and was enrolled in a graduate program when he died. By one benchmark—college completion rates—Brad was a success and soon-to-be-failure when he died.

What would test fairness have brought Brad? Likely little if we were to rely on measurement theory as a guide. Maybe more if we rely on articles such as those to which I now turn.

## PAST AS PROLOGUE

During most of the twentieth century, writing assessment researchers have had a love/hate relationship with the field of measurement. On one hand, researchers and teachers have long fought the over-reach of the testing industry into writing classrooms and programs. On the other hand, we have been exhorted by scholars within writing studies to adopt measurement theories related to validity, reliability, and fairness to improve the design and use of writing assessment. Those exhortations were strongest in the late 1990s into the early 2000s, yet today we see those theoretical connections —-citational pathworks—happening between measurement and writing studies. In these citational pathways, we can trace how researchers within any historical context have certain vantage points from which they see the social implications of assessment—i.e., the ways in which assessments are being used, the targets of assessment, and the ways assessment is connected to other institutional and social systems.

In documenting the work of William L. Smith at the University of Pittsburgh during the 1980s and 1990s, Peggy O'Neill situates Smith's work within "the larger context of educational measurement theories, placement testing, and holistic scoring" and argues that Smith's work is "an example of how systematic, ongoing validity inquiry can not only lead to better—more valid—local assessment but also contribute to the larger field of writing assessment" (p. 34). For everyone who has read his work, it is clear that Smith was an innovator; O'Neill saw that innovation and aimed to advance commonality. To make the case for the value of validity inquiry, O'Neill describes Smith's embrace of measurement theory:

> According to Smith (1998), there is a "paucity of validation research" (p. 3) in writing assessment, which stems from several different but interrelated problems: a lack of understanding of key concepts such as validity and reliability; an overemphasis on achieving reliability; a lack of understanding of what validation inquiry entails; and a failure to articulate the theoretical constructs underlying writing assessments. (p. 31)

O'Neill connects Smith's intellectual work with seminal measurement scholars Lee Cronbach, Samuel Messick, and Pamela Moss, especially in terms of their work on moving the field toward an argument-based model of validity.

The punchline for O'Neill is that "validation arguments are rhetorical constructs that draw from all the available means of support" (p. 32). From this vantage—in fact, a prescient one that illustrated the importance of interpretation and use of arguments advanced a decade later by Kane (2013)—she then draws a connection to writing studies scholar Brian Huot's work on writing assessment and validity. This citational pathway between measurement and writing studies ultimately allows O'Neill to claim that "this [interdisciplinary] approach to writing assessment would support the processes and theories associated with literacy, leading to more theoretical alignment between actual literate practice and the assessment of it (p. 33). In short, measurement theory, O'Neill proposed, would allow writing assessment researchers to theoretically align the teaching and assessment of writing.

The use of measurement theory for alignment between assessment and teaching is certainly evidenced in Smith's approach to assessment research at the University of Pittsburgh. At the University of Pittsburgh he investigated the local ways that test decisions were being made. He believed that the initial data on misplacement via teachers' readings of student essays were erroneous. A singular or double reading of student writing and replacement rates were insufficient. Student impressions were important as were teachers' perceptions, especially their perceptions over time:

> teachers' perceptions of students change considerably across the course of the semester. If gathered too early in the semester, teachers don't have enough evidence on which to base their decision; if gathered too late, teacher perception correlates very highly with the students' final grades, indicating that the students' actual performance is evaluated, not their potential. Smith concluded that teacher perception data should be collected during Weeks 3 through 5 of a 15–week semester. (p. 40)

In studies of rater reliability, Smith also found that raters' decisions varied by many factors, including raters' teaching experience, the course the rater most recently taught, when raters knew they were being tested, when raters scored as split-resolvers, when raters "made decisions about students, instead of merely judging texts," and when raters could not match students to a specific course (p. 58). Smith anticipated the later work of Dryer and Peckham (2014) and their emphasis on adopting an ecological view of processes in which, down to the level of the tables at which raters sat, differences occurred.

When Smith turned his attention to student performance, he "found that there were significant factors that influenced their performance, but that he could not control for them" (p. 41). Rather than pursuing studies of factors that influenced student performance, Smith focused on the programmatic context of writing assessment. He developed the expert-reader model in which raters place students into classes based on prototypes.

Regarding fairness, Smith's approach brings a longitudinal perspective. He allowed for judgments to change over time as teachers learned more about students. Yet, because he could not "control" for the factors that influenced student performance, perhaps including such things as testing histories, cultural context, and emotional well-being, Smith chose to not pursue further investigation. Valuable as his work was, it operated within a measurement paradigm of replicability in which further work was suspended for fear of contaminating the validity argument. Purpose pluralism was yet to come and, ironically, it was to come from a UK measurement researcher calling for assessment designs that should leverage "a multiplicity of assessment purposes simultaneously" (Netwon, 2017, p. 5).

## SITUATED ASSESSMENT

Published in 2005, Bob Broad and Michael Boyd's 2005 "Rhetorical Writing Assessment: The Practice and Theory of Complementarity" also focuses on innovation in the field of writing assessment, arguing that "writing portfolio assessment and communal (shared, dialogical) assessment are two of our field's most creative, courageous, and influential innovations" (p. 51). As is the case with O'Neill, Broad, and Boyd point to Huot to uncover the "'epistemological basis' . . . on which these new principles and procedures are built" (p. 54). In the twenty-first century, context would become everything.

Looking to advances in psychometrics—note that Broad and Boyd Note chose the term "psychometrics" in lieu of "measurement" as a way to emphasize the statistical quality of the research described by Pamela Moss and Lee Cronbach—they see promise in these changes akin to changes in classical physics and quantum physics in which Niels Bohr questioned the effect of "measuring instruments" on the phenomena being measured: "Quantum physics, in opposition to the classical version, accepts that ultimately all knowledge is indeterminate because the methods we use and the vantage points from which we obtain evidence substantially alters the evidence itself" (p. 55). Returning to measurement, they cite Egon Guba and Yvonne S. Lincoln's (1989) invocation of Bohr's complementarity principle as well as English Studies scholar Bernard Alford's dissertation in which he "draws on the work of quantum physicists Menas Kafatos and

Robert Nadeau to focus our understanding of the principle of complementarity" (p. 57). Broad and Boyd see Alford's work as a means to move "beyond objectivism and subjectivism" so that "we can verify postmodern claims to contingent truths through a process of bringing radically distinct constructs into dialogue with each other within established human communities" (p. 57).

It is from this citational path that Broad and Boyd argue, citing writing studies scholars James Berlin and Kathleen Yancey, that "the portfolio is a postmodern development" (p. 60) that "offered a way to move beyond grading of single pieces of writing to a process of 'collection, selection, reflection, and projection'" (p. 58). Communal writing assessment (CWA) they see as something even more radical: "The more radical shift is away from seeking and valuing homogeneity among judges to seeking and valuing diversity" (p. 68). In arguing for the potential of CWA, they note that CWA breaks from traditional notions of standardization in psychometrics.

Broad and Boyd refer to this epistemological change as a "velvet revolution in writing assessment" (p. 63) and argue that:

> [I]f we, the scholars and practitioners of writing instruction and writing assessment, hesitate further to develop and defend the epistemological base of these two practices, they will remain vulnerable to rear-guard actions by those still working within a positivist, a reactionary, or simply a budget-cutting framework. (p. 64)

Rear-guard action is a very real possibility, as Broad and Boyd caution that many measurement practitioners are reluctant to acknowledge such advances (p. 16). Ultimately, the theorization of writing assessment is a means to defend portfolios and CWA from "those wielding well developed and thoroughly institutionalized discourses such as those of positivist psychometrics" (p. 64).

In suggesting that assessment be about contradiction and multiplicity, Broad and Boyd point to a possibility "beyond the tired objectivist–subjectivist dichotomy" (p. 12). Communal writing assessment especially suggested the possibility of fairness with the multiplicity of readings and readers. Multiplicity in the ways that writing is assessed, however, does not extinguish power relations, invite understanding, or suggest pluriversal options. The difficulty of balancing community and multiplicity is nowhere more apparent than in Broad and Boyd's illusion to the Velvet Revolution. Like the Velvet Revolution in Czechoslovakia in 1989, whose reformers could not see the dissolution of the country four years later into two countries—the Czech Republic and the Slovak Republic—Broad and Boyd could not see that CWA would not become part of the mainstream discourse in writing studies. Yet, their belief in the value of CWA would give rise to many newer forms of assessment and would include core values of CWA. There was not to be a single way forward—how could there be—when context was the key.

## SOPHISTIC TURNS

Asao B. Inoue's (2007) "Articulating Sophistic Rhetoric as a Validity Heuristic for Writing Assessment" takes yet another approach in "bridg[ing] disciplines [of measurement and writing studies] by articulating validity in terms of rhetorical theory, and understanding ancient sophistic rhetorical positions as validity theory" (p. 67). Like O'Neill as well as Broad and Boyd, Inoue provides a citational chain through linkages of Cronbach, Messick, Moss, and Huot along with Lorrie Shepard, a classroom assessment researcher, to make the case of "validity as an argumentative activity" (p. 68). He goes on to argue that "conceptualizing validity as explicitly a rhetorical activity brings those doing writing assessment and educational measurement to the same table of theory" (p. 68). Inoue turns to sophistic rhetorical theory (the Sophists' articulations of *nomos–physis*) via Plato, Hippias and Antiphon, Thrasymachus, and Protagoras and Prodicus, arguing that sophistic rhetorical theory:

> offers a political sensitivity and philosophy of language that accounts for social contexts and cultural influences on individual readers/judges, allowing validity research to consider individual dispositions to judge in certain ways as consubstantial to larger cultural and historical milieus, creating a complex relationship that can be considered in our validity arguments. (p. 68)

Sophistic rhetorical theory provides Inoue an expansive theoretical framework, and in this way, he is the one writer in this section to dwell deeply in Western rhetorical theory for the theorization of writing assessment. For example, in making the case that "fairness is an investigation of the methods used and the social arrangements and decisions those methods produce (i.e., effects or outcomes)," he draws upon Protagoras: "Protagoras tells us that part of our need for agreement is that each stakeholder has something worthwhile to contribute, some kind of virtue to be tapped. So writing assessment needs more than stakeholder agreement. Writing assessment requires participation" (p. 81).

For Inoue, fairness is not something that is a universal truth; rather, it is "a construction of it, built into it by methods of evidence gathering and judging" (p. 76). Citing Guba and Lincoln (1989), he argues that fairness is "a reflexive method" and "a high level of fairness is achieved when judges/readers "solicit,' 'honor,' and compare various judgments/readings and their 'underlying value structures,' particularly ones that conflict." (p. 76) Again, returning to the sophists, Inoue writes, "For our heuristic, Prodicus calls attention to the healthy conflict within agreement. Agreement is not synonymous with consensus. It is a stance reached through differing readings and judgments, through hard work and *agon*, through disagreement, which could be debate, negotiation, or war" (p. 82). Like fairness, validity, then, "stems from stakeholder ability to participate in and accept decisions from participation" (p. 81).

Inoue's discussion of social implications is most interesting in his analysis of the contributions of classical rhetoric. On one hand, he does not address that the social conditions of classical rhetoric were far from equitable; women, children, foreign residents, and slaves could not participate in Greek democratic activities. On the other hand, readers can see him start to work through ideas about ideology and assessment that he would advance in later publications, such as his work on anti-racist writing assessment (Inoue, 2015). For example, his current work on habits of white language use (2021) is based on the argument that assessment standards are driven by underlying values, values that are based on white supremacy. In his 2007 article, readers can see evidence of his resistance to an ideal model or a standard against all are measured. As Inoue observes:

> Validating writing placement procedures, like validating grades on essays, is also a matter of recognizing clearly how close decisions come to ideal or correct decisions. Validity inquiry that appeals strictly to *physis* typically does not question the dominance of particular values, theoretical frameworks used to make inferences and decisions, or methods for data collection. (p. 73)

Further:

> Viable alternative interpretations and evidence have difficulty competing with dominant frameworks that make up our methods, what constitutes evidence, fairness, and participation in assessments. (p. 71)

And, in conclusion:

> How is the assessment and its results working toward the interests of those being assessed, namely students (and secondarily programs and faculty), and not simply reinforcing the interests of those with power (or those who control the "land" of assessment)? (p. 78)

Because Inoue is most interested in classroom writing assessment, he is attuned to the ways assessment can invite not just participation but also the negotiation of meaning and power. He does not construct the notion of validity, thus, as something about test design. Rather, he writes, validation "might be an inquiry into stakeholder interests and needs, the power created and used, and the assessment's consequences for stakeholder well-being" (p. 78). Such accounting for "individual ways of sensing and judging for those expectations" is an imperative for fairness and agency, rather than domination (p. 88). In the end, Inoue's position rests on agency and that we must have reflexivity in the knowledge to make choices, and the social structure to allow these choices to be made. For Inoue, the really important questions are about cultural hegemony that we reject in public but, in fact, practice within our classrooms. Thus, the really important answers are to be found in the direction of opening doors through our classroom assessment practices.

## ETHICAL DIMENSIONS

While O'Neill, Broad, and Boyd, and Inoue were negotiating the relationship of measurement and rhetoric in the early 2000s, by 2016 the field had changed. David Slomp's 2016 article "Ethical Considerations and Writing Assessment" (Chapter 14, this volume) evidences a different interdisciplinary moment. Slomp's article is the introductory article to a special issue of *JWA* on ethics and writing assessment, and the issue contained articles that drew from decolonial theory (Cushman, 2016), civil rights law (Poe & Cogan, 2016), politics (Broad, 2016), and philosophy (Elliot, 2016; Slomp, 2016). In his introduction, Slomp argues that "a theory of ethics compels attention beyond the question of technical competence towards broader questions of social consequences" (p. 97). Slomp's tone suggests that the contributors, of all writing studies researchers, had little interest in commenting on the need for an interdisciplinary landscape of writing studies and measurement. Instead, there was a more direct call to address limitations in measurement:

> Some might question the need for a theory of ethics. After all, the *Standards for Educational and Psychological Testing* (American Educational Research Association [AERA], American Psychological Association [APA], and National Council on Measurement in Education [NCME], 2014) already have defined technical requirements for assessment design and use. Throughout this special issue, however, we argue that technical competence/quality is only one component of ethical practice. Technical quality or feasibility may provide some justification for implementing

an assessment practice, but technical feasibility is not equivalent to moral or ethical justification for that practice. (p. 94)

In commenting directly on the field of measurement, Slomp and contributors no longer need to posit a relationship between writing studies and measurement. Instead, there is a move to shape measurement theory itself through humanistic intervention.

Slomp weaves ethics through each of the foundational principles of measurement theory—reliability validity, and fairness. In regard to reliability and the varied forms of evidence accompanying it, he argues that "the demonstration of high degrees of reliability can provide some technical justification for the use of an assessment without addressing deeper ethical questions" (p. 96). In regard to validity, Slomp takes on narrow interpretations of argument-use approaches to validity:

> Validity theorists, themselves, have consistently and explicitly narrowed the breadth of such arguments to focus solely on the uses and interpretations of test results. As such, these arguments are framed as technical ones. . . . We can trust [test scores] because they (a) have been shown to accurately predict future performance; (b) reflect similar scores achieved on similar parallel measures; and (c) accurately reflect the construct the instrument was designed to measure. (p. 96)

The restricted focus of validity arguments, thus, means that questions about construct representation and construct stability raises new questions: "can we defend the use of assessment results for tests that measure constructs we know little about or for where there is little consensus as to what the construct entails?" (p. 97).

In light of the 2014 revised *Standards* which elevated the status of fairness to validity and reliability, Slomp argues that "of the three guiding principles—validity, reliability, and fairness—fairness, with its attention to impacts of assessment practices on individuals, touches most closely on the need for new practices informed by moral philosophy" (p. 100). It is fairness that most attends to social conditions of test use: "In current times, large-scale high-stakes writing assessments may be designed to reflect principles of fairness for individual students while simultaneously being employed to both control and shape education systems" (p. 100).

As Slomp makes clear, none of the three core principles nor the *Standards* is sufficient as an ethical framework for assessment. In response to this gap, Slomp proposes "a theory of ethics for the field of writing assessment, one that advances such a framework toward new conceptualizations that better serve students" (p. 102). He offers six principles based on primary referential frames drawn from diverse stakeholders, exploration of issues related to reliability and validity from multiple perspectives, adoption of an ecological orientation; emphasis on an integrated approach to evidence, considerations of varied assessment genres, and actionable accountability. From Slomp's perspective, the question is not about the relationship between writing studies and measurement. Here, instruction and assessment as well as evidence of validity, reliability, and fairness are brought together not just through singular referential frames but, rather through ontological, epistemological, and axiological perspectives. The view is interconnected across sites of assessment, across communities of stakeholders, and makes test designers and test-users accountable to "how assessments shape systems of education, and how they impact stakeholders within those systems" (p. 103). In terms of assessment theory, there is no one answer, Slomp suggests. His aim is to trouble those who believe there is, a point he develops in future scholarship (Randall, Poe & Slomp, 2021; Slomp & Elliot, 2021).

## CONCLUSION

According to the CDC's Autism and Developmental Disabilities Monitoring Network "about 1 in 54 children has been identified with autism spectrum disorder (ASD)": ASD occurs in all racial, ethnic, and socioeconomic groups and 4 times more common in boys than in girls (Maenner et al., 2020). Now that neurological diversity is well-known in the field of writing studies (Yergeau, 2018), how will writing assessment change to make it more fair for such students? What lessons from history can we learn about what we can see today and what we cannot see? What can we say about fairness when it is acknowledged that substantial individual differences are part of any assessment? What difference does one person make?

If we think about assessment as situated historically, there are three lessons to be learned from the research contributions in this section of *Considering Fairness and Aspiring to Justice*. First, our understanding of construct—i.e., what is writing?—is always changing (not necessarily evolving); any claims drawn from assessment data are historically contingent. Thus, any claims about fairness must always be tempered by the acknowledgment that our understanding of lack of bias, equity, and justice are always contingent. Second, at each moment in history, assessment technologies and social condition are interlocking—in Brad's case, those technologies were developmental testing, IQ testing, classroom assessment, admissions, and warning systems meant to eliminate failures. The social conditions were social stereotypes, legacies of intergenerational poverty and linguistic discrimination, and whiteness. It was not one test that told a story of Brad's progress, potential, and failure. It was the interlocking of assessments, social conditions, and their consequences. Finally, advances in assessment technologies are never evenly distributed. We must never assume that any advancement in making assessment fairer will benefit all. There is always an injustice yet to addressed.

In re-reading these contributions spanning over almost two decades, we see the limits of history. Each piece is deeply contextualized within an historical moment, one that provides the exigence of a hopeful future for the authors but also limits what is unseen—advances that stall, historical narratives that are later challenged, and other roads taken. Published just four years apart, O'Neill, Broad, and Boyd, and Inoue were working at a historical moment when the discussion centered around the uses—or not—of measurement theory. In looking to measurement, writing studies researchers selected measurement researchers that seemed to fit the narrative that was needed for writing assessment—a rhetorical approach that invited community engagement.

But in crafting that narrative—an impulse to tell a history of assessment as one of waves (Yancey, 1999)—there was a subsequent erasure of other measurement histories. That history is now part of the racial reckoning that is happening in measurement through projects such as Stafford Hood and Rodney K. Hopson's "Nobody Knows My Name," an endeavor that retrieves "from near obscurity the work of early contributors and pioneering African American scholars who have been excluded from what is taught as the history of educational evaluation research in the United States" (p. 411). In writing about the work of Asa G. Hilliard, for example, Hood and Hopson (2008) write the idea of fairness has been central to such pioneers in the field:

> For nearly three quarters of a century, one issue has guided and driven the work of African American scholars of educational evaluation. Issues of fairness and equity were at the heart of their inquiry in the 1930s when the doctrine of the land mandated so-called separate but equal school systems for children of color. The issues of fairness and equity were central in their investigations of segregated schools during the pre-Brown and supposedly desegregated schools of the post Brown eras. The issue of fairness remains uppermost in our minds today as we investigate our woefully inadequate schools for Black children, other children of color, and children from economically oppressed backgrounds. (p. 413)

By the time that Slomp was writing in 2016, the need to legitimize the field of writing assessment was no longer needed (even if measurement researchers continued to fail in their citations of writing studies scholars; see Behizadeh & Engelhard, 2011). By 2016, researchers like Slomp were less interested in tracing advances in measurement than in demonstrating how writing assessment research could improve upon the shortcomings of those who continued to believe that standard gauges were the answer to all empirical challenges. By that same time, Inoue, too, had also sharply turned away from measurement as an epistemological orientation to assessment. Today a more tempered view is useful as we watch the standardizers lurch, absorbing notions like culturally and linguistically responsive assessment, but still resisting more radical transformations such as anti-racist assessment, translingual assessment, and neurodiverse validity. In all of it, I wonder what my brother would have felt.

## REFERENCES

American Educational Research Association, American Psychological Association & NCME. (2014). *Standards for educational and psychological testing*. American Educational Research Association.

Behizadeh, N. & Engelhard Jr, G. (2011). Historical view of the influences of measurement and writing theories on the practice of writing assessment in the United States. *Assessing Writing, 16*(3), 189–211.

Boyer, M. (2020). Fairness in educational testing: The role of values in addressing fairness in test purpose, use, and consequences. *Center for Assessment*. https://www.nciea.org/blog/educational-assessment/fairness-educational-testing.

Burke, K. (1950). *A rhetoric of motives*. Prentice-Hall.

Cleary, T. A. (1968). Test bias: Prediction of Negro and white students in integrated colleges. *Journal of Educational Measurement, 5*, 115–124.

Cushman, E. (2016). Decolonizing validity. *The Journal of Writing Assessment, 9*(1). https://escholarship.org/uc/item/0xh7v6fb.

Dorans, N. & Cook, L. (2016). *Fairness in educational assessment and measurement*. Routledge.

Dryer, D. B. & Peckham, I. (2014). Social contexts of writing assessment: Toward an ecological construct of the rater. *WPA: Writing Program Administration, 38*, 12–41.

Elliot, N. (2016). A theory of ethics for writing assessment. *Journal of Writing Assessment, 9*. https://escholarship.org/uc/item/36t565mm.

Educational Testing Service. (2014). ETS standards for quality and fairness. Educational Testing Service. https://www.ets.org/s/about/pdf/standards.pdf.

Educational Testing Service. (2016). ETS international principles for fairness review of assessments. Educational Testing Service. https://www.ets.org/s/about/pdf/fairness_review_international.pdf.

Gipps, C. & Stobart, G. (2010). Fairness. In B. McGraw, E. Baker & P. Peterson (Eds.), *International Encyclopedia of Education* (3rd edition, pp. 56–60). Elsevier.

Guba, E. & Lincoln, Y. (1989). *Fourth generation evaluation*. Sage.

Hannant, P., Tavassoli, T. & Cassidy, S . (2016). The role of sensorimotor difficulties in autism spectrum conditions. *Frontiers in Neurology, 7*, 124. https://doi.org/10.3389/fneur.2016.00124.

Hood, S., and Hopson, R. K. (2008). Evaluation roots reconsidered: Asa Hilliard, a fallen hero in the "Nobody Knows My Name" Project, and African educational excellence. *Review of Educational Research*, 78, 410–426. https://doi.org/10.3102/0034654308321211.

Huot, B. (2002). *(Re)Articulating writing assessment for teaching and learning*. Utah State University Press.

Inoue, A. B. (2015). *Antiracist writing assessment ecologies: Teaching and assessing writing for a socially just future*. The WAC Clearinghouse; Parlor Press. https://doi.org/10.37514/PER-B.2015.0698.

Inoue A. B. (2021). Above the well: An antiracist literacy argument from a boy of color. The WAC Clearinghouse; Utah State University Press. https://doi.org/10.37514/PER-B.2021.1244.

Kane, M. T. (2013). Validating the interpretation and uses of test scores. *Journal of Educational Measurement*, 50, 1–73.

Maenner, M. J., Shaw, K. A., Baio, J., Washington, A., Patrick, M., DiRienzo, M., Christensen, D., Wiggins, L., Pettygrove, S., Andrews, J., Lopez, M., Hudson, A., Baroud, T., Schwenk, Y., White, T., Rosenberg, C., Lee, L., Harrington, R., Huston, M., . . . Dietz, P. M. (2020). Prevalence of autism spectrum disorder among children aged 8 years—Autism and developmental disabilities monitoring network, 11 sites, United States, 2016. *MMWR Surveillance Summary*, 69(4), 1–12. http://dx.doi.org/10.15585/mmwr.ss6904a1external icon.

Nuwer, R. (2016). Autism's history holds lessons for today's researchers. *Spectru*m. https://tinyurl.com/mubd2d35.

Poe, M. & Cogan, J. A. (2016). Civil rights and writing assessment: Using the disparate impact approach as a fairness methodology to evaluate social impact. *Journal of Writing Assessment*, 9(1). https://escholarship.org/uc/item/08f1c307.

Poe, M., Oliveri, M. E. & Elliot, N. (2023). The standards will never be enough: A racial justice extension. *Applied Measurement in Education*, 36(3), 193–215. https://doi.org/10.1080/08957347.2023.2214656.

Randall, J., Poe, M. & Slomp, D. (2021). Ain't oughta be in the dictionary: Getting to justice by dismantling anti-Black literacy assessment practices. *Journal of Adolescent Learning and Literacy*, 48(3), 594–599.

Slomp, D. (2016). An integrated design and appraisal framework for ethical writing assessment. *Journal of Writing Assessment*, 9(1). https://escholarship.org/uc/item/4bg9003k.

Slomp, D. & Elliot, N. (2021). What's your theory of action? Making good trouble with literacy assessment. *Journal of Adolescent & Adult Literacy*, 64(4), 468–475.

Xi, X. (2010). How do we go about investigating test fairness? *Language Testing*, 27(2), 147–170.

Yancey, K. B. (1999). Looking back as we look forward: Historicizing writing assessment. *College Composition and Communication*, 50(3), 483–503.

Yergeau, M. (2018). *Authoring autism: On rhetoric and neurological queerness*. Duke University Press.

Zieky, M. (2016). Developing fair tests. In S. Lane, M. R. Raymond & T. M. Haladyna (Eds.)., *Handbook of test development* (pp. 81–99). Routledge.

CHAPTER 11.

# MOVING BEYOND HOLISTIC SCORING THROUGH VALIDITY INQUIRY

**Peggy O'Neill**
Loyola University, Maryland

*This essay re-examines the research into placement that William L. Smith did at the University of Pittsburgh during the 1980s and 1990s by situating Smith's work within the larger context of educational measurement theories, placement testing, and holistic scoring. I present the series of research studies that Smith conducted into Pitt's placement test as a case study in validation inquiry, arguing that his approach serves as a model for those who direct writing assessments. The implications of Smith's research reach beyond placement into first year composition: by approaching local writing assessment needs as Smith did, writing assessment professionals not only can create more effective assessments, but they also can contribute significantly to assessment theory.*

Since 1874 when Harvard introduced English composition as a subject in the battery of entrance exams prospective students completed in the application and admission process, writing assessments have become standard features of college entrance exams, playing a role in students' college curricula choices. Early writing tests—essays about literature—were typically evaluated by professors; however, during the 20th century, this practice gave way to more scientific methods, so that educational measurement theories and practices dominated writing assessment (White, 1998; Williamson, 1993). Tests of grammar, usage, and mechanics that required little or no writing (e.g., fill-in-the-blank, multiple-choice, editing) were popular, but by mid-century, instructors of writing and directors of writing programs had become increasingly disgruntled with these exams. Impromptu essay exams re-emerged as a popular method of placing students into the first-year composition program; however, these "new" essay exams depended on holistic scoring, a "scientific" and "objective" type of evaluation of student writing.

DOI: https://doi.org/10.37514/PER-B.2024.2326.2.11

Holistic scoring of timed essays quickly spread until it was assumed to be the best practice for placing students into the first-year writing curriculum. Edward White (1995a) explained that the popularity of the impromptu essay test, which was defended by English faculty because it replaced the use of multiple-choice exams, rested on the holistic scoring procedures, which were cost-efficient and produced valid and reliable results. Writing assessment practitioners and scholars assumed essay testing results valid because the test demanded students write instead of filling in scantron answer sheets, and reliability rates were acceptable as long as the readings were properly managed (White, 1998). The acceptance of holistic scoring as the cornerstone for direct writing assessment (Wolcott, 1998) continued as compositionists began to experiment—and favor—portfolios over impromptu essays for writing assessment. For example, Miami University used holistic scoring to evaluate portfolios submitted for advance placement in first-year composition (Beck, Dautermann, Miller, Murray & Powell, 1997). Holistic scoring of essays or portfolios typically went unquestioned as long as the interrater reliability coefficients were acceptable. Smith's (1992) response to the essay placement exam he inherited on his arrival at the University of Pittsburgh typifies this position: "It seemed to work, so there was no impetus to examine it, let alone change it. The incoming students were placed into our courses efficiently and with what appeared to be tolerable numbers of errors" (p. 314). However, although most compositionists remained complacent about using holistic scoring of timed essays for placement testing, Smith began to question the practice at his institution. Smith's tinkering with the placement testing during his association with the University of Pittsburgh's writing program produced not only several published research reports and numerous conference presentations but also demonstrated how systematic, ongoing validity research functions to enhance a particular local test and contributes—both theoretically and practically—to the scholarship of writing assessment.

By situating Smith's work within the larger context of educational measurement theories, placement testing, and holistic scoring and presenting it as a case study of validity inquiry, I argue that by approaching local assessment needs as Smith did, compositionists can create better assessments while contributing significantly to writing assessment theory.[1]

---

[1] I have relied heavily on the published work of William L. Smith (1992, 1993) as well as numerous informal communications with him about his research at the University of Pittsburgh where he served as the Composition Program's director of testing for more than a decade. Bill not only responded to my never-ending questions, but he also read and commented on multiple drafts of this article.

## VALIDITY

According to Smith (1998), there is a "paucity of validation research" (p. 3) in writing assessment, which stems from several different but interrelated problems: a lack of understanding of key concepts such as validity and reliability; an overemphasis on achieving reliability; a lack of understanding of what validation inquiry entails; and a failure to articulate the theoretical constructs underlying writing assessments. Correcting these deficiencies in the composition literature on assessment has begun (Huot, 1996; Moss, 1994, 1998; Smith, 1992, 1993, 1998; Williamson, 1993) but the confusion still exists, especially in our understanding of validity.

Validity has been—and continues to be—misconstrued in most of composition's assessment literature. White (1995a), one of the most prolific voices in composition's assessment community, wrote, "Validity means honesty: the assessment is demonstrably measuring what it claims to measure" (p. 40). In the revised edition of his popular book, Teaching and Assessing Writing, White (1998) stated: "Although validity is a complex issue—colleges offer advanced courses in it—one simple concept lies behind the complexity: honesty. Validity in measurement means that you are measuring what you say you are measuring, not something else, and that you have really thought through the importance of your measurement in considerable detail" (p. 10). Even more recent discussions have continued this misperception despite measurement theory and writing assessment literature that contradicts these simplified definitions. For example, Harrington (1998) explained validity this way: "A valid assessment is one which assesses what it sets out to assess (in this case, students' ability to write in relation to the local curriculum divisions)" (p. 59). Yancey (1999) asserted: "Validity means that you measure what you intend to measure" (p. 487). And Shane Borrowman (1999) quoted White when defining validity: "According to Edward M. White, 'Validity . . . has to do with honesty and accuracy, with a demonstrated connection between what a test proclaims it is measuring and what it in fact measures'" (p. 9). In discussing their self-placement system, Royer and Gilles (1998) sidestepped the issue of validity for the most part: "Our old concerns about validity and reliability are now replaced with something akin to 'rightness'" (p. 62). Although Royer and Gilles, Harrington (1998), and others acknowledged more complex considerations of validity, in addressing validity issues of their specific placement systems, they resorted to simplistic and faulty conceptions. Validity, however, is a complex notion in assessment that should not be distorted or simplified to fit individual agendas, nor should it be reduced to a one-sentence sound bite.

In the educational measurement community, debates and discussions about validity have been ongoing. Two of the most influential voices in these discussions have been Cronbach and Messick (Moss, 1992, 1995; Shephard, 1993), who each has written about the complexity of validity's theoretical nuances and practical applications for over three decades. Although there has been considerable debate in the assessment community, several scholars such as Lorrie Shepard (1997) and Pamela Moss (1992), argue that the Standards for Educational and Psychological Testing, which are the standards for research and measurement endorsed by the American Psychological Association, the American Educational Research Association, and the National Council on Measurements Used in Education, and the scholarly literature do in fact support the unified, complex notions of validity that have evolved more recently. According to Cronbach (1988), who was instrumental in drafting the original Standards, validity "must link concepts, evidence, social and personal consequences and values" (p. 4). Messick (1989) argued that validity uses "integrated evaluative judgment," supported by empirical evidence and theoretical rationales, "to support the adequacy and appropriateness of inferences and actions based on test scores and modes of assessment" (p. 5). In other words, validation arguments are rhetorical constructs that draw from all the available means of support. Validation studies include issues of reliability, construct definitions, consequences, and other empirical and sociopolitical evidence. Huot (1996), who drew on the work of Cronbach and Messick, concluded that "in writing assessment, the validity of the test must include a recognizable and supportable theoretical foundation as well as empirical data of students' work" (p. 550). Valid writing assessments, he continued, "need input from the scholarly literature about the teaching and learning of writing" (p. 550). In validating a writing assessment, Huot recommended that writing researchers also include inquiry into the use of the assessment results. These conceptions of validity, argued Huot, "look beyond the assessment measures themselves and demand that a valid procedure for assessing writing must have positive impact and consequences for the teaching and learning of writing" (p. 551). In placement testing, validation demands determining the adequacy of placement as well as investigation into other aspects of the test, such as the testing and scoring procedures, to determine if students are being placed in the course which best fits their needs. Ensuring adequate placement should allow more effective teaching and learning because teachers will be able to better meet the needs of students.

Although validity theory is the overarching issue in assessment, reliability has most often dominated discussions of writing assessment, especially in terms of holistic scoring. As with validity, misperceptions about reliability have a long history in direct writing assessment. Reliability has been construed as a simplistic notion in most of the holistic scoring literature, which has been marked by an inconsistency and confusion in defining and calculating reliability (see Cherry & Meyer for a detailed discussion). In many cases, reliability has been reduced to interrater reliability, the agreement between two independent readers, although "interrater reliability alone cannot establish holistic assessment as a reliable or valid procedure" (Cherry & Meyer, 1993, p. 114). In fact, many different facets of reliability are at issue in rating essays such as intrarater reliability, the degree to which raters agree with themselves; rater set reliability, the consistency of rating of two primary readers that constitute a set; and instrument reliability, the consistency of the test itself across successive administrations, which takes into account students, tests and scoring as potential sources of error (Cherry & Meyer, 1993). As Cherry and Meyer explained, "Regardless of how consistently raters assign scores to written texts, if the writing prompt (the test) is faulty or if examinees do not respond consistently to it, the holistic scores will not reliably reflect writing ability" (p. 115).

Coupled with the ongoing misunderstanding about what reliability entails is a failure to acknowledge that reliability contributes to a validity argument but is not itself enough to validate the results of a test. In fact, Moss (1994) turned to interpretive research traditions such as hermeneutics to argue for the inappropriateness of reliability as a key part of validation in some types of assessment. According to Moss, traditional assessment privileges standardization but it is inadequate in evaluating complex performances such as reading and writing. A hermeneutic approach would include "holistic, integrative interpretations" that would "privilege readers who are most knowledgeable about the context in which the assessment occurs," and "ground those interpretations not only in textual and contextual evidence available, but also in a rational debate among the community of interpreters" (p. 7). This approach to writing assessment would support the processes and theories associated with literacy, leading to more theoretical alignment between actual literate practice and the assessment of it. Moreover, a hermeneutic approach undermines the quest for "objective" rating of essays that supports the proliferation of holistic scoring as the preferred procedure for direct writing assessment.

Besides—and maybe because of—these problems with key assessment concepts of reliability and validity, there is a lack of rigorous composition research into placement methods. Although there are not many models to follow, Moss (1998a) explained that in composition placement

> a sound program of validity research begins with a clear statement of both the purpose and the intended interpretation or meaning of test scores and then examines, through logical analysis, the coherence of tests with that understanding. Without a clear sense of how validity and validation inquiry plays into the development and evaluation of a placement test, it is not possible to be sure that students are being placed into the appropriate course. (p. 117)

In the case of a placement exam, logical analysis of coherence must also encompass an understanding of the different courses as well as the outcome measures used to evaluate success in those courses. Directors of placement tests need to systematically collect a variety of data such as raters' decisions and interviews and surveys of participants, and analyze the data through multiple perspectives. Moss (1998a) also suggested that validity inquiry should include other methods such as critical linguistics (linguistic analyses of discourse that surrounds an event) or ethnographic studies (participant-observer research). Validity research involves a dynamic process that requires an examination of procedures and results, use of this information to revise and improve assessment practices, and an examination of revised practices in a never-ending feedback loop. In short, validity inquiry should be embedded in the assessment process itself, ongoing and useful, responsive to local needs, contexts or changes, something that is never really completed.

The work that William L. Smith, along with a cadre of graduate students, did for more than a decade during his tenure as director of testing for the University of Pittsburgh composition program during the 1980s and early 1990s is an example of how systematic, ongoing validity inquiry can not only lead to better—more valid—local assessment but also contribute to the larger field of writing assessment.

## PLACING STUDENTS VERSUS HOLISTIC SCORING

A key to understanding the validity research Smith conducted is to understand the difference between holistic scoring—a procedure for evaluating texts—and placement—the decision that is made about the writer based on the results of an evaluation. Although this distinction may seem obvious now, it wasn't always so clearly understood. Traditionally, compositionists have talked about writing assessments in terms of direct and indirect tests. Indirect tests do not use student writing as part of the test but rather extrapolate "writing ability or potential" indirectly from, for example, the students' SAT or ACT scores or other multiple-choice tests of language use such as the computer adaptive COMPASS or ACCUPLACER. The most recent published surveys of placement (Huot, 1994; Murphy et al., 1993) demonstrate that multiple-choice tests are still very popular methods of composition placement although students do not do any actual writing. Compositionists tend to favor direct measures because they use student writing as the basis for the assessment. Samples of student writing may be collected through impromptu essays given during a testing period, online writing submitted via the Internet, or portfolios of school or self-sponsored writing. Although the sampling methods may vary, most large-scale direct assessments are evaluated through holistic scoring (see White, 1998; Wolcott, 1998).

Although one way to describe writing assessments is by the sampling method (direct or indirect), a more productive way to look at an assessment is through its purpose: Why are we assessing student writing? Possible responses include program assessment, student proficiency, or placement. Another way to see a test is through its effect: What are the consequences of this test to students, programs, teachers? By posing these sorts of questions, we move beyond the sampling method to a more productive framework for identifying similarities and differences. Placement testing that uses writing samples has often been conflated with holistic scoring. For example, placement often uses timed impromptu essays to collect a writing sample, much like large-scale assessments such as National Assessment of Educational Progress. Additionally, placement rating is like holistic rating in that the readers use the basic holistic method: a single, quick reading leading to a single, overall judgment. Additionally, both types of assessment generally use two independent raters as the basic decision-making unit. However, placement rating is unlike holistic in some very important ways:

1. In holistic rating, the meaning of the points on the scale are internally derived; it depends on both the range finders and the range of the essays in the set to be rated. In placement rating, the points on the scale are externally derived because the scale is determined by the institutional context: the curriculum, the assumptions about composition, and the purposes of each course. The particular set of essays being rated does not influence these conditions and does not determine the scale.

2. In holistic scoring, an interval scale is used, which means that the distance between points on the scale is the same. That is, the range from Point 1 to Point 2 is equal to the range from Point 2 to Point 3. More importantly, the difference between a 2.5 and a 3.5 is equal to the distance between a 1.5 and a 2.5. A rater holistically scoring texts is ranking and comparing the texts along the scale. Because the text is being compared to the others in the set, summing of the primary raters' score or averaging of them is acceptable. A split-resolver's score can be averaged or substituted without problem. In other words, texts can receive scores along the continuum of the scale. However, in placement a categorical—also known as an ordinal—scale is used, which means that the distances between points is often more varied; consequently, the distance between the midpoints is not equal. The placement scale is actually determined by the curriculum with each scale point representing a curricular choice (e.g., basic writing, composition 1, honors composition). The range for the point that represents

the standard first-year course is usually wider than other courses such as developmental or honors. Because the scale is categorical, texts need to be slotted into one category or another; therefore, differences among raters cannot simply be averaged because between-course scores can result. In fact, it is to be expected that some students, through their writing sample, will exhibit characteristics of more than one course, not fitting neatly into any course (or any point on the scale, any one category) although they have to be placed into one course.

3. In holistic scoring, the scale is defined by the set of student texts being evaluated; therefore, the texts "fit" the scale. In placement, however, the scale is pre-set by the curriculum, so the students have to fit the scale, which isn't always the case. This feature affects the distribution of students. Because the scale is not set by the pool being evaluated but is predetermined, the distribution of students along the scale should vary from year to year. If the distribution does remain constant it is highly likely that either students are being placed in order to fill seats in classes, not to put them in the most appropriate class, or there is a very stable pool of students.

4. In holistic scoring, the focus is on the text and locating the text on a scale. In placement, the focus is on the student and placing the student in the appropriate course. There are very real consequences in placement and raters have explained that even if a holistic scale is used, they make judgments about students not just texts (e.g., Pula & Huot, 1993; Smith, 1993).

Holistic scoring, then, is not the most appropriate method for placement although it may be useful for other situations, for example, when the results of the test are used to evaluate a program, not individual writers.[2] In this scenario, the scale points can be determined according to what the test giver desires to learn, such as whether or not the program's outcomes are being met. In this type of testing, the features of the written text can provide answers to the research questions, and the results are reported for the group with no consequence to the individual writers. Placement, by its very nature, has consequences for individuals and it needs to be distinguished from holistic scoring. Besides all of these differences, several issues that influence its design and implementation are unique to placement. Practical issues, such as administration and processing of placement essays (especially in reference to turn-around time), have to be

---

2  I realize that many programs claim to use "holistic scoring," but my point is that often what is called holistic scoring is actually placement, as I explained earlier.

negotiated with other campus parties, such as the orientation coordinator and the advisement center. Composition curricula, enrollment patterns, first-year student demographics, orientation demands, and funding may also be influential factors in designing individual placement systems. Other elements such as the pool of available readers or the size of the set to be read also need to be considered.

All placement methods, however, assume that different courses are needed to meet the needs of different students, and all acknowledge the need for some type of sorting mechanism for matching students to the appropriate courses. Because our placement methods sort students, as professionals it is imperative that we validate our placement assessments: [W]e have an obligation to make certain (i.e., conduct research) that our testing is fair and valid, in elicitation methodology, in the scales used, in the ways we make judgments on the writings, in the ways we analyze, interpret, and use the results, and in the ways and forms in which we publish those results . . . only through rigorous forms of validation research can we really construct assessments that accurately and ethically assess our students and programs. (Smith, 1998, p. 3) Besides ethical and professional obligations, we should be concerned with our ability to legally defend our assessments if challenged. William Lutz (1996) explained that few academics realize that there are enough legal precedents to indicate there is liability associated with assessment, even institutional testing such as placement and exit. To be prepared for a legal challenge and to ensure we act ethically and professionally, Lutz (1996) and Smith (1998) recommended similar approaches: We need to conduct systematic, ongoing research into our methods, procedures, and programs. In most cases, however, very little rigorous research has been conducted to determine the validity of placement decisions.

## A CASE STUDY OF VALIDATION INQUIRY

As Smith (1992) explained, when he started at Pitt he inherited a method for placing students that was standard and consistent with what other universities used. Most of the placement occurred over the summer during orientation sessions. Students wrote their essays in large group sessions spread over the summer months. Because the composition program was based on the interrelation of reading and writing, students were given a passage to read and a series of questions designed to focus their response. The prompts closely resembled the assignments students experienced in the composition courses. Students were given 2 hours to complete the task. The essays were rated immediately after students finished by composition faculty who were trained raters and experienced teachers. The rating system consisted of two primary raters who scored the essay independently. The scale corresponded to the curriculum: a rating of A, B, C, coincided with the three composition courses, and D rating indicated "exempt."[3] If the two primary raters agreed, the student was placed into that course; if they disagreed, a third rater, a "split-resolver" was used.

Although Smith acknowledged his initial complacency with the placement test he inherited, he began to feel uneasy about it so he embarked on a series of research projects, which he conducted for more than a decade. Data sources for these projects included surveys of faculty and students; interviews with students, teachers and raters; think aloud protocols of raters; analyses of rater and rater-set decisions; grade distributions; placement distributions; and statistical analyses. Although he designed and conducted a series of distinct studies, Smith found that his interpretations and conclusions depended on the accumulated knowledge and experience he garnered from the ongoing nature of

---

3   Understanding Smith's validation inquiry requires some sense of the University of Pittsburgh's Composition Program because this type of research is local and contextualized. Smith (1993) described Pitt's Composition Program as being based on four concepts:

- Writing is an effort to make meaning;
- Writing is closely related to reading;
- To make meaning, a writer must develop a sense of authority; and
- Students gradually come to a sense of authority.

Consequently, in all of their courses, students respond to a sequence of assignments on a central topic (see Bartholomae, 1983; Coles, 1981; Bartholomae & Petrosky, 1987, for more detailed expositions of the basis for the program). It is important to note that composition courses were not considered "service" courses; consequently, students were not required to write research papers or papers in various modes (description, narration, etc).

Because students have varied abilities along the four dimensions, the first year composition program consisted of three courses, each addressing different writing problems and abilities. Course A was designed for students with serious problems with writing that indicate problems with reading and appropriating a text they have read. These students' essays lack development of ideas, lack coherence, are not well-organized, and do not address the issue. Commonly, these students inadequately summarize what they are asked to read or make general statements about the issue or topic, but they do not interrelate what they have read with their own ideas. These students also typically have patterns of surface level errors caused by their inability to proofread. Students who successfully complete this course take Course C.

Course B is also designed for students who have significant writing problems such as coherence, organization, or development of ideas, but these problems are not related to their ability to read. Instead, they indicate a lack of a sense of text and a lack of authority. Surface error is common in their texts, typically caused by their lack of a sense of text. If asked whether they read their own texts as they read other ones, they will say they do not, and if pressed for reasons, they will say that their own reading does not merit such reading. Students pass from this class into Course C.

Course C is designed for students who have the ability to read and make meaning but need more experience in developing their abilities, particularly in dealing with problematic texts and in using writing as a means for working their way through complex problems. Some students are exempted from any composition course because the writing ability they demonstrate suggests that these courses would not be of significant value to them (pp. 144–145).

his work.[4] In other words, he did not keep reworking and revising his research until he got the placement process "right"; instead, his research helped him to form new research questions, revise his research approach or focus, and revise the placement procedures. Ultimately, it led Smith to develop new placement assessment methods, which he continued to research until he left Pitt.

## Determining Adequacy of Placement

Smith realized that he had no solid evidence that the placement system was working—that students were appropriately placed. Like most composition placement systems, Pitt's seemed to be adequate because the error rate—the number of misplaced students—appeared relatively low. Determining the error rate depended on an essay written during the first week of class. Based on this essay, teachers identified students they believed misplaced, and a senior faculty member would read the essays, moving students into different courses if necessary. The first-week essay check, reasoned Smith, provided only marginal evidence about how many students were misplaced. He suspected that the error rate was seriously underestimated: teachers were reluctant to have students transferred out (which meant others may transfer in), some students were absent for the first-week essay, and students' attitude toward their placement (and the specific class and teacher) may have effected their effort on the first-week essay.

Because Smith wasn't content with the procedures for determining adequacy of placement, he spent 3 years developing methods for figuring out if students were being placed adequately or not. He concluded that adequacy of placement depended on triangulating several different data sources, none of which was sufficient by itself:

- The number of students moved to a new course during the first week.
- Student's final course grades; student's impressions—collected during and especially after the course—of the degree to which the course met their needs.
- Teachers' impressions of how well the students fit the course.
- Exit exams or posttests.

Alone, each of these measures has problems. For example, grades could be influenced by factors such as attendance and promptness that are unrelated to

---

[4]  There are three published articles about this research (Smith, 1992, 1993; Smith et al., 1985). Much of the research went unpublished, although "Assessing the Reliability and Adequacy of Holistic Scoring" (Smith, 1993) reports in detail on several years worth of research focused on raters. In addition, Smith, often with graduate students, presented several conference papers about this placement testing research.

the appropriateness of the course. An exit exam or posttest might often depend on just one writing sample that may not adequately represent students' abilities; or as at Pitt, not all courses required exit exams. After surveying teachers and students, conducting interviews with teachers and students, and analyzing the results, Smith determined that teacher perception is the single best measure of whether students belong in the course. Smith also found that teachers' perceptions of students change considerably across the course of the semester. If gathered too early in the semester, teachers don't have enough evidence on which to base their decision; if gathered too late, teacher perception correlates very highly with the students' final grades, indicating that the students' actual performance is evaluated, not their potential. Smith concluded that teacher perception data should be collected during Weeks 3 through 5 of a 15-week semester.

## Causes of Errors in Placement

Besides developing procedures for determining a more accurate error rate, Smith focused on investigating the possible causes for error. He identified several potential sites of error: the writing prompts, the conditions under which the students write, the writers not writing essays that accurately represent them, raters not making good decisions, and an inadequate rating scale. He also acknowledged that as the director of testing, he was another source of error because he was the one who decided on the testing procedures, hired the raters, and evaluated the system. After specifying these potential sources of error, Smith began systematic inquiry into each one.

The first area for investigation was the writing prompts. The placement prompt required students to read a short text and then respond to it. Smith and his coresearchers conducted a series of studies where they varied the format of the prompt and analyzed the writing that students produced.[5] They examined three different types of prompts with writers at different ability levels. The writers responded in class within the time period allotted for the placement. After analyzing the results for types of errors, frequency of errors, and fluency, Smith concluded that the prompt they were using was adequate because it differentiated writers appropriately for the courses offered in Pitt's writing program.

The second series of studies investigated the placement exam conditions. Did it make a significant difference if students wrote their essay in large groups or small groups? Was the 2–hour time limit a factor? Did "warm-up" exercises make a difference in students' writing? Did it matter if a "real" composition teacher, who explained Pitt's composition program to the test takers, administered the test? According to Smith's studies, time and group size were not

---

[5] Part of this research was reported by Smith et al., 1985.

factors while warmups and teachers made only slight differences. These differences were only apparent for the weaker writers, and the differences were not consistently positive. Smith concluded that the testing conditions were not very influential factors.

Smith next turned to looking at the writers and found that there were significant factors that influenced their performance, but that he could not control for them. For example, Smith found (to no one's surprise) that many students—especially males—are distracted when they take the placement exam by the new setting, new people, and new freedom they encounter in their trip to campus. However, administering the test during another time was not feasible.

The rating scale was another factor that Smith had no direct control over. Placement rating scales should be determined by the courses in the composition program, so that at Pitt, the 4–point scale corresponded to the three composition courses and an exemption from composition option. Finally, Smith's research led him to focus on the raters, which yielded not only a wealth of information but helped Smith revise the placement system.

## Focusing on the Raters

Smith set out on a series of studies focusing on the raters and rating system he used for placement. The raters were teachers in the composition program who, as paid volunteers, scored placement essays during the summer. All raters had experience teaching Course C, whereas some had experience with Course A and/or B, but during a given semester teachers only taught one course (because most raters and teachers were graduate students, this was done so they had only one course preparation per term). All placement essays were read by two raters and if they disagreed, another rater (split-resolver) decided the rating. The second rater did not know the first rater's score; the split-resolver knew he or she was a split-resolver, not a primary rater. In this system, each rater was responsible for making multiple decisions: Does the student belong in Course A, Course B, Course C, or should the student be exempt from composition altogether?

In conducting his studies of raters, Smith relied for the most part on records of rater decisions collected as they rated, rater profiles of teaching experience, and think-aloud protocols. His experience with the raters and the placement system were also valuable sources of information. By keeping meticulous records of the rating decisions for each essay and re-rating of certain essays, Smith was able to collect detailed information about how raters scored. He used these procedures to conduct a series of studies that examined rater reliability (interrater and intrarater), rater-set reliability, and split-resolver rating patterns. His research led him to examine how raters' profiles correlated with reliability rates and eventually how placement decisions were influenced by raters' teaching experience. (For an in-depth account of these studies see Smith, 1993). Smith's conclusions also resulted from his willingness to re-examine and rethink his approach and the data. For example, instead of merely focusing on trying to get raters to agree more consistently, Smith looked at when raters disagreed, determined if the disagreements were reliable (they were) and then tried to figure out why. In making hypotheses and testing them, Smith did not neglect to go back to what prompted the studies in the first place: Were students' placements valid? He used the procedures for adequacy of placement, most importantly teacher perception, that he had developed to see if students were indeed being appropriately placed.

Based on these studies, Smith made some conclusions about placement research and procedures that may be useful for other researchers:

- *When raters knew they were being tested, they responded differently*: In placement research, that means that dry runs, "staged" placement sessions, or other uses of holistic scoring may not be adequate representations of what raters do in "real" placement. Recirculating essays without the raters knowledge is necessary to get an accurate sense of rater reliability.
- *Raters who are split-resolvers rate differently than when they are primary raters:* Placement for students who fall between courses is not the same as those who fit the scale more easily, which means interrater reliability is affected because raters and rating are not consistent.
- *Raters made decisions about students, instead of merely judging texts*: In think-aloud protocols and informal conversations about placement reading, raters often referred to their classrooms and the student writer instead of the text. Because raters are deciding what course a student should take, and not judging the text itself, raters can disagree about quality but agree on placement. However, disagreement, whether about quality or placement, is to be expected. Holistic scoring, on the other hand, actually tries to eliminate or minimize disagreement, focusing instead on consensus or agreement.
- *Some students didn't fit into any course*: It is reasonable to assume that not all students will fit neatly into one of the composition courses because the scale is predetermined by the curricula. This is a potent source for disagreement.
- *Using traditional methods for determining reliability did not accurately portray what raters actually did nor how reliable their judgments were*: Reliability in most writing assessments has been determined by interrater reliability alone, which represents how often raters agree with each other; however, this statistic masks other important aspects of reliability: Is a rater consistent with him or herself? Is a rater-set

consistent? Are raters consistent in their disagreements? Do split-resolvers rate consistently? Unpacking reliability complicates determining whether a placement test is reliable, but it provides more information for determining if the test results are valid because it provides multiple perspectives and data, allowing the researcher to get a more nuanced understanding of what the raters and the rating process.

- *Raters' teaching experience affected their rating, perhaps even more than calibration*: Raters were all experienced teachers and depended on that experience and knowledge in determining placement. It proved to be more powerful than calibration or practice sessions in their decision making.
- *The course the rater most recently taught affected the rater's decision:* Ultimately, when comparing the rater's most recently taught course experience to their rating decisions, raters were most consistent in placing students into the course they had most recently taught. Their consistency decreased the further away they were in terms of experience from the course. For example, a teacher who most recently taught Course C placed students into Course C more reliably than in Course B, but Course B placements were more reliable than those for Course A.

## THE EXPERT MODEL

Based on these conclusions, Smith changed the placement procedures to what he called the "expert model." In this system, raters were assigned to rate for one course only, the one they most recently taught. They made only a binary decision: Accept the student for their course or reject him or her. Depending on the course for which they were rating, they could reject high or reject low. The basic process was as follows:

> If the first reader accepts, the next reader has the same course-taught expertise (CTE).
>
> If a CTE-(Course) A rejects high, the next reader is CTE-C (because most students ended up in C).
>
> If CTE-B rejects low, the next reader is a CTE-A.
>
> If CTE-B rejects high, the next reader is CTE-C.
>
> If CTE-C rejects low, the next reader is CTE-B.
>
> If CTE-C rejects high, the next reader is CTE-D.

Of course, because Course D represents exemption, there can be no CTE; instead a panel of expert teachers read the essay and decided if the student should be exempted from all composition or take Course C. Inevitably, as Smith found out, some students did not fit neatly into a particular course; he called them "'tweeners" because they fell between courses. All essays were read at least twice until they were located on the following scale:

> Course A
>
> Between Courses A & C
>
> Course B
>
> Between Courses B & C
>
> Course C
>
> Between Course C & D (exempt)
>
> Exempt

Smith's research indicated that raters reliably rated tweeners between courses. Smith also found that in the traditional placement system, which used split-resolvers, tweeners' placement was affected by the split-resolvers' most recent course taught experience so that tweeners were not reliably placed. In the expert model, Smith determined that all tweeners would go to the next highest course except for those between Course C and exemption; they would take Course C. Analysis of the adequacy of placement of tweeners found that they did not have a higher failure rate than students placed directly into the course although teachers continued to identify them as marginal, not an exact fit for the class. (Interestingly, the perception as a tweener continued once the student passed through Courses A or B and into C). The overall rate of error—the number of misplaced students—was less than 3% with the expert model, but even more importantly, the number of prototypic students for each course increased (there were less marginal students in each course). Smith, of course, acknowledged the need for more research to test the expert model. For example, would the practice of moving tweeners to the higher course ultimately affect the teachers' perception of the prototypic student? Would the reliable placement of students through the expert model prove itself through multiple years of inquiry? Before he could address these questions, Smith left Pitt. However, his work has made a considerable contribution to not just placement research and procedures but also to writing assessment in general.

## CONCLUSIONS AND IMPLICATIONS: FROM LOCAL APPLICATIONS TO ASSESSMENT THEORY

Smith's placement research was grounded in Pitt's composition program, not necessarily universally applicable. For example, Pitt had a composition program with clearly articulated assumptions about writing and teaching writing that were shared by the faculty. Furthermore, the expert model depends on having teachers teach all sections of the same course in a semester. In many composition programs, this isn't possible so teachers may be teaching two or more of the first year composition courses would have more than one most recently taught course, which may be a factor in their placement decisions. Although the particulars of Smith's research, conclusions, and revised placement procedures will not fit another program exactly. His conclusions and procedures can help other placement directors design studies and procedures, and the implications of the work reach beyond placement to other forms of writing assessment.

One of the most important aspects of an assessment is validity, yet it is also an area that is under researched and misunderstood in composition's assessment literature. Smith's work not only illustrates how to conduct validation research but also how writing specialists need to understand the complexities—both theoretical and practical—that validity involves. Validity inquiry needs to focus on the purpose and use of the test's results and requires more than a quantitative analysis of the results. As Moss (1994) argued, traditional standardized, objective approaches to assessment are inadequate for evaluating complex performances such as reading and writing. A hermeneutic approach would include "holistic, integrative interpretations" that would "privilege readers who are most knowledgeable about the context in which the assessment occurs," and "ground those interpretations not only in textual and contextual evidence available, but also in a rational debate among the community of interpreters" (p. 7). Smith's expert model enacted this approach: He allowed experienced, expert teachers to make holistic, integrated judgments about student placement, and he grounded these decisions with a variety of evidence and rational debate. This approach to writing assessment endorses the approach to reading and writing supported by composition scholarship, and it undermines the quest for an "objective" rating of essays that accompanies holistic scoring, the most popular procedure for direct writing assessment. In placement testing, validity rests on determining that the students are being adequately placed, a task that is more involved than most programs acknowledge. In exit testing or competency testing, validity inquiry will take different forms. Local context, including faculty, curricula, student populations, come into play in collecting and analyzing data and building a validation argument.

Smith's work also reminds compositionists that reliability is complex and multidimensional. Composition as a field has often relied on interrater reliability in determining reliability, but that distorts the notion of reliability. Readers' disagreements are an important source of information that needs to be unpacked. Resorting to a simplified reliability coefficient can mask important aspects of a rating system, of reliability, or of validity. By examining when readers disagreed,

Smith realized that readers can reliably disagree. There may also be factors that influence reliability, which Smith discovered he could control for. In Pitt's placement program, teachers' most recent course taught experience was a significant factor in reliability of ratings; in other programs, there may be other factors such as education or background. In other types of writing assessments, such as competency testing or exit testing, reliability may be influenced by different factors specific to the test's purpose, the curriculum or other contextual variables. In short, individual writing assessments and the requisite validation inquiry that should accompany them need to be sensitive to local context.

The ongoing research conducted by Smith highlights the demands of writing assessment, which is a specialized field that requires practitioners to understand composition theory as well as assessment theory. Smith's work not only legitimizes assessment work as discipline defining and knowledge-generating but also as something that demands specialized knowledge and education. Writing assessments, after all, play an important role in identifying values and assumptions about writing, evaluation, and teaching of writing. Unfortunately placement (or other assessment demands) are most often viewed as part of administration or service, requiring no specialized knowledge or education. Huot (1994) found that only 14% of schools' using direct writing assessment for placement had a director with a terminal degree in composition or publications in writing assessment. In other words, many of the professionals designing, implementing, and evaluating placement tests are not writing specialists, let alone writing assessment specialists. By allowing assessment to be controlled by professionals without the necessary knowledge and experience, we are in effect allowing our field to be dominated and defined by those outside the field.

Likewise, as long as compositionists continue to separate themselves from the larger educational assessment community (Huot, 2002), we run the risk of merely adopting assessment methods and approaches that are inconsistent with our assumptions that literacy is a complex, contextual activity. Writing assessment specialists need to critically examine assessment theories and practices, and if necessary adapt them to fit particular purposes, or develop new approaches that are consistent with our understanding of writing, reading, and teaching. Holistic scoring as traditionally defined came out of the measurement community and reinforces an approach to reading and writing that is acontextual and objective. Psychometric theory, which is used to "validate" holistic scoring, assumes traits and abilities are normally distributed throughout the population, an assumption that is antithetical to what composition theory supports. These traits or abilities, according to traditional psychometrics are isolatable, quantifiable, and unchanging. Writing specialists, however, define writing as a contextual, communicative activity that is not transferable across time and place. Composition theory also assumes that writing "abilities" are influenced by instruction. These fundamental differences are significant and should not remain hidden or unarticulated but rather need to be addressed directly. By integrating experience and knowledge of composition, teaching, and psychometrics and confronting paradigmatic conflicts, Smith was able to create new approaches to assessment that honored composition scholarship and assessment demands.

Since the mid-1980s, there seems to be an accumulating body of composition research about placement (i.e., Borrowman, 1999; Decker, Cooper & Harrington, 1993; Harrington, 1998; Haswell & Wyche-Smith, 1994; Huot, 1994; Lowe & Huot, 1997; Robertson, 1994; Royer & Gilles, 1998; Sommers, Black, Daiker & Stygall, 1993). Unfortunately, the level of systematic and ongoing inquiry into these programs has been inconsistent, or at the very least inconsistently reported: Haswell and Wyche-Smith's (1994) work has developed into a comprehensive writing assessment system and a rich source of scholarship and ongoing research (e.g., Haswell, 1998, 2001; Haswell, Johnson-Shull & Wyche-Smith, 1994; Haswell & McLeod, 1997). Yet other placement systems, such as the self-placement system used at Grand Valley State University (Royer & Gilles, 1998) or the small-group teaching model reported by Robertson (1994), provided very little rigorous research to support them and demonstrated lack of awareness of the complex assessment theories involved in designing and directing placement programs, but were legitimized through publication. Innovating and reconceptualizing placement can be important sources of knowledge, providing improved ways of meeting students' needs; however, without the appropriate inquiry, which demands an understanding of the complexity of the theories and assumptions informing writing and assessment practices, there is no way to justify revising or maintaining assessment procedures.

As a field, college composition has been quick to embrace new assessment practices—such as holistic scoring, portfolios, and directed self-placement—without sufficient understanding of the theories and assumptions that support them. When assessments are adopted and promoted without appropriate validation inquiry, we are not only jeopardizing our students' opportunities for learning and success—after all, writing assessments often function as institutional barriers—but we are ignoring a significant site of power and knowledge, undermining the legitimacy and professionalism of composition.

## REFERENCES

Bartholomae, D. (1983). Writing assessments: Where writing begins. In P. L. Stock (Ed.), *Forum: Essays on theory and practice in the teaching of writing* (pp. 300–312). Boynton/Cook.

Bartholomae, D. & Petrosky, A. (1987). *Ways of reading: An anthology for writers.* Bedford/St. Martin's Press.

Beck, A., Dautermann, J., Miller, C., Murray, K. & Powell, P. R. (1997). *The best of Miami University's portfolios 1997.* Department of English, Miami University.

Borrowman, S. (1999). The trinity of portfolio placement: Validity, reliability, and curriculum reform. *WPA: Writing Program Administration, 23*(1/2), 7–27.

Cherry, R. D. & Meyer, P. R. (1993). Reliability issues in holistic assessment. In M. M. Williamson & B. A. Huot (Eds.), *Validating holistic scoring for writing assessment: Theoretical and empirical foundations* (pp. 109–141). Hampton Press.

Coles, W. E., Jr. (1981). *Composing II: Writing as a self-creating process.* Hayden Book.

Cronbach, L. J. (1988). Five perspectives on validity argument. In H. Wainer (Ed.), *Test validity* (pp. 3–17). Erlbaum.

Decker, E., Cooper, G. & Harrington, S. (1993). Crossing institutional boundaries: Developing an entrance portfolio assessment to improve writing instruction. *Journal of Teaching Writing. 12*(1), 83–104.

Harrington, S. (1998). New visions of authority in placement test rating. *WPA: Writing Program Administration, 22*(1–2), 53–84.

Haswell, R. H. (1998a). Multiple inquiries in the validation of writing tests. *Assessing Writing, 5*(1), 89–109.

Haswell, R. H. (Ed.). (2001). *Beyond outcomes: Assessment and instruction within a university writing program.* Ablex.

Haswell, R. H., Johnson-Shull, L. & Wyche-Smith, S. (1994). Shooting Niagara: Making portfolio assessment serve instruction at a state university. *WPA: Writing Program Administration, 18*(1–2), 44–54.

Haswell, R. H. & McLeod, S. (1997). WAC assessment and internal audiences: A dialogue. In K. B. Yancey & B. Huot (Eds.), *Assessing writing across the curriculum: Diverse approaches and practices* (pp. 217–236). Ablex.

Haswell, R. H. & Wyche-Smith, S. (1994). Adventuring into writing assessment. *College Composition and Communication, 45*(2), 220–236.

Huot, B. (1994). A survey of college and university writing placement practices. *WPA: Writing Program Administration, 17*(3), 49–67.

Huot, B. (1996b). Toward a new theory of writing assessment. *College Composition and Communication, 47*(4), 549–566.

Huot, B. (2002). *(Re)Articulating writing assessment for teaching and learning.* Utah State University Press.

Lowe, T. J. & Huot, B. (1997). *Using KIRIS writing portfolios to place students in first-year composition at the University of Louisville.* Kentucky English Bulletin, 20, 47–64.

Lutz, W. D. (1996). Legal issues in the practice and politics of assessment in writing. In E. M. White, W. D. Lutz & S. Kamusikiri (Eds.), *Assessment of writing: Politics, policies, practice* (pp. 33–44). Modern Language Association.

Messick, S. (1989a). Meaning and value in test validation: The science and ethics of assessment. *Educational Researcher, 18*(2), 5–11.

Moss, P. A. (1992). Shifting conceptions of validity in educational measurement: Implications for performance assessment. *Review of Educational Research, 62*(3), 229–58.

Moss, P. A. (1994). Can there be validity without reliability? *Educational Researcher, 23*(2), 5–12.

Moss, P. A. (1998). Response: Testing the test of the test. *Assessing Writing, 5(1),* 111–122.

Murphy, S., Carlson, S. & Rooner, P. with the CCCC Committee on Assessment. (1993). *Report to the CCCC executive committee: Survey of postsecondary writing assessment practices.* Unpublished manuscript.

Pula, J. J. & Huot, B. A. (1993). A model of background influences on holistic raters. In M. M. Williamson & B. A. Huot (Eds.), *Validating holistic scoring for writing assessment: Theoretical and empirical foundations* (pp. 237–265). Hampton Press.

Robertson, A. (1994). Teach not test: A look at a new writing placement procedure. *WPA: Writing Program Administration, 18*(1–2), 56–63.

Royer, D. & Gilles, R. (1998). Directed self-placement: An attitude of orientation. *College Composition and Communication, 50*(1), 54–70.

Shephard, L. (1993). Evaluating test validity. *Review of Research in Education, 19,* 405–450.

Shepard, L. A. (1997). The centrality of test use and consequences for test validity. *Educational Measurement: Issues and Practice, 16*(2), 5–8, 13, 24.

Smith, W. L. (1992). The importance of teacher knowledge in college composition placement testing. In R. J. Hayes (Ed.), *Reading empirical research studies: The rhetoric of research* (pp. 289–316). Ablex.

Smith, W. L. (1993). Assessing the reliability and adequacy of placement using holistic scoring of essays as a college composition placement test. In M. M. Williamson & B. A. Huot (Eds.), *Validating holistic scoring for writing assessment: Theoretical and empirical foundations* (pp. 142–205). Hampton Press.

Smith, W. L. (1998). Introduction to Special Issue. *Assessing Writing, 5*(1), 3–6.

Smith, W. L., Hull, G. A., Land,, R. E., Jr., Moore, M. T., Ball, C., Dunham, D. D., Hickey, L. S. & Ruzich, C. W. (1985). Some effects of varying the structures of a topic on college students' writing. *Written Communication, 2*(1), 73–89.

Sommers, J., Black, L., Daiker, D. D. & Stygall, G. (1993). The challenges of rating portfolios: What WPAs can expect. *WPA: Writing Program Administration, 17*(1–2), 7–29.

White, E. M. (1995a). Apologia for the timed-essay. *College Composition and Communication, 46*(1), 30–45.

White, E. M. (1998). *Teaching and assessing writing* (2nd edition). Calendar Islands.

Williamson, M. M. (1993). An introduction to holistic scoring: The social, historical, and theoretical context for writing assessment. In M. M. Williamson & B. A. Huot (Eds.), *Validating holistic scoring for writing assessment: Theoretical and empirical foundations* (pp. 1–44). Hampton Press.

Wolcott, W. & Legg, S. M. (1998). *An overview of writing assessment: Theory, research, and practice.* National Council of Teachers of English.

Yancey, K. B. (1999). Looking back as we look forward: Historicizing writing assessment. *College Composition and Communication, 50*(3), 483–503.

# CHAPTER 12.
# RHETORICAL WRITING ASSESSMENT: THE PRACTICE AND THEORY OF COMPLEMENTARITY

**Bob Broad**
Illinois State University

**Michael Boyd**
Morton High School, Morton, IL

*Writing portfolio assessment and communal (shared, dialogical) assessment are two of our field's most creative, courageous, and influential innovations. Because they are also relatively expensive innovations, however, they remain vulnerable to cost-cutting by university administrators and to attacks from testing corporations. This article lays a theoretical foundation for those two powerful and valuable practices in teaching and assessing writing. Building on the concept of "complementarity" as developed in the fields of quantum physics (Bohr, 1987; Kafatos & Nadeau, 1990) and rhetoric (Bizzell, 1990) and adapted for educational evaluation (Guba & Lincoln 1989, 2000), we provide some of the "epistemological basis," called for by Huot (1996, 2002), on which portfolio and communal assessment are based and by which those practices can be justified. If we must look to science to validate our assessment practices (and perhaps we must), we should not settle for outdated theories of psychometrics that support techniques like multiple-choice testing. Instead, from more recent scientific theorizing we can garner strong support for many of our best practices, including communal and portfolio assessment. By looking to the new science—including the new psychometrics (Cronbach, 1988; Moss, 1992)—we can strengthen and protect assessment practices that are vibrantly and unapologetically rhetorical.*

The past 20 years has brought many remarkable innovations to the forefront of writing assessment. Among the most prominent of these developments are writing portfolios and communal writing assessment (CWA). The rise of portfolio assessment has been especially dramatic: dozens of writing programs (including Miami University, State University of New York- Stonybrook, University of Cincinnati, Washington State University) now use portfolios to place students in composition courses or to certify students' writing competency, and the trend appears to be growing. CWA has grown with somewhat less fanfare; no books or conferences have yet focused on the nuances of group evaluation as many already have on portfolios. Nevertheless, the dynamics of CWA have attracted significant attention in recent journal articles and books (Allen, 1995; Broad, 1997, 2000, 2003; Huot, 2002).

Proponents of both these practices claim they afford sweeping benefits to students' learning and instructors' professional development. Literally dozens of articles and books trumpet the glories of portfolio assessment. Although CWA has not yet received this kind of attention, the scholarship just cited strongly advocates what Allen (1995) calls "shared evaluation" for the sake of improved validity and ethics in assessment decisions as well as the professional growth of instructor-evaluators. Broad (2003) claims that dialogical group judgment has fostered a "new [democratic] politics of inquiry" in writing assessment.

This is the good news. The potentially bad news is that both CWA and portfolios are expensive practices, and expensive practices tend to disappear once the initial flush of enthusiasm has faded from their practitioners' faces. As Mike Williamson (1994) has pointed out, educational assessment practices in the 20th century United States were less likely to be educationally beneficial and theoretically sound than to be quick and cheap. Thus, the ongoing dominance of the cheap and quick method par excellence, the multiple-choice test (Williamson, 1994), despite nearly universal condemnation of such tests from every corner of assessment scholarship and practice. Now that teachers of writing have developed, nurtured, and propagated the more educationally fruitful approaches of employing multiple evaluators (CWA) to judge multiple performances (portfolios), how can we better understand these two innovations in writing assessment and protect them from the omnivorous shredding machine of efficiency ideology? To support these sophisticated and vulnerable assessment practices, we need to look to ascendant theories of language, knowledge, and value. The difficulty is that writing assessment practice historically has shown excessive timidity and even loathing toward theory and philosophy. But what if neglecting theory also meant losing the two most exciting and productive innovations in a century of writing assessment? Perhaps in that case theorizing these practices would rate a second look.

## THE POSSIBILITIES OF THEORY IN WRITING ASSESSMENT

In his 1993 "An Introduction to Holistic Scoring: The Social, Historical, and Theoretical Context for Writing Assessment," Williamson dared to dream of a new paradigm in writing assessment distinguished by its, "tearing itself loose from the theoretical foundations of psychometric theory and establishing itself with a foundation based in a theory of writing." (p. 38) Surveying the competing interest groups who vie for control of writing assessment, however, Edward M. White (1996) subsequently wondered whether Williamson's prophetic vision was "perhaps too hopeful." In "Power and Agenda Setting in Writing Assessment," White voiced considerable skepticism that we could ever persuade government officials or testing agencies to explore new theoretical possibilities, stating flatly that "it is a waste of time to urge commercial testing firms to accommodate poststructuralist theories of reading" (p. 23).

If Bernard E. Alford (1995) is right, however, we ought not to dismiss too quickly Williamson's prediction that theory might transform our practices.

> In the theories of language that have emerged in this century, English has the tools to challenge rather than run from the hegemony of science. It has the tools to reclaim from positivist and supposedly objective discourses the right to critique and define what it means to know something. (p. 64)

Alford strongly suggests that at the start of the 21st century, the moment may indeed have arrived for an end to the "hegemony of science" in writing assessment practice and the establishment of a new, rhetorical, approach.

As a matter of historical fact, the entire (presumably hopeless) project of "persuading" the resistant group White invokes may prove superfluous. No doubt White is correct in stating that the eyes of those employed by testing corporations would glaze over if we urged them openly to embrace poststructuralist or postmodern theories of language meaning and value. However, while we writing assessment specialists have wondered anxiously about when, whether, and how a poststructuralist, postmodern theory of writing assessment would ever arrive, it quietly entered the scene without our even noticing. The widespread implementation within the past decade of two distinctly rhetorical writing assessment practices—portfolios and CWA—preceded any sustained articulation of the rhetorical theory for which Williamson called.

This practice–theory time delay should hardly surprise us. Brian Huot (1990) pointed out more than a decade ago that theoretical awareness in writing assessment usually lags behind practice.

It is not unusual to find assessment techniques used before they have received proper theoretic research attention. Faigley et al. have noted that, "of necessity, practice has far outrun theory in writing assessment" (p. 205) and Gere has observed that "the theoretical basis of evaluation remains unarticulated." (p. 201)

At the close of this article we return to Huot's analysis of the temporal gap between practice and theory in writing assessment. For the moment, it will suffice to note that we have all been tapping into a new theory of writing assessment for years but are only now beginning to grasp its scope and character. If Alford (1995), Huot (1990, 1996, 2002) and Williamson (1993) are correct, we need not invent a new theory of writing assessment. It already exists, and has already been put to use. What we now urgently need to do—what this article helps to do—is further develop and strengthen that new paradigm through study of its theoretical roots and of the specific assessment practices that enact it.

Fortunately, much of the groundwork for naming and developing a theory of rhetorical writing assessment has already been laid. Huot's (1996) "Toward a New Theory of Writing Assessment" examines descriptions of five assessment programs and draws from their practices five shared principles of rhetorical writing assessment. Huot reveals that a rhetorical theory of writing assessment calls for practices that are: site-based, locally controlled, context sensitive, rhetorically based, and accessible.

The crucial question Huot's (1996, 2002) investigation leaves unanswered is the specific epistemological basis (Huot's term) on which these new principles and procedures are built. Part of our project is to connect Huot's (1996, 2002) analysis of principles and programmatic practices to their epistemological bases, and answer the urgent question: "When we leap from the theoretical foundation of positivism, on what, if anything, do we land?" The resounding answer offered by Alford (1995), Guba and Lincoln (1989), and Bizzell (1990) (discussed later) is complementarity, a rhetorical and democratic process for establishing knowledge, truth, value, meaning, and everything else for which we once relied on positivism and foundationalism.

Once we have traced the theoretical roots of rhetorical writing assessment, we then want to examine some of its fruits. We explore how portfolio assessment and communal writing assessment already embody the new theory of writing assessment to which Huot (1996, 2002) recently called our attention. These two practices enact the very break with traditional psychometrics and the shift toward a rhetorical conception of writing assessment for which Williamson (1993) called. Borne of writing teachers' and administrators' frustration and anger at the damage psychometric testing did—and continues to do—to students, teachers, and learning, compositionists quietly developed and institutionalized alternative assessment practices more to their satisfaction. Without announcing it, they ushered in a new paradigm in writing assessment, which has been propagated across the country by such scholar-practitioners as Haswell (2001), Smith (1993), Yancey (1992, 2004) and others.

## THE PRINCIPLE OF COMPLEMENTARITY

Niels Bohr's 1958 essay entitled "Quantum Physics and Philosophy: Causality and Complementarity" (Bohr, 1987) describes the theoretical differences that were beginning to emerge between classical physics and quantum physics. "Within the scope of classical physics," he claims, "all characteristic properties of a given object can in principle be ascertained by a single experimental arrangement" (p. 4). Under the new paradigm of quantum physics, the central tenets of classical physics are problematized:

> In quantum physics . . . evidence about atomic objects obtained by different experimental arrangements exhibits a novel kind of complementary relationship. Indeed, it must be recognized that such evidence which appears contradictory when combination into a single picture is attempted, exhausts all conceivable knowledge about the object. Far from restricting our efforts to put questions to nature in the form of experiments, the notion of complementarity simply characterizes the answers we can receive by such inquiry, whenever the interaction between the measuring instruments and the objects forms an integral part of the phenomena. (p. 4)

The theoretical differences between classical physics and quantum physics stem from the epistemological problem Bohr describes in this essay. Although classical physicists were convinced that adequate data and knowledge about a particular object or phenomena were ascertainable from the results of a single experiment, quantum physics complicates this notion by claiming that the "measuring instruments" have as much impact on the measurement as the phenomena being measured. The dichotomy evoked here is one of determinism and indeterminism.

Quantum physics, in opposition to the classical version, accepts that ultimately all knowledge is indeterminate because the methods we use and the vantage points from which we obtain evidence substantially alters the evidence itself. Bohr even alludes to "the irrevocable abandonment of the ideal of determinism" (p. 5), before attempting to predict what new practices scientists will employ in order to adequately represent the situations they study.

Because "measuring instruments" impact the object of study, Bohr predicts that "multivalued logics [are] needed for a more appropriate representation of the situation" (p. 5). More succinctly, Bohr claims, "a completeness of description like that aimed at in classical physics is provided by the possibility of taking every conceivable experimental arrangement into account" (p. 6). Not only does Bohr's theory of complementarity recognize the role of subjectivity in the collection and interpretation of data, it also abandons an obsession with reliability by acknowledging that differing experimental arrangements will sometimes yield contradictory evidence.

Studying the behavior of atomic particles is different from studying the rhetorical strengths and weaknesses of written texts or a reader's ability to evaluate those texts. Nevertheless, both fields share parallel epistemological problems as well as solutions. In both cases, the theory of complementarity can help to make meaningful and useful a body of data that preceding paradigms would have viewed as contradictory or chaotic. Bohr's theories substantially altered the practice of atomic physics; they have also influenced the field of writing assessment.

Two texts portray the principle of complementarity as directly relevant to the field of writing assessment. Egon Guba and Yvonne S. Lincoln (1989) draw on complementarity in developing the multiperspectival, highly contextualized, and continuously evolving method of evaluation named in the title of their book, Fourth Generation Evaluation. Their work emerges form the field of education and organizational evaluation and measurement. The other text on which I draw here is firmly rooted in English Studies. Alford's (1995) Modern English and the Idea of Language: A Potential Postmodern Practice disentangles weak and strong versions of postmodernism to present a transformative and coherent postmodern theory and pedagogy of literacy. Like Guba and Lincoln, Alford extensively draws on—and further develops—Bohr's analysis.

For Guba and Lincoln, the principle of complementarity serves chiefly to remind researchers and evaluators that the act of inquiring unavoidably shapes the outcome of any inquiry:

> The Bohr Complementarity Principle . . . argued that the results of any study depended upon the interaction between inquirer and object. . . . That is, the findings depended as much on the nature of the questions asked . . . as on any intrinsic properties of a "real" reality "out there." (p. 66)

Like most post-positivist critique, this analysis helps to show the weakness of foundationalist and objectivist approaches. Guba and Lincoln move on to develop their method of "fourth-generation evaluation" as a way of practicing evaluation without assuming or claiming access to context-free or pure truths. Whatever truths their approach to evaluation yields will be contingent—partial, positioned, and rooted in belief as human knowledge must be, but also multiple and diverse. Thus, multiplicity and difference within community provide the legitimizing process and features of fourth generation evaluation.

Alford (1995) helps to develop and clarify why difference and multiplicity within community (i.e., complementarity) are so important to postmodern claims to truth. It is not enough to throw out objectivism, for human communities (e.g., schools and universities, for-profit organizations, and governmental units) still need a public process for sorting out competing claims on truth and value. Even under postmodernism, we still need to make judgments that can be documented and supported. Subjectivism is typically offered as the necessary and only alternative to objectivism, but few among us feel confident implementing high-stakes judgments labeled "subjective," although in truth the process of reading and therefore evaluating texts is always subjective, because it is based on an individual's ability to construct the text she is reading. Drawing on work in postmodern theory and complexity theory in the physical sciences, Alford (1995) conclusively moves the important debate about truth claims beyond the tired objectivist–subjectivist dichotomy:

> Alford draws on the work of quantum physicists Menas Kafatos and Robert Nadeau (1990) to focus our understanding of the principle of complementarity. Alford (1995) explains the following: Kafatos and Nadeau use the principle of complementarity . . . as a way of explaining how categories that exclude each other in any particular action or example (particle/wave) are still linked in any understanding of the whole system at work. (p. 86)

In other words, a particular category or perspective offers its own distinct value in understanding or assessing any object of inquiry. If we wish to strengthen and verify that understanding, however, we need to introduce one or more categories or perspectives that are not merely additional to the first but also radically different from it. Alford goes on to quote Kafatos and Nadeau directly:

> One [category or construct] excludes the other in a given situation or act of cognition in both operational and logical terms, and yet the entire situation can be understood only if both constructs are taken as the complete view of the situation. (cited in Alford, 1995, p. 86)

Alford shows that by moving beyond objectivism and subjectivism, we can verify postmodern claims to contingent truths through a process of bringing radically distinct constructs into dialogue with each other within established human communities. (For further useful discussion of such paradigmatic issues of validation, see Guba & Lincoln, 2000.)

Before we examine how portfolios and CWA enact complementarity, we need to clarify an important link between the principle of complementarity and the field of contemporary rhetoric. Specifically, we need to explain why we have referred to writing assessment that embodies complementarity as rhetorical writing assessment:

> In "Beyond Anti-Foundationalism to Rhetorical Authority: Problems Defining 'Cultural Literacy,'" Patricia Bizzell (1990) wrestled with the challenges of antifoundationalist and postmodern processes for assessing truth claims. Her analysis yielded a process of judgment that looks a good deal like Guba and Lincoln's and Alford's. Bizzell, however, named her alternative process "rhetoric" and its outcome "rhetorical authority." We must help our students, and our fellow citizens, to engage in a rhetorical process that can collectively generate trustworthy knowledge and beliefs conducive to the common good. (p. 671)

According to Bizzell, we need not panic as the house of foundationalism crumbles before our eyes. For once we have dispensed with foundationalism we will rely on what we have, in fact, always relied upon: persuading one another through a process of disputing conflicting truth claims and negotiating contingent, communally sanctioned truths through discourse. In other words, we will rely on rhetoric. Let us now turn to the two practices we mentioned at the outset and explore how they both enact a rhetorical theory of writing assessment rooted in the principle of complementarity.

## PORTFOLIOS AND COMPLEMENTARITY

Portfolios in classroom settings mark a significant but not radical departure from the practices they displaced: grading several discrete writing performances over a semester or year (Yancey, 1992). In most writing classrooms, students already compose a variety of texts for a variety of audiences, and they take each piece through processes of drafting, response, research, revision, editing, and publication. The movement in such classrooms to portfolio assessment adds "collection, selection, reflection, and projection" (Yancey, 2004) to teaching and writing—a significant, but not radical, shift in pedagogy.

Portfolios are a more dramatic departure from past practices in the area of large scale writing assessment. Most often to certify "writing proficiency" and somewhat less often to determine appropriate placement in composition courses, large-scale assessment has over the past two decades moved steadily away from assessment of single writing performances, usually the "timed impromptu" (White, 1995), and toward diverse collections of writing performances, that is, toward portfolios. The move from single to multiple artifacts or perspectives is often represented as a postmodern move (Berlin, 1994). However, multiplicity alone does not necessarily constitute a theoretical shift. When combined with the positive valuing of differences and diversity, however, multiplicity becomes potentially transformative. It is the combination of multiplicity and difference in what portfolios present that connects them with the principle of complementarity. Along with multiplicity, portfolios call for difference both within and among collections of students' rhetorical performances.

Timed impromptu tests strongly imply a single quality or characteristic in a writer called writing ability (Purves, 1995). Much of the elaborate process of developing, piloting, and refining prompts for writing tests centers on the goal of eliciting the single performance that will most accurately represent the test-taker's writing ability. Portfolio assessment, because it requires not only multiplicity of, but also differences among, the performance(s) to be assessed, highlights the speciousness of the singular conception of writing ability.

In fact, portfolios make it difficult for anyone—writer or evaluator—to overlook that there is no single writing ability. Instead, we expect different writers to bring different strengths to different rhetorical efforts. At Miami University, for example, incoming students submit a portfolio of four pieces so they may be placed on one of three institutional tracks related to first-year composition. Portfolios for placement at Miami include the following:

- a reflective letter
- a story or description
- an explanatory, exploratory, or persuasive essay, and
- a response to a written text

Indeed, as in most places, students at Miami University are awarded a single score and their academic fate depends on that score. The assessment outcome therefore remains strikingly singular. The assessment process, however, deconstructs the fiction of writing ability and acknowledges that the university cares about and is responsible to each student as multiple rhetors: the supplicant to the university bureaucracy (in the reflective letter); the rhetorical aesthete who will entertain her readers and/or stimulate their senses and imaginations (in the story or description); the presenter and interpreter of information and the changer of minds (in the explanatory, exploratory, or persuasive essay), and the master of literary interpretation and taste (in the response to a written text). Reflecting on all this proliferation of rhetorical roles in "The Subversions of the Portfolio," James Berlin (1994) credits portfolios with deconstruction of "the unified, autonomous, self-present subject of liberal humanism," one of the key features on the basis of which he claims that "the portfolio is a postmodern development."

In the same essay Berlin applauds the "de-standardizing" effects of differences among students' portfolios. In composing portfolios, students undertake projects whose topics and angles they chose and shaped; they are not submitting to "standardized" assignments. The same writing "assignment" (e.g., public, persuasive nonfiction) can be fulfilled through two or more dramatically different choices of genre, data, tone, and topic. This variability among portfolios based on writers' knowledge, needs, interests, and choices can make writing assessment decisions more valid, for we are assessing rhetorical performances that authors not only choose and shape but about which they therefore have the opportunity to care. Isn't that what we really want to know when we assess a writing performance? Not how someone writes when she doesn't know or care, but when she does. In this way, we can argue that anything less than self-initiated, self-selected multiple texts underrepresent the ability to write (Cherry & Witte, 1998). This quality of investment and caring is necessarily scarce in standardized tests of writing, for test takers play a drastically diminished role in shaping their responses to a test. And test makers, for their part, work to ensure that every test taker's level of interest in the testing prompt is low, because high-interest topics often generate texts that evoke diverse, therefore "unreliable," scores from evaluators.

Recognizing the necessary inadequacy of gauging writing ability in response to a single performance, compositionists championed portfolios. They called for students to shape the diverse contexts and contents of those portfolios, and they required students to demonstrate their abilities playing multiple rhetorical roles. The conscious and stated reasons for this movement are summed up by Peter Elbow (1991):

> We all sense . . . that we cannot trust the picture of someone's writing that emerges unless we see what he or she can do on various occasions on various pieces. (pp. xi-xii)

Teachers and scholars of writing sensed their own unease with the constraints placed upon writing assessment by psychometricians, and—despite repeated warnings from influential voices in our field—we embraced portfolios, a technology that shrugged off those constraints. The danger is that the warnings of doom for portfolio assessment could prove true after all. For the complex and expensive practice of portfolio assessment to survive, it will likely not be enough to refer to our sense of what we can and cannot "trust" in evaluating writing. We will need to articulate the "epistemological base" to which Huot (1996, 2002) refers. Complementarity provides that base, and thus provides theoretical and political shelter for portfolio assessment.

## COMMUNAL WRITING ASSESSMENT AND COMPLEMENTARITY

Even more dramatically than portfolios, the growing practice of CWA enacts the transformative power of rhetorical writing assessment and the principle of complementarity. As in the case of portfolios, the move from the single judge of writing performance to multiple judges is only the first step in the theoretical and practical transformation. The more radical shift is away from seeking and valuing homogeneity among judges to seeking and valuing diversity; however, before we look at this radical shift as it is enacted in CWA, we need to examine how similar shifts are taking place in psychometric approaches to writing assessment.

In the history of large-scale writing assessment, multiple evaluators have long been a key to ensuring the validity of the measure (Diederich, French & Carlton, 1961; White, 1994). Note, however, the difference between the psychometric uses of multiple homogeneous raters—to ensure accurate detection of the "true score" for each performance—and the rhetorical uses of multiple and diverse readers. Within traditional psychometric assessment, multiple evaluators were urged, indeed required, to produce identical scores. Standardization procedures attempted to make each evaluator's judgments identical; those who could not make their judgments homogeneous were excluded from the process. Although many psychometricians choose to ignore innovations in their own field, postmodern and antifoundationalist theory is continuing to impact the field of psychometrics. For instance, Pam Moss (1992) points out that some psychometricians have expressed "philosophic concern with the epistemological foundations of positivism" (p. 233). Moss even quotes Cronbach, a psychometrican, with claiming that "it was pretentious to dress up our immature science in positivist language" (cited in Moss, 1992, p. 233).

Moss also reveals a movement within the field of psychometrics to "redesign" its approach to writing assessment. This new design, developed by Wolf, Bixby, Glenn, and Gardner (1991), proposes assessment practices that "promote serious thought" by abandoning rubrics and considering the "possibility of multiple paths to excellence" (p. 63). They also proposed a revision to "our notions of high-agreement reliability as a cardinal symptom of a useful and viable approach to scoring student performance" (p. 63). One interesting thing about Wolf, et al.'s redesigned approach to assessment is that it begins to move in the direction of rhetorical writing assessment and away from the impulse to ensure that evaluators make identical judgments. Cronbach himself articulates even more succinctly this trend within psychometrics toward rhetorical and discursive approaches to assessment. "Cronbach (1988) suggested that readers think of validity inquiry as the building of an argument that 'must link concepts, evidence, social and personal consequences, and values' (p. 4)" (cited in Moss, 1992, p. 242). What is encouraging about Moss' discussion of the "shifting conceptions of validity" in the field of psychometrics is the realization that psychometricians are abandoning their obsession with foundationalist, positivist science and looking more toward rhetorical strategies in creating, using, and interpreting assessments. What is less encouraging is the fact that most practicing psychometricians have completely ignored these most recent advances in their field. Moss (1992) claims that "the practice of validity research typically has not done justice to the modern views of validity" (p. 245). Having taken into account some psychometricians' refusal to acknowledge progress in their own field, we can now turn to our examination of CWA and rhetorical writing assessment.

Recent innovations in CWA radically overturn the homogenizing impulse of traditional psychometric assessment. Certain assessment programs actively seek out variations among evaluators' backgrounds and frames of knowledge. One of those is the first-year English program at "City University" documented and analyzed by Broad (1997).

According to Broad, faculty at City University did what old-school psychometricians would consider foolish: they juxtaposed evaluations of judges who, by virtue of their distinctive positions within the university and the profession, are sure to assess students' writing differently each from the other.

- *Administrators* bring to assessment discussions their special concerns regarding "rigor" and "standards" within the program. They also wield considerable disciplinary knowledge, citing from the scholarly literature during "norming" sessions.
- *Teachers* bring their strong commitments to teacher autonomy in writing assessment and their richly contextualized knowledge of students' efforts, progress, and attitudes. Holding as it does many secrets of the teacher–student relationship, their "Teachers Special Knowledge" places them in a position in the program at once powerful and suspect.
- *Outside evaluators* bring their knowledge based on teaching the same course, but with no knowledge of the particular student whose writing

is under discussion. Outside instructors' judgments are known and valued at City University as "cold readings."

Weaving these three distinct perspectives into the same assessment program makes for some volatile evaluative dynamics. It also makes for a more trustworthy, more democratic truth than the old model of evaluative orthodoxy could provide.

City University's reciprocal authorities find justification in the principle of complementarity. Recall that, according to Kafatos and Nadeau (Alford, 1995), under complementarity "the entire situation can be understood only if both constructs are taken as the complete view of the situation." Instructors and administrators at City University found that a "complete view" of students' writing proficiency required not two but three constructs, each of which to some extent "excluded each other." Also significant is that they answered Bizzell's (1990) call for "a rhetorical process that can collectively generate trustworthy knowledge and beliefs conducive to the common good." The rhetorical processes found in the extensive, sometimes fiercely conflictual, talk of norming sessions and trio sessions at City University enacted just such a rhetorical process for writing assessment.

## A VELVET REVOLUTION IN WRITING ASSESSMENT

In 1990, Brian Huot pointed out in "Reliability, Validity, and Holistic Scoring: What We Know and What We Need to Know" that, contrary to the claims of several prominent commentators, the dominant practice of holistic scoring in writing assessment had a clear theoretical base: positivist psychometrics. At that time, Huot (1990) also introduced questions regarding where writing assessment—and its rhetorics—might go next. In 1996, he surveyed a cluster of assessment programs and articulated a set of patterns or themes that characterized contemporary assessment practice and, Huot (1996) claimed, pointed "Toward a New Theory of Writing Assessment." What remained was to explicate the "epistemological basis" of this new theory and to explore ties between that theory and the face-to-face, moment-by-moment practices supported by it.

Perhaps it is the destiny of writing assessment always to practice first and theorize last. Indeed this may be a good thing. Advocating what he calls a "post-intellectual" practice of teaching English studies, Alford argues that practice belongs first.

This [post-intellectual] approach would signify a change in the relationship between theory and practice because it would put practice first and return theory to a reflective role. That is, instead of predetermining the order of events and the priority of focus, this approach would emphasize the performative aspect of culture, the point at which identity and understanding are constructed (Alford, 1995, p. 138).

This article has reflected on a particular "performative aspect" of the culture of teaching and assessing writing. Compositionists felt a need for new approaches to assessment, and met that need by developing writing portfolios and communal writing assessment, among other practices. Later, the theory they enacted could be named, contextualized, and developed.

The stakes are higher, however, than deciding or documenting whether theorizing precedes or follows practice. Without the intellectual work of theorizing, practices like portfolios and communal writing assessment remain vulnerable to critique from those wielding well developed and thoroughly institutionalized discourses such as those of positivist psychometrics. Let us not dismiss lightly Edward M. White's (1996) warnings regarding reactionary testing corporation employees and legislators. We would like to think that the new practices are well enough entrenched to withstand the storms of efficiency ideology and scientism that are likely to rage against them when the money gets tight or when people catch on to their full implications. History suggests otherwise, however, so we have endeavored to connect Huot's (1996, 2002) framework for a new theory of writing assessment with its theoretical roots and its practical fruits.

If we, the scholars and practitioners of writing instruction and writing assessment, hesitate further to develop and defend the epistemological base of these two practices, they will remain vulnerable to rear-guard actions by those still working within a positivist, a reactionary, or simply a budget-cutting framework. Note, for example, Huot's alert that statewide portfolio programs in Vermont and Kentucky have struggled for years to meet demands for interrater reliability and other questionable psychometric requirements of "standardization."

It is imperative that we at the college level continue our experimentation and expand our theorizing to create a strong platform for new writing assessment theory and practice, so that we can see the emergence of rhetorical and contextual writing assessment for all students. (Huot, 1996, pp. 563–564)

This article has expanded our theorizing in support of our two most creative, courageous, and influential assessment experiments. If as a result our political vulnerable parts are now better protected, then we can proceed with new experiments and move forward with the project of rhetorical writing assessment.

# REFERENCES

Alford, B. E. (1995). *Modern English and the idea of language: A potential postmodern practice.* Unpublished doctoral dissertation, Michigan State University, Lansing.

Allen, M. S. (1995). Valuing differences: Portnet's first year. *Assessing Writing, 2*(1), 67–89.

Berlin, J. A. (1994). The subversions of the portfolio. In L. Black, D. A. Daiker, J. Sommers & G. Stygall (Eds.), *New directions in portfolio assessment: Reflective practice, critical theory, and large-scale scoring* (pp. 56–67). Boynton/Cook.

Bizzell, P. (1990). Beyond anti-foundationalism to rhetorical authority: Problems defining "cultural literacy." *College Composition and Communication, 52*(6), 661–675.

Bohr, N. (1987). Quantum physics and philosophy: Causality and complementarity. *Essays 1958–1962 on atomic physics and human knowledge.* Ox Bow Press.

Broad, B. (1997). Reciprocal authorities in communal writing assessment: Constructing textual value within a "new politics of inquiry." *Assessing Writing, 4*(2), 133–167.

Broad, B. (2000). Pulling your hair out: Crises of standardization in communal writing assessment. *Research in the Teaching of English, 35*(2), 213–260.

Broad, B. (2003). *What we really value: Beyond rubrics in teaching and assessing writing.* Utah State University Press.

Cherry, R. D. & Witte, S. P. (1998). Direct assessments of writing: Substance and romance. *Assessing Writing, 5*(1), 71–87.

Cronbach, L. (1988). Five perspectives on validity argument. In H. Wainer (Ed.), *Test Validity* (pp. 3–17). Erlbaum.

Diederich, P. B., French, J. W. & Carlton, S. T. (1961). *Factors in the judgment of writing quality.* Educational Testing Service.

Elbow, P. (1991). Foreword. In P. Belanoff & M. Dickson (Eds.), *Portfolios: Process and product* (pp. ix-xxi). Boynton/Cook.

Faigley, L., Cherry, R. D., Jolliffe, D. A., Skinner, A. M. (1985). *Assessing writers' knowledge and processes of composing.* Ablex.

Gere, A. R. (1980). Written composition: Toward a theory of evaluation. *College English, 42(1),* 44–58.

Guba, E. G. & Lincoln, Y. S. (1989). *Fourth generation evaluation.* Sage.

Guba, E. G. & Lincoln, Y. S. (2000). Paradigmatic controversies, contradictions, and emerging confluences. In N. Denzin & Y. S. Lincoln (Eds.), *Handbook of qualitative research*, 2nd ed. (pp.133–155). Sage.

Haswell, R. H. (2001). *Beyond outcomes: Assessment and instruction within a university writing program.* Ablex.

Huot, B. (1990). Reliability, validity, and holistic scoring: What we know and what we need to know. *College Composition and Communication, 41*(2), 201–213.

Huot, B. (1996). Toward a new theory of writing assessment. *College Composition and Communication, 47*(4), 549–566.

Huot, B. (2002). *(Re)Articulating writing assessment for teaching and learning.* Utah State University Press.

Kafatos, M. & Nadeau, R. (1990). *The conscious universe: Part and whole in modern physical theory.* Springer.

Moss, P. A. (1992). Shifting conceptions of validity in educational measurement: implications for performance assessment. *Review of Educational Research, 62*(3), 229–258.

Purves, A. C. (1995). Apologia not accepted. *College Composition and Communication, 46*(1), 549–550.

Smith, W. L. (1993). Assessing the reliability and adequacy of using holistic scoring of essays as a college composition placement technique. In M. M. Williamson & B. A. Huot (Eds.), *Validating holistic scoring for writing assessment* (pp. 142–205). Hampton Press.

White, E. M. (1994). *Teaching and assessing writing* (2nd edition). Jossey Bass.

White, E. M. (1995). An apologia for the timed impromptu essay test. *College Composition and Communication, 46*(1), 30–45.

White, E. M. (1996). Power and agenda setting in writing assessment. In E. M. White, W. D. Lutz & S. Kamusikiri (Eds.), *Assessment of writing: Politics, policies, practices* Modern Language Association.

Williamson, M. M. (1993). An introduction to holistic scoring: The social, theoretical, and historical context for writing assessment. In M. M. Williamson & B. A. Huot (Eds.), *Validating holistic scoring for writing assessment* (pp. 1–43). Hampton Press.

Williamson, M. (1994). The worship of efficiency: Untangling theoretical and practical considerations in writing assessment. *Assessing Writing, 1*(2), 147–173.

Wolf, D., Bixby, J., Glenn, J. & Gardner, H. (1991). To use their minds well: Investigating new forms of student assessment. *Review of Research in Education*, 17, 31–74.

Yancey, K. B. (1992). Portfolios in the writing classroom: A final reflection. In K. B. Yancey (Ed.), *Portfolios in the writing classroom: An introduction* (pp. 102–116). National Council of Teachers of English.

Yancey, K. B. (2004). Postmodernism, palimpsest, and portfolios: Theoretical Issues in the representation of student work. *College Composition and Communication, 55*(4), 738–761.

# CHAPTER 13.
# ARTICULATING SOPHISTIC RHETORIC AS A VALIDITY HEURISTIC FOR WRITING ASSESSMENT

**Asao B. Inoue**
California State University, Fresno

*This essay develops a validity inquiry heuristic from several Elder Sophists' positions on the* nomos–physis *controversy of the fifth and fourth century B.C.E. in Greece. The* nomos–physis *debate concerned the nature and existence of knowledge and virtue, and maps well to current discussion of validity inquiry in writing assessment. Beyond rearticulating validity as a reflexive, agency-constructing, rhetorical act, this article attempts to bridge disciplines by articulating validity in terms of rhetorical theory, and understanding ancient sophistic rhetorical positions as validity theory.*

What kind of theoretical framework best supports a rhetorical relationship between teaching and writing assessment? For several years now, there have been calls for writing assessment and composition theory (particularly pedagogical theories) to be articulated together (Huot, 2002), for writing assessment to incorporate "language-based theories" (Williamson, 1993), and for test validation to provide "validity arguments," that is, to be understood as more rhetorical (Cronbach, 1988; see also Kane, 1992; Shepard, 1993). These calls stem from a growing recognition that our ways of talking about and teaching language and our theories and methods of writing assessment should be theoretically closer to one another, or at least in conversation. A common theoretical language can build disciplinary bridges in composition and rhetorical theory (generally speaking) and writing assessment theory, as Williamson (1993) and Huot (2002) have suggested. This article attempts to do this multidisciplinary work by articulating contemporary assessment theory, especially validity, as a sophistic rhetorical practice.

The practice of assessment, particularly the reporting of test results and test validation, has long been understood as a rhetorical endeavor. In fact, Cleo

DOI: https://doi.org/10.37514/PER-B.2024.2326.2.13

Cherryholmes explained that Cronbach and Meehl's original work on construct validity begins to argue construct validation as not just an interpretation of test results and its supporting nomological network (Cronbach & Meehl, 1955, p. 300) but as "explicitly discursive" (Cherryholmes, 1988, p. 102). By 1971, Cronbach promoted validation as an investigation that becomes rhetorical "in the sense of making persuasive arguments" (Cherryholmes, 1988, p. 103). And eventually, Cronbach argued an explicit rhetorical notion of construct validity, as well as one that is empirical and logical (Cherryholmes, 1988, p. 107; Cronbach, 1988, 1989). In his comprehensive discussion of the subject, Samuel Messick's (1989) famous explication of validity focused on "integrated evaluative judgment," "inductive summary," and the interpretation and use of "inferences" and "actions" from test results (p. 13).[1] In short, Messick revealed validity as a rhetorical endeavor. Finally, Brian Huot (2002) draws on Cronbach (1988), Moss (1992), and Lorrie Shepard (1993) to explain validity as an argumentative activity:

> Not only does validity as argument pose more of an interest to those with a strong sense of rhetoric, it also give[s] them a rhetorical heuristic for learning to construct validity arguments that contain a strong consideration of alternate views as well as an understanding of how to create arguments that are compelling to various audiences. (p. 56)

According to Huot, validity arguments can be "familiar, understandable and valuable" to those in English departments who are "isolated from . . . educational measurement" (p. 56). Conceptualizing validity as explicitly a rhetorical activity brings those doing writing assessment and educational measurement to the same table of theory. Additionally, sophistic rhetorical theory offers a political sensitivity and philosophy of language that accounts for social contexts and cultural influences on individual readers/judges, allowing validity research to consider individual dispositions to judge in certain ways as consubstantial to larger cultural and historical milieus, creating a complex relationship that can be considered in our validity arguments. In this project, a neosophistic orientation is offered to provide teachers, writing program administrators, assessment specialists and validity researchers a framework to address the formidable issues they face.[2] The Sophists' understanding of how rhetoric, culture, and agents

---

1   Samuel Messick's (1989) definition is important to my discussion and is assumed throughout. He stated it as: "Validity is an integrated evaluative judgment of the degree to which empirical evidence and theoretical rationales support the adequacy and appropriateness of inferences and actions based on test scores or other modes of assessment" (p. 13).

2   Invoking Edward Schiappa's (1991, 2003) distinction between research on the Sophists that is either "historical reconstruction" or "contemporary appropriation," Bruce McComis-

function to produce and validate decisions through *agon* explicitly accounts for the ways power and privilege are distributed; such understanding offers insights for validity theory and assessment at all levels. In the following discussion, I first give a brief account of ancient Hellenic Greek society and its culture of *agon* (i.e., contest or struggle that results in a winner). This section explains the historical origins and purposes of sophistic rhetoric that's important to understanding the social and cultural grounds of the *nomos–physis* debate. Second, I discuss primarily three sophistic positions on *nomos–physis* in order to produce a validity heuristic that offers reflexive inquiry that agrees with much existing validity theory. This heuristic offers three important areas of inquiry that focus on concerns about methods and fairness, well-being of stakeholders, and participation and agreement. Third, I conclude by suggesting how the *nomos–physis* validity heuristic reinforces sophistic notions of agency through reflexivity in ways more comprehensive than postmodern accounts. I end my discussion by explicating Protagoras' human-measure doctrine in order to connect individual ways of judging to the validity inquiry that the *nomos–physis* validity heuristic provides. This last aspect of validity highlights the importance of any inquiry's need to examine carefully hegemonic power arrangements and socialized tastes that develop from writing assessments.

## HELLENIC SOCIETY AND *AGON*

Ancient Hellenic societies of the fifth and fourth centuries might be best characterized as burgeoning cultures of mandatory civic participation. Civic decisions were debated openly, thus contentious debates were explicitly about making decisions that were acceptably valid. Shortly after the overthrow of the tyranny of Sicily in 446 B.C.E., all citizens were expected to participate in civic decisions, represent themselves in the law courts when necessary, and serve in a variety of public capacities (e.g., serving in the Assembly, acting as a juror, or providing military support, etc.; Bizzell & Herzberg, 2001, p. 21; Jarratt 1991, p. xv; Kennedy, 1994, pp. 3, 15). This Athenian democratic movement was aided by the Periclean constitutional reforms in Athens around 462–461 B.C.E. (Bizzell & Herzberg, 2001, pp. 20–21; Kerferd, 1981, p. 16; Plutarch, Cimon 15.2; Thucydides II.37.1), and these factors "created the need for a kind of

---

key's (2002) definition of "neosophistic appropriation" seems to offer the best explanation for my project (pp. 7–11; 55–56). McComiskey explained that neosophistic appropriation culls "sophistic doctrines and historical interpretations . . . for theories and methods that contribute solutions to problems in contemporary rhetoric" (p. 55). These ancient theories and doctrines then "travel" to modern contexts, and "are remolded in ways that the exigencies of the original historical contexts might not have suggested or even allowed" (p. 56).

secondary education designed to prepare young men for public life in the polis" (Jarratt, 1991, p. xv).³ Those who first filled this need for training youth for civic service were the Sophists, traveling teachers of rhetoric, Corax and Tisias (c. 467 B.C.E.) being the first. A Sophist would travel from town to town, gathering and teaching small groups of young men the art of rhetoric, or the "art of politics" for a fee (Plato, Protagoras 319a; Marrou, 1956, p. 50). Some Sophists, in fact, are said to have written the laws (*nomos*).⁴ However, teaching rhetoric was considered by some to be ethically questionable since it suggested one could teach, arête (virtue), which was often assumed to be natural, innate, and reserved for a few elite individuals, as Plato argues in his dialogues (see Gorgias and Protagoras).⁵ From this contention around the art of rhetoric,⁶ we get the *nomos–physis* controversy.

The key to making decisions in Hellenic civic rhetoric was *agon* (i.e., contest, struggle).⁷ For many Hellenes, *agon* determined one's virtue (arête) and knowledge/truth (which for Plato was episteme, or a singular Truth linked to *physis* or one's nature). Competition was the primary method for determining right

---

3   The term polis refers to the Greek city-state, and maybe more importantly to the citizens that make—through their bodies and rhetoric—that city-state.

4   G. B. Kerferd (1981, p. 18), Susan Jarratt (1991, p. 98) and Edward Schiappa (2003, pp. 13, 52, 179) argued that many Sophists, like Protagoras and Gorgias, were instrumental in developing and writing the initial laws and codes of various Hellenic city-states.

5   The arguments against the Sophists that Plato makes through Socrates in his dialogues are more complicated and nuanced than this. One can find philosophical/ethical, practical, xenophobic, and elitist/aristocratic-based arguments made by Plato. George Kennedy (1994) offered a brief account of Plato's Phaedrus and Gorgias (pp. 35–43), and Gregory Vlastos (1956) gave a detailed accounting of Protagoras in the Prentice-Hall edition of the dialogue. G.B. Kerferd (1981) also gave an account of Plato's hostility toward the Sophists in chapter 2 of his book. I am mindful of the controversy around the use of the Greek term rhetoric (rhêtorikê) as a descriptor of what the Sophists said they taught. Edward Schiappa (2003) said the term does not even appear in the literature of the fifth century, and only rarely is it present in that of the fourth century (p. 42). He argued a more appropriate term might be logos (word, argument, logic) (pp. 54–55, 58). I retain "rhetoric" in this discussion for convenience.

6   I am mindful of the controversy around the use of the Greek term rhetoric (rhêtorikê) as a descriptor of what the Sophists said they taught. Edward Schiappa (2003) said the term does not even appear in the literature of the fifth century, and only rarely is it present in that of the fourth century (p. 42). He argued a more appropriate term might be logos (word, argument, logic) (pp. 54–55, 58). I retain "rhetoric" in this discussion for convenience.

7   The Oxford English Dictionary defines *agon* as "a public celebration of games, a contest for the prize at those games" and "a verbal contest or dispute between two characters in a Greek play." Liddell and Scott's Greek lexicon offer several definitions of the term: "gathering, assembly," particularly to see the Greek games; an "assembly of the Greeks at the national games"; a "contest for a prize at the games"; "generally, struggle," as in a "battle" or an "action at law, trial"; a "speech delivered in court or before an assembly or a ruler"; the "main argument of a speech"; "mental struggle, anxiety"; and "divinity of the contest."

and wrong, good and bad, just and unjust. Prior to Hellenic democratic times, the earlier aristocratic culture was one dominated by individual virtue, military training, and training in athletic contest (e.g., boxing, wrestling, long jump, javelin and disc throwing, running, etc.). In fact, sport and "physical training occupied the place of honour" in education and culture (Marrou, 1956, p. 40). Hellenic society was "based on a system of contests that centered on fame, competitive achievement, and envy . . . [there was] a conviction that fame must be earned in a contest, not inherited" (Petrochilos, 2002, p. 605). This cultural heritage constructed virtue as a material sign, like physical beauty, muscularity, and athletic prowess, attained and proven through *agon*, all of which is illustrated in the conception of the "perfect and just" man (kalos kagathos) that George Petrochilos (2000) discusses.[8] Thus, Hellenic agonistic logic followed a predicable pattern: Civic decisions are validated by contest because contest reveals the strongest and best people, arguments, and decisions. As the mechanism for making Hellenic decisions, *agon* produced empirical evidence, such as the javelin thrown farther or the first man across the finish line, as signs of virtue that then tacitly signify an individual's merit, worth, or status.

Hellenic society reveals a very contemporary writing assessment issue. If *agon* creates merit, worth, and virtue in our society, then as Kurt Spellmeyer (1996) argued in a different way, (1996), assessment as *agon* is a political struggle for power that defines culture, literacy, the "haves," and the "have-nots." *Agon* is also important to the validation of writing assessment decisions, and students' virtue and social opportunity are at stake in its success. Putting aside a discussion of assessment as an *agon* among students, validity inquiry and research often require *agon* in order to test assessments and their results. Yet our theoretical frameworks, like assessment rubrics and assumptions implicit in norming procedures, which are often taken for granted, construct what is evidence in student writing. Viable alternative interpretations and evidence have difficulty competing with dominant frameworks that make up our methods, what constitutes evidence, fairness, and participation in assessments. Hellenic society's use of *agon* shows us that validity inquiry is about more than establishing the degree to which theoretical frameworks and empirical evidence appropriately and adequately determine results and decisions. It is about investigating the social consequences of our assessments and the *agon* that produces those consequences for their fairness and equity. If our inquiries don't directly address this issue, as Pamela Moss

---

8   David Rosenbloom's (2004) discussion of Ponêroi and Chrêstoi, two economic and social classes seen as opposites, also suggest that those born in certain classes and trades would not have the opportunity to be judged as kalos kagathos; however, arête (virtue) is still understood in these two classes as manifested through Conspicuous material signs one's profession and dress, which the *agon* of life, markets, and history create.

(1998) asks us to by questioning our "taken-for-granted theories and practices," then validation may simply reinforce inequalities and social imbalances that our assessments often create. The sophists' positions on *nomos–physis* articulate a validity heuristic that addresses the above issues in validation. If reformulated as a three-part heuristic, the various sophistic positions on *nomos–physis* investigates the *agon* of the inquiry itself. It examines the construction of fairness in an assessment, the use of power for various stakeholders' interests and well-being, and the participation of stakeholders and their agreement on decisions.

## *NOMOS–PHYSIS* AS A HEURISTIC FOR VALIDITY

The ongoing philosophical and political debate of *nomos–physis* stems from accusations that the Sophists were corrupting the young men they taught by teaching them how to argue for the wrong things, or that the gods didn't exist.[9] In one sense, they were accused of teaching ways to validate untruths and unjust decisions, and this criticism assumed the primacy of *physis* in the binary. G. B. Kerferd (1981) defined *physis* as "nature," or "characteristics appropriate to a thing as such, that it possesses in its own right, or of its own accord" (p. 111). James Herrick (2001) defined *physis* as, "[t]he law or rule of nature under which the strong dominate the weak," and as Gutherie (1971) pointed out, is taken from Plato's Callicles in Gorgias (1990) and in his Laws ( 1956b). For our discussion, the concept of *physis* is a position that promotes the customs, conventions, and values of a community as universal and natural by their dominance or hegemonic use in the culture.

Plato clearly embraced the concept of *physis*. His description of the soul in Phaedrus is an apt illustration of where he stood on *nomos–physis*. Plato's Socrates describes physical beauty as the easiest to see of the soul's past perfection because sight is the "clearest of our senses" (p. 250c-d). He concludes that the image of beauty alone can be recognized as such (p. 250d). As illustrated in the soul's perfection, Platonic Truth is static, eternal, and empirical. For even after the soul has fallen from its perfect state in heaven to earth, losing its immediate knowledge of wisdom and Truth, Socrates says that it can still glimpse wisdom empirically from the "godlike face or form which is a good image of beauty." When this happens, the beholder sweats and produces "unwonted heat . . . beauty enters him through the eyes, [and] he is warmed." The dormant feathers that once allowed his soul to soar are softened and begin to grow back

---

9   In Plato's Apology, Socrates (Plato's teacher) attempts to defend himself against the accusations (mainly by Meletus, Anytus, and Lycon) of being a "villainous misleader of youth" and for "teaching things up in the clouds and under the earth, and having no gods, and making the worse appear the better cause," all of which were accusations of being a sophist.

(p. 251a-b). For Plato and his Socrates, the truth of *physis* is revealed empirically (yet lies dormant within the soul), and is described not-so-ironically as a product of internal *agon* in labor, sweat, and heat. Thus, some will be able to recognize Truth, others won't, which justifies unequal social arrangements—some are more capable of making civic decisions because of their inherent virtue. So the validity of any decision about reality or Truth, like the dialogue itself, can be tested in an agonistic dialectic that deduces the significance of empirical signs from static truths (theoretical frameworks) agreed upon by all. The true lover of wisdom will recognize the Truth from the *agon*. *Physis*, for Plato, always makes the cream rise to the top, and this fact is empirical.

For Plato, there is a perfect student paper. There exists a static set of writing constructs usable for deducing both truth and the distance from it. Platonic philosophy, particularly the assumption of an episteme (a singular Truth), is part of a tradition that later would yield logical positivism, itself a vision that "argued that the goal of science was to speak correctly about the world" (Cherryholmes, 1988, p. 100; Shapiro, 1981).[10] If everyone works from the same universal ideals, then validating decisions Platonically is simply a matter of recognizing or acknowledging Truth when it shows itself. Validating writing placement procedures, like validating grades on essays, is also a matter of recognizing clearly how close decisions come to ideal or correct decisions. Validity inquiry that appeals strictly to *physis* typically does not question the dominance of particular values, theoretical frameworks used to make inferences and decisions, or methods for data collection. *Physis* assumes those who achieve in the system have inherent "merit," so the frameworks used, methods established, and evidence collected are "correct." As a validity concept, *physis* calls attention to how theoretical frameworks (regardless of how they are defined), as Messick's validity definition points out, are necessary to read empirical signs and make inferences. Additionally, Plato's position on *physis* implies for a postmodern audience that part of validity inquiry is understanding the nature of what we investigate. In other words, the writing performance by a student is one thing; the significance or meaning of that performance as judgments made by individuals is another. What's between are competing theoretical frameworks.

Many of the sophists, on the other hand, often argued from a position of *nomos*, or socially derived customs, conventions, or rules agreed upon by the

---

10  Plato's need for episteme (a singular Truth) stems from two places: first, his own philosophical idealism that locates episteme outside of human affairs and the world in a static realm ready to be rediscovered by the lover of wisdom, which is exemplified in his theory of the divided line, the cave allegory (Republic Books 6 and 7), and his description of the soul as a charioteer and two horses (Phaedrus, pp. 246a-249c); and second, his belief in the power of dialectic (roughly speaking, philosophy or philosophical inquiry) over rhetoric for the discovery of episteme.

citizenry (Herrick, 2001, p. 38, 279). In the strictest sense, an understanding of *nomos* as agreed upon convention or custom constructs values not as inherent, static, or universal, but as relative to context, people, and situations. In effect, cultural and social customs evolve through agreement and decisions made in communities, which are its laws and conventions, or *nomoi*. *Nomos*, then, is "always prescriptive and normative and never merely descriptive," providing direction "affecting the behaviour and activities of persons and things" (Kerferd, 1981, p. 112). *Nomos* is not the Truth or right course of action, like *physis*. *Nomos* is local and political, and is about agreement on what is the fairest and best course of action. There are no universals by which to compare results. Truth, per se, is not what's at stake, only actions and decisions that a community accepts, only exigency and opportunity. So, as many validity researchers tell us today (Cronbach, 1988; Huot, 2002; Moss, 1998; Shepard, 1993), revealing various positions and arguments in the validation of decisions is critical. These "validity arguments" (Cronbach, 1988) might be loosely understood as *nomoi* that map out the available judgments and decisions that a community regards at a given historical moment in their assessments.[11] Not all Sophists, however, held the same position concerning how *nomos* and *physis* could be applied to rhetoric. Each position on *nomos-physis* articulates a set of concerns in validity inquiry.

## HIPPIAS AND ANTIPHON: CONCERNS ABOUT METHODS AND FAIRNESS

The Sophist Hippias of Elis held to a theory of "absolute *physis*," in which "[t]he law of nature [*physis*] . . . is . . . something more objective, universal and morally binding than *nomos*" (Untersteiner, 1954, p. 281). Hippias would have decisions validated through controlled *agon*. The Hippias of Plato's Protagoras implores Protagoras and Socrates not to "quarrel," but instead "to come to terms arranged, as it were, under our arbitration" and "to choose . . . [a] supervisor . . . who will keep watch for you over the due measure of either's speeches" (pp. 337c-338b).[12] Hippias wishes to level the field of contest, so that all rhetoric can be fairly judged and the result of the *agon* will be *physis*. The morally superior natural law will conspicuously win, and there will be empirical evidence to back

---

11   I use "historical moment" to suggest that kairos (the "right moment") indeed is a part of this debate, affecting the outcome of any *agon*, and generally is a component of sophistic rhetoric, as Gorgias the Sophist illustrates in his Encomium of Helen (cf. DK 82B 11.11), and as Bruce McComiskey (2002) explained in chapter 1 of his discussion of Gorgias. However, because of my scope in this article, I cannot engage deeply with kairos or Gorgias.

12   "DK" refers to the Diels-Kranz translations and numbering system for various fragments of the ancient Greek texts, which are commonly used and found in Sprague (2001) and Freeman (1966).

up convention and laws. In this sense, *physis* validates *nomos* through controlled *agon*. This assumption of *physis* as an origin for what's right, and articulated in communities, is similar to Antiphon's position, only his was one of "enlightened self-interest" (Gutherie, 1971, p. 107), and it didn't assume *physis* to be present in communities, nor that communities establish valid *nomoi*. You should obey laws when there are witnesses, otherwise do what benefits you most. In On Truth, Antiphon states: "[T]he demands of the laws are artificial, but the demands of nature are necessary . . . Laws lay down what the eyes may see and not see, what the ears may hear and not hear . . . When justice is brought in to assist in punishment it is no more on the side of the sufferer than of the doer" (DK 87B 90 fr. A). Cynically echoing Democritus,[13] Antiphon attacks social conventions, deciding for might as right, but acknowledges that local *nomos* does not always agree with *physis*. The natural strength of one's arguments and one's ability to get away with selfish (but enlightened) acts validate decisions through *agon*.

Hippias' and Antiphon's positions on *nomos-physis* allow us to see that part of inquiring into validity is questioning and articulating the methods used to gather evidence and make ethical decisions in assessment. I'll call this attention to methods and ethics fairness because at the heart of Hippias and Antiphon's positions are decisions meant to be fair for all. Consequently, an important aspect of both fairness and "due measuring" by judges is the test itself, which in Hippias' case is the rhetorical *agon* in Plato's dialogue. But as Antiphon shows (if we read him positively), sometimes we know the best decision to make but our methods (e.g., the test as a method for evidence gathering and the methods of judging that evidence) may prohibit an ethical decision or outcome, so there may be occasions where arguments can be made to circumvent the test to keep a decision fair. In this way, "fairness" does not equate to "consistency." Instead, fairness is an investigation of the methods used and the social arrangements and decisions those methods produce (i.e., effects or outcomes). Seen in this way, fairness is conceived in a more complex and contextual way than Edward White's (1995) use of the term to define "reliability" (p. 22).[14] We might rely on the first two of Guba and Lincoln's (1989), "authenticity criteria" for evaluation, which they term "fairness" and "ontological authenticity." For them fairness

---

13  Democritus' famous fragment states: "Sweet exists by convention, bitter by convention, colour by convention; atoms and void (alone) exist in reality. . . . We know nothing accurately in reality, but (only) as it changes according to the bodily condition, and the constitution of those things that flow upon (the body) and impinge upon it" (DK 68B 9).

14  I agree with Liz Hamp-Lyons and William Condon's (2000) argument that reliability can not be equated to fairness because an assessment might create consistent judgments "across time and among readers," but may still produce unfair results. One example they offer is a program that teaches "writing as a process but testing only the writer's ability to draft quickly" (p. 13).

is a reflexive method (pp. 245–246), and a high level of fairness is achieved when judges/readers "solicit," "honor," and compare various judgments/readings and their "underlying value structures," particularly ones that conflict (p. 246). Ontological authenticity is achieved through methods and techniques that allow judges/readers to evolve and improve their understanding of other competing judgments, which matures their own (p. 248). Just as Hippias pleads for proper methods of supervision of the *agon* in order to come to fair conclusions, Guba and Lincoln's criteria also focus on methods that allow competing readings to co-exist and even affect each other.

For example, let's examine a decision to pass a particular student's writing portfolio in a composition course. Some judges have read it as not demonstrating writing of passing quality, whereas others argue the portfolio embodies competency. Each decision might be a fair one if all readings, and their readers' "enlightened interests," are examined carefully as *nomoi* with particular value structures, each offering ethical rationales that need articulation. How and why is the evidence read differently? In what ways is each decision ethical or fair? What various external criteria are being considered in each reading that make it fair? Also, the various methods of the assessment are implicated in this sophistic inquiry: How well does the portfolio itself, as a method that a student must use to demonstrate writing proficiency, allow that student to demonstrate what various judges are looking for in student writing? How well does it allow the student to demonstrate the external criteria a judge uses in her reading? How does the assessment's method of decision making by readers account for the inevitably diverse set of external criteria that they applied to their readings of those portfolios?[15] In a concise way, this sophistic *nomos-physis* position highlights the concerns that Messick (1989) said are involved in content and criterion-related validities (pp. 16–17), but it does so by focusing on more tangible inquiries, those concerning methods for testing and judging, and the value structures that make various decisions fair.

Mostly, Hippias and Antiphon compel us to see larger concerns about methods and fairness. How do our assessment's various methods construct fairness? How do the rationales we use that form our readings of student writing and ethical decisions construct fairness? In short, Hippias and Antiphon call attention to the ways in which fairness is not inherent or outside of any system, but is a construction of it, built into it by methods of evidence gathering and judging. Fairness isn't inherent in any particular kind of assessment, like portfolio-based procedures or holistic readings, but is itself a design feature that needs articulation and supervision.

---

15   In effect, this is the focus of Bob Broad's (2003) inquiry.

## THRASYMACHUS: CONCERNS OF POWER AND THE WELL-BEING OF STAKEHOLDERS

The Sophist Thrasymachus provides a second validity concern for our heuristic. Thrasymachus has been described as an "amoral realist," who understood justice, moral standards, and conventions as depending on "equality of power: the strong do what they can and the weak submit," thus *nomos* embodies group or individual "interests" rather than some ideal "justice" (Gutherie, 1971, p. 85). Kerferd (1981) agrees and explained that Thrasymachus' *nomoi*, and their paternalistic creators, would look out for the interests of the weak (those being ruled) (p. 121). In Plato's Republic, Thrasymachus makes clear how *nomoi* are validated through rulers' power: "[I]n all states alike 'right' has the same meaning, namely what is for the interest of the party established in power, and that is the strongest . . . 'right' is the same everywhere: the interest of the stronger party" (Book I, p. 338). Thrasymachus' position perhaps works from an older notion of *nomos*. Susan Jarrett (1991) explained that *nomos* derived from an older term, nomós, meaning "pasture." In Pindar it referred to "habitation," then later it shifted to signify "habitual practice, usage, or custom" (p. 41). What's important in this etymology is the term's close association to rhetoric as "a process of articulating codes, consciously designed by groups of people," and connected to the ways ancient communities managed property, made judgments in law courts, and decided upon civic issues (Jarrett, 1991, p. 42). In effect, *nomos* was the production of power, which ratified future decisions and solidified particular groups' dominance, particularly through land ownership. Thrasymachus' position on *nomos* reveals that those in positions of power in an assessment (e.g., test designers and policymakers) also typically determine the interests for assessing and of the assessed, and that the assessment itself is in fact a way for a dominate group to solidify its dominance and interests over others. These interests determine not just how a portfolio is read, but what writing constructs, or "explanatory concepts" (Messick, 1989, p. 16), are used as qualities a test measures and/or predicts as future achievement.

More specifically, Thrasymachus' position suggests several questions: How and why are particular interests, and the agents and groups associated with them, being used to conduct assessment and validation? What rationales construct decisionmakers' power, and in turn, determine what's "right" in an assessment, who judges student writing, who makes decisions, and who determines methods? How is the assessment and its results working toward the interests of those being assessed, namely students (and secondarily programs and faculty), and not simply reinforcing the interests of those with power (or those who control the "land" of assessment)? Are the interests and needs of students being represented by students, or are these interests merely represented for them? How is each stakeholder allowed an inquiry in validation processes? I'm not suggesting that power arrangements will be equal or can be in writing evaluation in and outside the classroom, or that all groups' interests are in conflict all the time. What I am suggesting is that assessment should not be based on the altruism of elite decision makers. Stakeholder silence, like the silence of our students, should not be assumed as acquiescence. Consideration of the well-being of all stakeholders should be a factor in the invention, arrangement, and style of any writing assessment.

Guba and Lincoln's (1989) fairness criteria addresses some of the concerns Thrasymachus' position reveals, but their "tactical" and "educative" authenticity criteria provides a fuller articulation of the issues of stakeholder interests and power. Guba and Lincoln's discussion examines how the various testimonies of stakeholders are "appreciated" and "negotiated" (pp. 248–249), making the evaluation process "educative" for participants. Their participation should also empower all participants to act, or to make the decisions that the assessment might produce (p. 250). This means that validity inquiry is about making arguments for the ways in which power is used and by whom, and how the well-being of stakeholders is addressed through this power. These arguments might also take into account how power in the assessment (re)produces particular interests while ignoring others. Validating a classroom's evaluation processes, for example, may involve a classroom inquiring into the interests represented in an evaluation rubric, whom the rubric serves, and what reasons can be given for their use. Furthermore, the class might look at the results of the decisions made from the rubric. Did half the class fail the assignment? What feedback did the assessment offer students and how did they understand that feedback? What grade distribution did it produce, and how do students understand its meaning and significance for their learning? For Thrasymachus, then, validation might be an inquiry into stakeholder interests and needs, the power created and used, and the assessment's consequences for stakeholder well-being.

Richard Haswell (1998a) argued for a similar kind of validation inquiry in his discussion of the need for "multiple inquiry in the validation of writing tests." He asked: If the writing test "is social, then what (fallible) humans run it for what (debatable) ends and (more or less) how well, and how do the (vulnerable) people who are labeled by it feel (they think) about the process?" (p. 92). His multiple inquiry identifies several stakeholder groups that form Washington State University's efforts at validating their writing placement program, such as students, teachers of writing courses, teachers of other courses, central administrators, higher administration, among others. Although Haswell discussed each in terms of their different interests and uses of collected data, he does not address how power is unevenly distributed, which affects the plausibility of any possible validity arguments a group might make, or the usefulness of the data. For instance, his discussion of central administrators, focuses on delivering data for their use and possible responses, which could gesture to student interests and well-being but these validity concerns are not articulated at all. Haswell discussed how the data can be used to help departments reflect on how they perform compared to other departments (p. 103), and what courses seem to offer students profitable writing practice within a department (p. 104), but he does not say how multiple inquiry can be used to investigate how the interests of those making decisions (and the power those decisions have) affect the well-being of students. How is power and the interests it (re)produces checked in the system? How is the assessment not simply an enactment of "might is right"?

Additionally, each stakeholder group's relative power in the institution affects how each might use, understand, and comment on data collected, offer rival hypotheses for judgments, or make validity arguments. Each group's position in the institution often dictates what they can say, or how influential their voices will be. A Board of Regents will have stronger voices, and more power to act and make related decisions, than teachers of writing courses. And students may not be listened to carefully when they argue that their assessments are "unfair" or "too strict" or "inconsistent," especially when writing teachers argue contrary positions. Additionally, Haswell's chairs don't seem to be a part of any data collection or substantive inquiry; instead, he speaks of them as using the data collected for departmental purposes, or understanding it as justifications for assessment results. Thrasymachus' position suggests that chairs and other stakeholders might be involved in decisions about methods and data collection since these things dictate what kinds of information are understood as data for future analysis and validation.[16] As Haswell (1998a) pointed out, what higher administration might find most useful in validating a test, like costs and "distinctive outcomes" (p. 104), may seem completely irrelevant to a teacher of writing or a student, thus not data worth collecting. While acknowledging that multiple-method inquiry allows for program improvement through various stakeholders' input, Pamela Moss (1998) in her response to Haswell identified a similar concern about stakeholder interest and power in Haswell's writing program example: "it appears that validity evidence was not used to illuminate biases of those responsible for the writing program,

---

16   This last comment is somewhat unfair to Haswell because he did gesture toward this, and having worked within the assessment program he speaks about, I acknowledge that stakeholder participation is encouraged and usually welcomed.

but rather to persuade the stakeholders that they should see things differently" (p. 118). Moss used this analysis to make her point about "challenging biases" of an assessment (p. 118), or questioning "the beliefs and practices of researchers," which she later identified as "epistemic reflexivity," taken from Bourdieu (p. 120). Challenging the biases of various stakeholders amounts to analyzing the use of power as a way to construct self-conscious data and evidence, a lesson Thrasymachus offers as well. In short, the data worth collecting and analyzing are products of power, associated with those who wield it, and contribute to stakeholder well-being.

## PROTAGORAS AND PRODICUS: CONCERNS OF PARTICIPATION AND AGREEMENT

Perhaps the strongest position for *nomos* is that of Protagoras. Protagoras saw *nomos* as a social force that improved *physis*. Kerferd (1981) explained that the myth attributed to him in Plato's Protagoras offers "a fundamental defense of *nomos* in relation to *physis*, in that *nomos* is a necessary condition for the maintenance of human societies" (p. 126).[17] There are no "ultimate moral standards" for Protagoras, instead, similar to Antiphon's position, *nomoi* "teach . . . citizens the limits within which they may move" in their society (Gutherie, 1971, p. 68). Protagoras' creation myth illustrates the evolutionary aspect of humanity, accomplished by *nomoi* that protect humans, first from the elements and starvation, next from the wild beasts who would kill them, and finally from each other (war and civil discord) (Plato, Protagoras, pp. 320c-323a). Yet it takes Zeus to intervene, providing humanity with "reverence and justice" as "ordering principles of cities and the bonds of friendship and conciliation." So while humanity develops *nomoi* as prescriptions for security and well-being, each person is guided by his own divinely bestowed *physis*, but this *physis* does not designate static virtue or a "true" course of action, instead it indirectly regulates individual agency that produces fair decisions through society's *agon*. Protagoras provided the thread that sews together all three validity concerns. Just as Guba and Lincoln's (1989) authenticity criteria promote full stakeholder involvement (pp. 245–250), Protagoras' democratic participation by all stakeholders is the key to the validity of civic decisions.[18] In fact, validity,

---

17  Some have argued that the myth attributed to Protagoras in Plato's Protagoras (pp. 320c-323a) may not be authentically a position of the Sophist; however, I find Untersteiner's (1954, endnote 24, pp. 72–73) and Schiappa's (2003, pp. 146–147) arguments for its authenticity compelling.

18  Protagoras' use of sophistic antilogic, or the use of contrary arguments (logos) that form the rhetoric of debate and finally of civic decisions, which is often discussed as a rhetorical method

generally speaking, requires agreement to function. Researchers agree to the meaningfulness of the correlation that any validity inquiry provides, yet Protagoras tells us that part of our need for agreement is that each stakeholder has something worthwhile to contribute, some kind of virtue to be tapped. So writing assessment needs more than stakeholder agreement. Writing assessment requires participation.

Although Protagoras' teachings offer much more for validity researchers, here it is enough to say that he promotes a process of civic decision making as a rhetorical *agon* that, similar to Guba and Lincoln's methods, asks for competing arguments (logoi), which embody competing *nomoi* and the interests of well-being for each stakeholder involved. Because all have a share in virtue, which Protagoras traces to Zeus' gift, a community's *agon* will produce valid decisions, not because *physis* dictates winners and what's right or true, but because agreement and participation allow choices and decisions to be accepted. Thus for Protagoras, the level of participation and agreement correlates to understanding validity. Validity, then, stems from stakeholder ability to participate in and accept decisions from participation.

Prodicus offers an even clearer rendition of this last concern in our *nomos-physis* heuristic. For him *nomos* perfected *physis*, which is exemplified in his fragment, "Heracles at the Crossroads" (DK 84B 2).[19] Untersteiner (1954) explained Prodicus' position: "*physis* acquires its value as a result of the use made of it, by the *nomos* which interprets it. . . . Virtue is therefore a *nomos* which interprets *physis*" (p. 217). In this way, sophistic rhetoric supports the emphasis on test use for considering validity issues. Virtue's speech to Heracles provides a clear illustration of this *nomos–physis* position:

The gods give no real benefits or honors to men without struggle and perseverance: to obtain the gods' favor you must serve them; to get abundant fruit from the earth one must cultivate it; to earn wealth from livestock one must learn to care for them; to prosper in war, to gain the power to succor friends and best one's enemies, one must study the techniques of warfare from its masters and exercise oneself in their proper employment—and finally, if you should wish to enjoy physical vigor, it is to the mind that the body must learn subjection, and discipline itself with hard work and sweat (DK 84B 2).

---

for "seeing both sides on every subject" (Gutherie, 1917, p. 24), is the essence of democratic participation (see Kerferd, 1981, pp. 61– 64).

19. This doctrine of nature (*physis*) developed or cultivated by nurture (*nomos*) appears to be common. It is also articulated in the Anonymous Iamblichi (DK 896), the Dissoi Logoi (DK 90 6), Demosthenes' speech XXV, Against Aristogeiton, and the Sophist Isocrates' *Against the Sophists*, in which he argued that valid civic decisions and *nomoi* are accomplished through the rhetoric of the orator with natural talent (*physis*), which would have been honed by training and experience (Isocrates, 1929, p. 294).

It is significant that Virtue speaks to Heracles because he is the personification of humanity's "opposing tendencies," as Untersteiner (1954) tells us (p. 217). These tendencies are articulated in *nomos–physis*, and Heracles' is the ultimate illustration of the binary. His kernel virtue (*physis*) is an in-born strength, athletic prowess, and power, which represents a "primitive state of conscience" (p. 217), but this raw strength will not be enough to allow him to succeed. His *physis* needs perfecting through *nomos*, hard work, *agon*, and civilized training. Virtue in this scene explains that he must cultivate and perfect his natural abilities to succeed in his life's labors and work. For Prodicus, like Protagoras, *nomoi* are conventions, like the ethics of "hard work and sweat," agreed on by communities to cultivate the natural virtue within each person. And assumed in this cultivation of *physis*—assumed in *nomos*—is not just *agon* but others who form the *agon*. One must compete against someone else (it is telling that Virtue ends her speech with examples of war, military training, and athletic contest). Thus, part of participation, and agreement in any contest is tension, conflict, struggle, difference, and disagreement, which are all important to Prodicus' sense of *nomos-physis* in fair civic decisions.

For our heuristic, Prodicus calls attention to the healthy conflict within agreement. Agreement is not synonymous with consensus. It is a stance reached through differing readings and judgments, through hard work and *agon*, through disagreement, which could be debate, negotiation, or war. Like Haswell's (1998a) multiple inquiry, validation might involve a process that allows for various stakeholders to voice opposing arguments for a student's placement in a writing course, thus disagreement is necessary to test the decisions made and their adequacy. Because all are assumed capable in some way, even students can be brought into these decisions since validation inquires into who can and should make decisions and how all stakeholders are a part of decision making. For the writing classroom, inquiring into participation and agreement might mean a teacher and her students investigate ways to allow for multiple readings and evaluations of writing to be considered in grades. A class might ask how "stake" can be given to students in the evaluations and grades of their writing. Reflective activities and group discussions that examine student writing and multiple evaluations of it can be conducted as inquiries of stakeholder biases, evaluative frameworks, and interests, as well as the processes themselves that produce evaluations of student writing. Importantly, in the classroom a teacher and his or her students together would construct consciously participation and agreement.

When unified, the *nomos–physis* validity heuristic achieves the "epistemic reflexivity" that Moss (1998) encouraged, which she called a "courageous act of opening the details of a program of research to critical public review" (p. 120).

Through its inquiries into "how" assessment is constructed and decisions are made, and by whom, the *nomos–physis* heuristic provides reflexivity for researchers, teachers, and students. And reflexivity is a defining feature of sophistic rhetoric and agency. Reflexivity can also explain how the *nomos–physis* heuristic investigates the (re)production of hegemony, accounts for individual judgment as more than just reflections of social dispositions, and articulates/theorizes individual agency as a constitutive part of any assessment decision.

## PROTAGORAS' HUMAN–MEASURE: A CONCLUSION ON AGENCY

Table 3.1 illustrates one way the positions on *nomos–physis* can be represented. It shows the three areas of concern that *nomos–physis* articulates as validity inquiry: methods and fairness, power and the well-being of stakeholders (particularly those with less power), and the ways participation and agreement are constructed. This heuristic, however, also extends postmodern positions on subjectivity that affect the construction of socialized judgment and decision–making in assessments. *Nomos–physis* renders personal and local dispositions to read and judge in certain ways as gestalts that are made from, and make, larger histories of *agon* that maintain or alter a community's intellectual property, sense of its culture, and privilege while also preserving a sense of individual agency by holding on to both ends of the *nomos–physis* binary.[20]

Lester Faigley's (1992) *Fragments of Rationality* provides a good case in point. Faigley looked at the evaluations of student essays submitted for the College Entrance Exam Board in 1929 and essays from William Coles and James Vopat's (1985) anthology of student writing, What Makes Writing Good. Faigley argued that teachers evaluate writing through their historically contextual and culturally defined tastes, and by implication, their distastes (pp. 119–130). In the 1980s, these tastes were governed by the essayistic use of "confession" as truth-telling, which "emerge," or come "out of," historical values shared broadly by academic culture (p. 111).[21] He concluded that teachers must consider the relations of power (using Foucault) inherent in their evaluation practices if they are going to create better assessments with "more equitable relations of power" (p. 131). Faigley's excellent account reminds us that who assesses determines what values and tastes power will embody and promote, and that those with power tend to

---

20  As the previous sophistic positions suggest, I use "gestalt" to imply agency in the individual, because the term suggests that there is more to one's disposition to judge than her training and socio-historical and contextual influences.

21  Faigley (1992) also explicated the Latin roots of "evaluation" (ex + valere) to illustrate how judgment of writing comes "out of" values (p. 113).

hold tastes that define and give them power. But as Faigley himself acknowledged in his conclusion (pp. 238–239), this postmodern account of judgment and tastes do not explain well individual agency on the part of teachers and validity researchers, nor ways to resist, or participate if an agent works from a marginal position.[22] Faigley's account does remind us not to obscure the ways in which culturally and historically defined tastes control value, student interests, and the production of subjectivity. The Sophists, on the other hand, tell us that not only must there be tastes governed by larger stable ideas, values, and patterns of behavior—or *nomoi* developed from *physis*—but those who control assessment control the construction of fairness, well-being, and agreement (i.e., control what we take for granted and what we investigate in/through our decisions). These "controls" influence tastes and power, but do not wholly govern individual judgments.

The Sophists' articulations of *nomos–physis* both acknowledge the socialized aspects of our tastes and decisions, and reinsert agency into the agent's act of judging by calling attention to how its formed and situated. Sophistic agency is not a modernist agency, not an "individual struggling against the constraints and conforming pressures of society" (Faigley, 1992, p. 230), nor the agency of "Liberalism" that is "motivated only by its [the self's] desires" (p. 231); instead, the Sophists offer an agency that is defined by reflexivity (through the "how" questions in the heuristic). Agency is constructed through individual articulations of fairness, of interests, tastes, and well-being, and through conscious participation and negotiation in decisions. This is not simply, as Faigley favored in his conclusion, a subjectivity that works from Lyotard's differend, or a rhetorical and material space in which parties in conflict disagree about "the relevant rule of justice" (Faigley, 1992, p. 233). Lyotard's subjectivity, according to Faigley, created an agency defined by "ethical decisions" that are "a matter of recognizing the responsibility of linking phrases" (p. 237). But agency still seems undefined and presumed in Lyotard's account: How is one's recognition of linking phrases achieved? What constitutes "ethical"? In writing assessment decisions, how exactly are hegemonic dispositions and readings interrogated? Since there are no universal values or "external discourse to validate choice" (p. 237), no *physis*, only multiple *nomoi*, Lyotard's differend makes agency a mysterious, inherent aspect of agent, but not something easily consciously constructed.

---

22   I realize that Faigley was not making claims about writing assessment researchers; however, I believe teachers and validity researches share fundamental issues concerning how judgments are made on student writing and their sources.

## Table 3.1. A *Nomos-Physis* Validity Heuristic

| Sophists | Characteristics | Key Investigations | Validity Concerns |
|---|---|---|---|
| Hippias and Antiphon | Absolute *physis*<br><br>By their natural right and abilities, the strongest will achieve<br><br>Assessment decisions can be supervised and empirically verified | How does the assessment's methods for gathering evidence construct fairness?<br><br>How are fair results ethically determined, supervised and articulated? | Methods and Fairness |
| Thrasymachus | Amoral realist; *physis* produces *nomos*<br><br>Altruistic power governs conventions and "rightness"<br><br>Assessment decisions are made by stakeholders in power based on the interests and needs of those the assessment serves (weaker stakeholders) | How does power work to validate decisions?<br><br>What are the interests and needs of students and other stakeholders involved and who articulates them?<br><br>How do our assessments serve our students, their needs, and well-being? | Power and the Well-being of Stakeholders |
| Protagoras and Prodicus | *Nomos* cultivates *physis*<br><br>All stakeholders have the ability and right to participate in assessment since they all share in the virtue of the community<br><br>Antilogical methods performed by all stakeholders | How is agreement constructed and by whom?<br><br>Who is affected by the results of the assessment decision and how are they involved in decisions?<br><br>How are various adjustments accounted for before a decision is made? | Participation and Agreement |

Sophistic agency, however, provides for ethics through reflexive discourse. By acknowledging the full binary, the Sophists' articulations of *nomos–physis* leave room for decisions that are un-evitable, counterhegemonic, ambiguous, indecisive, radical, inevitable, hegemonic, clear, and decisive. So unlike Lyotard and Faigley, the Sophists do not allow assessment researchers and teachers to use vague notions of "ethics" to govern decisions. Instead their positions on *nomos–physis* acknowledge that even ethics are constructed in practice, yet there may be some universal ideas, or larger patterns of truth, that govern *nomos* in particular contexts, such as the ideal of democratic participation, the need for equality in effects, and the necessity of honoring of all voices in debate.

At its most fundamental level, sophistic agency theorizes how individuals make decisions, and it is best located in Protagoras' Human-Measure doctrine.[23] As suggested in Protagoras' position on *nomos–physis*, his rhetoric generates *nomoi*, and is "the mechanism allowing for the functioning of social organizations," or "how group values evolve out of custom or habit as 'pragmatic solutions to temporal and historical needs'" (Jarratt, 1991, p. 10). These *nomoi* articulate and stem from various senses of fairness, justice, and well-being that citizens voice in democratic debate and decide upon. Agency, then, is understood as partly the *physis* that grants citizens their abilities to participate in decisions, partly the *agon* of society itself, and partly the reflective ability inherent in democratic participation and rhetoric.

Protagoras' human-measure fragment embodies all of these components in a theory of individual judgment.

Protagoras' human-measure fragment can be stated as follows: "Of everything and anything the measure [truly is] human(ity): of that which is, that it is the case; of that which is not, that it is not the case" (Schiappa, 2003, p. 121).[24] According to Protagoras, what is "measurable" is limited socially, locally, and discursively. The agent's measuring is understood as consubstantial to the *nomos* of his or her larger social context. Judgment is shaped through democratic *agon* (agreement from difference). In one sense, Protagoras' doctrine states that a teacher's reading of writing is a product of various readings voiced already (or those the teacher is aware of). These other readings, like Faigley's tastes, influence a teacher's reading practices. There is no clear line between how, for instance, a teacher's judgment of a student's essay is "honest" and "persuasive," and what that teacher's larger historical and academic context prescribes as "honesty" and "persuasiveness" in student writing. And yet, sophistic agents are not simply conduits for *nomoi* and social tastes, which could be concluded from Faigley's

---

23 This fragment has traditionally been known as the "man-measure" doctrine, but as Edward Schiappa (2003) pointed out in his discussion of it, the Greek term used by Protagoras (anthrô-pos) actually can refer to individual human beings or to humanity as a whole, which includes women. I favor Schiappa's use of "human measure" as the preferred nonsexist term (p. 131).

24 Herrick (2001) stated the fragment this way: "man is the measure of all things, of things that are not, that they are not; of things that are, that they are" (p. 42). He took this version from Plato's Theaetetus (pp. 151a-152a). Sextus gives this version of the doctrine: "of all things the measure is man, of things that are that they are, and of things that are not that they are not" (Diels, 1972, p.10).

and other postmodern accounts of power and socialized tastes. Human-measure, on the other hand, promotes a reflexive theory of judgment, and this reflexivity defines agency in assessment.

Cynthia Farrar (1989) helps make clearer how human-measure's notion of agency works. She said that human measure theorizes how an orator can articulate only "the way things are" for the polis through his own eyes. "Of the things that are f, he measures that they are f," Farrar explained (p. 49). This means that what an agent experiences is all the agent can know. Additionally, Farrar said that "measuring is not limited to perceiving an object or feature of the world but includes the rendering of judgments," so a teacher may read a student essay, but the teacher also renders judgments, or makes inferences. Together, sensing and judging create a teacher's measuring. Farrar (1989) continued, "man the measurer is both what we would call a 'sensing' and 'judging' being, and his standard is his own. . . . The man-measure doctrine makes a claim about all men; but it does not claim that the measure is the species man, except in so far as such a unified view could emerge from the experience of individual men" (p. 49). So although Farrar emphasized the singular "man" measuring in Protagoras' doctrine, as she discussed later in the article, this man is social, or a man-in-the-polis and not simply an isolated man. One's decisions and judgments—one's measuring—are always guided by social and civic ends. But, as with Lyotard's differend, we run into a problem: Where do these ethics or values come from by which an agent judges? What or who defines proper social and civic ends? How do we account for the agent's own standard?

Farrar said that human measure promotes a "unified view" that "emerges from the experience of individual men" (p. 49). So in Farrar's reading, teachers create readings of student writing that become hegemonic to some degree. These hegemonic readings in turn create communal dispositions, such as "good development" in student writing, or what a particular department or rubric designates a "passing" portfolio. Farrar explained how individuals arrive at judgments about student writing. Her reading of human measure assumes an individual has agency simply because he or she can sense and judge, because he or she is the measure of all things. This account does not really explain agency. It simply asserts it much like Lyotard's account. Furthermore, Farrar's reading may be too *physis*-centered, thus less critical of how social dispositions are constructed. When a teacher agrees with others' readings of student writing, the teacher's agency is affirmed by his or her access to socialized tastes. The teacher's use of them confirms his or her position in the community of teachers (the community of power). In this paradigm, agency is indistinguishable from an adherence to the status quo.

To solve this problem, we need only adjust slightly Farrar's logic. Human-measure can be read to state that the agent who measures does so from "standards" and "senses," or tastes and dispositions, that are simultaneously socially sanctioned and products of individual reflective participation. We have our own share of innate virtues, as Protagoras claims in his origin myth, yet they are each cultivated differently in society's *agon* (as Prodicus' Heracles illustrates). So an individual's measuring is consubstantial to his larger social milieu, but never identical to the ways others have of measuring. Additionally, individual ways of measuring help constitute the social milieu in which those individuals measure. Calling attention to this dialectic in one's rhetoric provides the agent with self-conscious, reflective claims that construct his or her agency and acknowledges social influences and hegemony. This reflexive component is seen in the second part of Protagoras' doctrine. An agent's rhetoric must acknowledge what and how he or she knows what he does. This positions the agent socially in the *agon* and accounts for the three concerns that the *nomos-physis* validity heuristic focuses on. In short, an individual's level of agency comes from his or her reflexive understanding that the individual can make choices about methods and fairness, select from a variety of tastes and theoretical frameworks by which to make judgments about his or her own well-being and that of others, and be guided by his or her ethical obligation to participate in the *agon* that produces decisions.

Additionally, by creating the agent as the sole origin of judgment, Farrar's account displaces the powerful influence social tastes (*nomoi* as prescriptions and past decisions) have on individual "sensing" and "judging." We get our ideas about things from contextual and historical sources that can be located, as many validity researchers have already discussed (e.g., Edgington, 2005; Huot, 1993; Pula & Huot, 1993), but we choose from these sources unevenly, and perhaps at times randomly or unpredictably, often revising social tastes for our individual uses. Decisions are social, but the individuals who make up the various judgments that construct those decisions are more than simply socially constructed. Agency, then, in my reading of human measure does not come from inherently using one's own standard (as Farrar suggests), but from the ability to choose, change, and affect socialized standards and tastes reflectively. Thus, human measure would explain how a rubric may still represent departmental expectations but not account for individual ways of sensing and judging for those expectations, making the continual revisiting of expectations an integral part of program assessment, the rearticulation of its values, and validation.

Perhaps the *nomos–physis* heuristic and human-measure doctrine mostly offer validity researchers a reflexive rhetorical stance toward validity inquiry. In her response to Haswell's "Multiple Inquiry in the Validation of Writing Tests," Moss promoted this reflective aspect of validation, calling it an "epistemic reflexivity" (taken from Bourdieu in Bourdieu & Wacquant, 1992) that compliments Haswell's multiple method approach, which she acknowledged (Moss, 1998, p.

112). In fact, Haswell's (1998a) work defined assessment in a contextual, local way, one that requires reflexive practices from multiple methods of inquiry (pp. 91–92).[25] Loïc J. D. Wacquant identifies three characteristics of Bourdieu's epistemic reflexivity that enrich an understanding of the reflexive qualities promoted by the *nomos–physis* heuristic. First, epistemic reflexivity targets the "social and intellectual unconscious embedded in analytic tools and operations," that is, it is a conscious articulation of the constitutive *nomos* of researchers and their methods for assessing and validating, which might also include how fairness is constructed; second, it is a "collective enterprise," one of dialogue in a community that assumes participation and the sharing of power by various stakeholders; and third, it supports "the epistemological security of sociology," searching for ways to understand current results and theoretical constructs, validating and justifying them when possible (Bourdieu & Wacquant, 1992, p. 36), which means it inquires and justifies current interests and power embodied in the theories and assumptions that are stable in any field of study. In these three ways, the *nomos–physis* heuristic makes epistemic reflexivity a defining feature of the discourse of validation, and the human-measure doctrine accounts for this reflexivity at an individual level, making validation endeavors that can do more than simply affirm the status quo.

John Trimbur (1996), reflecting on the politics of writing assessment, said that when we talk about assessment, we are really talking about "conflicts of interest, asymmetrical relations of power, hidden motives, and unforeseen consequences." The goal then, in "analysis," or validity research, is to "read between the lines, so we see what's really going on in writing assessment" (p. 45). Trimbur's penultimate question is a sophistic one: "I simply want to ask why assessment is taken for granted as a necessary part of the study and teaching of writing. What are the politics that authorize the assessment of writing?" (p. 47). Politics, in fact, is much of what the *nomos-physis* heuristic investigates in reflexive ways. It allows researchers and teachers to acknowledge openly that assessment is surveillance, that it reproduces social arrangements by privileging certain dispositions, but it can also establish self-consciously new social arrangements. This kind of validity inquiry, in turn, allows for broader institutional questions: How do the dispositions to judge writing in certain ways distribute power in our classrooms? What material effects might our validity rhetorics have on the academy and

---

25  Haswell (1998) explained the contextual and local nature of assessment: "an institutionalized writing test [is] a social apparatus that applies a nomenclature (specialized and provisional language) in order to classify and label people for certain public uses" (p. 91). This implies, as his long list of questions suggest (p. 92), that validation must be reflective and interpretive by nature. This inference is backed up by Haswell's own "rationales for multiple inquiry" (pp. 93–94).

our students in terms of their educational access and opportunity? How might our assessment practices radiate from (contested/able) concerns for intellectual property, privilege, and power? From what socio-historical sources do our dispositions come, and how do our social and private methods for measuring work in concert with, or against, these sources and dispositions? Furthermore, given the social arrangements and uneven distributions of power already, what kinds of validity arguments are more important to make and for what ultimate social goals and stakeholder well-being? What are our ethical responsibilities toward those left out of our *nomos* and the academy, those who define our distastes (which not so ironically help define our tastes), as assessment practitioners and theorists, teachers and guardians of culture? Ultimately, I believe, the sophists' positions on *nomos–physis* and Protagoras' human-measure doctrine ask us to reconsider continually our own relationships to the cultural hegemony we often say we resist as intellectuals, but clearly must work within as teachers, assessors, validity researchers, and citizens, which in turn asks us to find ways to open the academy's doors a little wider.

# REFERENCES

Bizzell, P. & Herzberg, B. (Eds.). (2001). *The rhetorical tradition: Readings from classical times to the present* (2nd edition). Bedford/St. Martin's.

Bourdieu, P. and Wacquant, L. J. D. (1992). *An invitation to reflexive sociology*. University of Chicago Press.

Broad, B. (2003). *What we really value: Beyond rubrics in teaching and assessing writing*. Utah State University Press.

Cherryholmes, C. H. (1988). *Power and criticism: Poststructural investigations in education*. Teachers College Press.

Cronbach, L. J. (1971). Test validation. In R. Thorndike (Ed.), *Educational Measurement* (2nd edition, pp. 443–507). American Council on Education.

Cronbach, L. J. (1988). Five perspectives on validity argument. In H. Wainer (Ed.), *Test Validity* (pp. 3–17). Erlbaum.

Cronbach, L. J. (1989). Construct validity after thirty years. In R. Linn (Ed.), *Intelligence: Measurement, theory, and public policy*. University of Illinois Press.

Cronbach, L. J. & Meehl, P. E. (1955). Construct validity in psychological tests. *Psychological Bulletin*, *52*(4), 281–302. https://doi.org/10.1037/h0040957.

Diels, H. (1972). The older sophists: A complete translation by several hands of the fragments. In R. K. Sprague (Ed.), *Die fragmente der vorsokratiker*. University of South Carolina Press.

Edgington, A. (2005). What are you thinking?: Understanding teacher reading and response through a protocol analysis study. *Journal of Writing Assessment*, *2*(1), 125–147. https://escholarship.org/uc/item/8dt3v2vh.

Faigley, L. (1992). *Fragment of rationality*. University of Pittsburgh Press.
Farrar, C. (1989). *The origins of democratic thinking: The invention of politics in classical Athens*. Cambridge University Press.
Freeman, K. (Ed.). (1966). *Ancilla to the pre-Socratic philosophers*. Harvard University Press.
Guba, E. & Lincoln, Y. (1989). *Fourth generation evaluation*. Sage.
Gutherie, W. K. C. (1971). *The sophists*. Cambridge University Press.
Haswell, R. (1998a). Multiple inquiry in the validation of writing tests. *Assessing Writing, 5*(1), 89–109. https://doi.org/10.1016/S1075-2935(99)80007-5.
Herrick, J. A. (2001). *The history and theory of rhetoric: An introduction* (2nd edition). Allyn & Bacon.
Huot, B. (1993). The influence on holistic scoring procedures on reading and rating student essays. In M. M. Williamson & B. A. Huot (Eds.), *Validating holistic scoring for writing assessment: Theoretical and empirical foundations* (pp. 206–236). Hampton Press.
Huot, B. (2002). *(Re)articulating writing assessment for teaching and learning*. Utah State University Press.
Jarratt, S. C. (1991). *Rereading the sophists: Classical rhetoric refigured*. Southern Illinois University Press.
Kane, M. T. (1992). An argument-based approach to validity. *Psychological Bulletin, 112*(3), 527–535.
Kennedy, G. A. (1994). *A new history of classical rhetoric*. Princeton University Press.
Kerferd, G. B. (1981). *The Sophistic movement*. Cambridge University Press.
Marrou, H. (1956). *A history of education in antiquity* (G. Lamb, Trans.). University of Wisconsin Press.
McComiskey, B. (2002). *Gorgias and the new sophistic rhetoric*. Southern Illinois University Press.
Messick, S. (1989). Validity. In *Educational measurement* (3rd edition). The American Council on Education and the National Council on Measurement in Education.
Moss, P. (1992). Shifting conceptions of validity in educational measurement: Implications for performative assessment. *Review of Educational Research, 62*(3), 229–258.
Moss, P. (1998). Testing the test of the test: A response to "multiple inquiry in the validation of writing tests." *Assessing Writing, 5*(1), 111–122.
Petrochilos, G. A. (2002). Kalokagathia: The ethical basis of Hellenic political economy and its influence from Plato to Ruskin and Sen. *History of Political Economy, 34*(3), 599–631.
Plato. (1956a). *Protagoras* (B. Jowett & M. Ostwald, Trans.; G. Vlastos, Ed.). Prentice-Hall.
Plato. (1956b). *Republic* (F. M. Cornford, Trans. and Ed.). Oxford University Press.
Plato. (1990). *Gorgias* (W. R. M. Lamb, trans.). In P. Bizzell & B. Herzberg (Eds.), *The rhetorical tradition: Readings from classical times to the present*. Bedford.
Plato. (2000a). *Apology* (B. Jowett, Trans.). In D. C. Stevenson (Ed.), *Internet classics archive*. http://classics.mit.edu/Plato/apology.html.
Plato. (2000b). *Phaedrus* (B. Jowett, Trans.). In D. C. Stevenson (Ed.), *Internet classics archive*. http://www.perseus.tufts.edu/cgi-in/ptext?lookup=Plat.+Phaedrus+250d.

Pula, J. J. & Huot, B. (1993). A model of background influences on holistic raters. In M. M. Williamson & B. A. Huot (Eds.), *Validating holistic scoring for writing assessment: Theoretical and empirical foundations* (pp. 237–265). Hampton Press.

Rosenbloom, D. (2004). Ponêroi vs. chrêstoi: The ostracism of hyperbolos and the struggle for hegemony in Athens after the death of Perikles, part I. *Transactions of the American Philological Association, 134,* 55–105.

Schiappa, E. (2003). *Protagoras and logos: A study in Greek philosophy and rhetoric* (2nd edition). University of South Carolina Press.

Shapiro, M. J. (1981). *Language and political understanding.* Yale University Press.

Shepard, L. A. (1993). Evaluating test validity. In L. Darling-Hammond (Ed.), *Review of research in education* (pp. 405–450). American Educational Research Association.

Spellmeyer, K. (1996). Response: Testing as surveillance. In E. M. White, W. Lutz & S. Kamusikiri (Eds.), *Assessment of writing: Politics, policies, and practices* (pp. 174–181). Modern Language Association.

Sprague, R. K. (Ed.). (2001). *The older sophists.* Hackett.

Trimbur, J. (1996). Response: Why do we test writing? In E. M. White, W. Lutz & S. Kamusikiri (Eds.), *Assessment of writing: Politics, policies, and practices* (pp. 45–48). Modern Language Association.

Untersteiner, M. (1954). (Freeman, K., Trans.). *The Sophists.* Philosophical Library.

White, E. M. (1995). An apologia for the timed impromptu essay test. *College Composition and Communication, 46*(1), 30-45.

Williamson, M. M. (1993). An introduction to holistic scoring: The social, historical and theoretical context for writing assessment. In M. M. Williamson & B. A. Huot (Eds.), *Validating holistic scoring for writing assessment: Theoretical and empirical foundations* (pp. 1–43). Hampton Press.

# CHAPTER 14.
# ETHICAL CONSIDERATIONS AND WRITING ASSESSMENT

### David Slomp
University of Lethbridge

*Large-scale writing assessment has become ubiquitous in North American education. Students at the K-12 level in Canada and the United States are virtually guaranteed to be subjected to any number of large-scale writing assessments at some point in their education. Lazarin's (2014) study of testing in 14 large school districts in seven US states found, for example, that students write as many as 20 (and an average of 10) standardized tests a year. A study conducted by the Council for the Great City Schools, composed of superintendents and school board members from the nation's largest urban school systems, found that students in the 66 sampled districts were required to take an average of 112.3 tests between pre-K and grade 12—a total that does not include diagnostic, school, or teacher developed tests). More specifically, in the 2014–2015 school year, students in the 66 urban school districts sat for tests more than 6,570 times (Hart, Casserly, Uzell, Palacios, Corcoran & Spurgeon, 2015). Faced with increasing opposition, the Obama administration admitted that testing had gone too far and, as the NY Times reported, acknowledged its role in test proliferation (Zernike, 2015). In its reauthorization of the Elementary and Secondary Education Act of 1965 on January 6, 2015, the Every Child Succeeds Act (S.1177) substantially limits the role of the federal government in education and restores to the states the responsibility for federal test use, with additional support for locally developed assessments.*

The stakes associated with these assessments have and will vary from low to extreme, from locally-developed and school-based to standardized and federally-sponsored. Their impacts on students, teachers, and systems of education will vary also. It is within this shifting and contingent environment that the present special issue of the Journal of Writing Assessment—that begins to articulate a theory of ethics for the field—is situated.

Some might question the need for a theory of ethics. After all, the Standards for Educational and Psychological Testing (American Educational Research Association [AERA], American Psychological Association [APA], and National Council on Measurement in Education [NCME], 2014) already have defined technical requirements for assessment design and use. Throughout this special issue, however, we argue that technical competence/quality is only one component of ethical practice. Technical quality or feasibility may provide some justification for implementing an assessment practice, but technical feasibility is not equivalent to moral or ethical justification for that practice.

Consider, for example, recent problems with large-scale writing assessments in Alberta, Canada, and Nevada. In both cases the platforms that housed new computer-based literacy tests crashed while students were trying to log in to write their exams. In Alberta, assessment officials made the decision to use regression analysis as a tool for generating a replacement (or fake) grade for all the students who were affected by the crash of the exam platform. Rather than receiving a grade for actual performance on the writing exam these students received a grade that was based on the statistical manipulation of three sets of data: (a) students' scores on their reading comprehension exam; (b) students' school awarded marks; and (c) a statistical analysis that compares (a) and (b) against the performance of other students in the province who completed the writing exam.

The decision to generate replacement grades was justified on the basis of three core principles articulated in the Standards. First, this approach was fair because it attempted to mitigate in as equitable a fashion as possible, the negative impacts for students caused by the exam's crash. Second, this approach is reliable "providing the 'best predictor' of how these students would have performed on [the writing exam] if they actually wrote the examination" (Alberta Education, 2015). Third, this approach generates valid scores:,

Multiple regression is a method used by Alberta Education to estimate/predict the unknown mark (in this case, part A). It is based on statistical analysis to determine the relationships among three variables (Part A, Part B and School-awarded marks) of unaffected students. These calculated relationships are used to generate the unknown mark for affected students who are requesting a partial exemption (Alberta Education, 2015).

However, even though the solution is technically feasible and was justified to some degree using arguments related to fairness, reliability, and validity, the ethical questions remain. Is it ethical to generate a proxy grade for students on a high-stakes exam? Is it ethical to use replacement grades on high-stakes exams to determine eligibility for a high school diploma, for high school and university scholarships, and for post-secondary admissions? What are the consequences of this practice for students, teachers, and systems of education? Are these consequences justifiable?

As illustrated by this example, a theory of ethics compels attention beyond the question of technical competence towards broader questions of social consequences. Additionally, the theory of ethics we are developing recognizes that technical standards are themselves social constructions, designed by a community of stakeholders out of a particular perspective and to serve specific purposes. As such, it calls for a critical engagement with those standards, perspectives and purposes.

In this introductory article, I set the stage for the arguments that follow in each of the contributions to this special issue. First, I critically examine the three pillars of the current Standards—fairness, validity, and reliability—exploring briefly how on their own each concept is insufficient to guiding ethical practice. Then I briefly examine the Standards themselves highlighting their limitations in guiding ethical practice. Finally, I provide a brief introduction to the various dimensions of the theory of ethics we are developing in this special issue.

## SOURCES OF EVIDENCE AND THE STANDARDS

Each of the authors of this special issue recognizes that no assessment program is neutral. Whether by intention or by fact of their implementation, all such programs have an effect on the individuals and systems to which they connected. Recognizing this fact, the educational community has worked hard over the years to establish conceptual and technical guidelines for managing the influence of assessment programs. The Standards for Educational and Psychological Measurement (AERA, APA & NCME, 2014) defined technical qualities that are essential to the evaluation of tests, testing practices, and test use. These technical standards have evolved over time to reflect advances in research and to address changes in practice and uses of assessments. Historically, technical quality of assessment programs has been defined by these Standards in terms of both the concepts of reliability and validity; more recently the concept of fairness has received additional attention. Because of the importance of these key terms and the concepts they suggest, attention to each is warranted.

## RELIABILITY AS CONSISTENCY

Broadly speaking, reliability is concerned with the social and scientific values of dependability, consistency, accuracy and precision (Parkes, 2007). As such, reliability is essentially a facet of the concern for construct validity; low reliability indicates that construct-irrelevant variance is in some way reducing the precision of test scores, and by extension, their dependability. In this way, reliability can also be understood as a form of fairness. An instruments' capacity to produce scores that consistently reflect a precise measurement of the construct enables test users to make fair decisions and inferences about students and their ability. Similar to issues of validity, the demonstration of high degrees of reliability can provide some technical justification for the use of an assessment without addressing deeper ethical questions. Historically, for example, selected response tests that measured writing ability demonstrated high degrees of reliability. In some respect, such instruments also demonstrated certain degrees of validity, yet in the 1960s and 1970s these were largely replaced by tests that measured samples of actual student writing because such tests were seen to be more valid. From the perspective of social consequences, such tests also seemed to better support more effective practices with respect to teaching and learning in schools. In the 1980s and 1990s this shift from selected response test formats for writing toward performance-based assessments of writing saw the development and introduction of portfolio-based writing assessments. The strengths of portfolio assessment are that they enabled test developers and users to capture a broader more complex sample of the writing construct. Their weakness, however, is that they often demonstrated weak measures of reliability. As a consequence, many state assessment programs have abandoned their portfolio assessment programs. Parkes (2007) associates this history with a major problem with reliability theory: The measurement community has for too long conflated the social values underpinning reliability with the narrow set of methods established for measuring the degree to which such values have been captured by a set of test scores.

## VALIDITY AS DEFENSE

Validity has historically been understood as the primary concern for evaluating the integrity of assessment programs. While the concept itself has evolved over time, it currently refers to the defensibility, and thus to the appropriateness, of our uses and interpretations of assessment results. Huot (2002) has made much of the fact that this current conception of validity places the concept within the domain of rhetoric. In the process of validation, assessment developers and users must construct an argument that defends the uses and interpretations of assessments results. Validity, then, hinges on one's ability to construct an argument. Validity theorists, themselves, have consistently and explicitly narrowed the breadth of such arguments to focus solely on the uses and interpretations of test results. As such, these arguments are framed as technical ones. The questions they are designed to answer is, "On the basis of their technical merits, can we justify the uses and interpretations of these test results?" Historically, answers to this question have been framed in several ways. We can trust them because they (a) have been shown to accurately predict future performance; (b) reflect similar scores achieved on similar parallel measures; and (c) accurately reflect the construct the instrument was designed to measure.

Such questions, however, tend to ignore the broader ethical questions associated with the concept of defensibility. In spite of the fact that (a), (b), and (c) may be true, can we defend the use of assessment results for tests that measure constructs we know little about or for where there is little consensus as to what the construct entails? Can we defend the use of assessments that measure well the construct they intended to measure, but that are measuring the wrong construct or facets of the construct so narrow that they are irrelevant? Can we defend the use of assessments that only measure the narrow aspects of the construct that can easily be measured by tests?

In Ontario, Canada for example, the Ontario Secondary School Test (OSSLT) was designed to measure the construct of basic literacy. Even if such a test measured the construct of basic literacy perfectly, could it be justified when the very construct "basic literacy" is itself so hotly contended? Can the use of such a test be justified if it fails to capture the broader literacy construct as it is understood both in the Ontario curriculum and in the academic literature? Can the use of such a test be justified if it has been shown to have negative impacts on the broader system of education, on teachers' sense of professionalism, on student self-perception, or on the breadth of the literacy curriculum taught in Ontario schools (Slomp, 2014)? Validity theory as it has currently been constructed provides no answers to these questions. For this reason, Schendel and O'Neill (1999) argued that valid use is not that same as ethical use. They wrote:

> Although validity is often a part of discussions of assessment, the ethical dimension is often missing. To ensure that our assessment practices are both ethical and valid, we should engage in critical examination of the processes and consequences of asking students to assess their writing as well as the rhetoric we use to talk about [assessment] practices. (p. 200)

Messick's work in the 1980s advocated a return to the ethical aspect of validity by calling for assessment developers and users to examine both the actual and potential consequences of assessment design and implementation (Mike, 2013). Yet, while Messick's move to make construct validity the central concern in validity theory has been widely accepted within the field of educational measurement, his simultaneous move to fuse concerns for construct validity with concerns for the consequences of test use have not received the same level of acceptance. As is the case with reliability, validity can only take us so far in making decisions about the ethical use of assessments.

## FAIRNESS AS VALIDITY

The most recent version of the Standards marks a radical step forward from earlier editions, by elevating the concept of fairness to a level equal to that of the concern for both reliability and validity. A concern for fairness, however, has been an overt goal of most large scale assessment programs dating as far back as the Imperial Chinese examination program. However, because assessment always involves a power imbalance between those who ask questions and those who are required to answer them, Spolsky (2014) argues that other unstated purposes have often been the true drivers of such assessment programs: In imperial China assessment was used to control the less privileged, and to select among them; in 19th Century England, the civil service examination was designed to replicate the social order of the day; in the 1950's Australia's immigration test was designed to control immigration patterns for certain ethnic groups; in the 1960s the TOEFL was also used to "control the immigration loophole" (p. 1575). Spolsky's history makes clear that fairness, understood as a technical concern, should not be equated with ethical practice. The Imperial Chinese civil service exam may have been designed to select as fairly as possible candidates for the civil service while concurrently operating as an instrument of social control. In current times, large-scale high-stakes writing assessments may be designed to reflect principles of fairness for individual students while simultaneously being employed to both control and shape education systems. In such cases, these assessment programs may be technically sound while also being morally debatable. As such, the definition of fairness in the Standards (AERA, APA & NCME, p. 2014)—that a fair test that is fair minimizes variance that "would compromise the validity of scores for some individuals" (p. 219)—seems quite beside the point both in its self-referential solipsism and silence on consequence.

## LIMITATIONS OF THE STANDARDS

Each of these concepts have been defined and updated repeatedly in *the Standards*. *The Standards* themselves have been designed created to guide assessment design and use and will continue to play an important role in educational measurement in general and writing assessment in particular.

*The Standards*, however, are nevertheless insufficient for guiding ethical decision making: They reflect a narrow epistemological, ontological and axiological standpoint, they focus narrowly on intended uses and interpretations of test scores, and they handle key technical issues such as validity, reliability, and fairness as siloed concepts. An important flaw in *the Standards* is that they are designed to reflect the perspectives and interests of the dominant stakeholder group—those who design and use large-scale assessments (Maul, 2014, p. 40)—while simultaneously excluding the perspectives of classroom teachers (Plake & Wise, 2014). As a result, they failure to attend to the broader social consequences that Messick advocated attention to.

While the *Standards* acknowledged that reliability, validity, and fairness are related concepts, it treats them independently of one another while at the same time calling on test users and developers to make integrated judgments regarding assessment design and use. Unfortunately, the Standards provide only the vaguest of guidance on how such integrated judgments should be structured:

> [A] test interpretation for a given use rests on evidence for a set of propositions making up the validity argument, and at some point validation evidence allows for a summary judgment of the intended interpretation that is well supported and defendable. (AERA, APA & NCME, 2014, p. 22)

What the field requires is a more cohesive, integrated framework that provides more concrete guidance for assessment design and use.

Taken as a whole, *the Standards* pay little attention to a systems-level perspective on the role of assessment in education (Diaz-Bilello et al., 2014). In the United States educational policies such as No Child Left Behind (NCLB) and Race to the Top (RTTT) have created an environment in which testing has become an apparatus within larger systems of accountability. This phenomenon is not unique to the American context, as systems of education around the globe are increasingly administered within rigid accountability frameworks. Within such accountability systems, technical quality of testing instruments becomes increasingly important. The Standards play an important role in this respect. However, technical quality in itself is insufficient; accountability systems themselves need to be critically evaluated, their impact on the systems over which they have been imposed need to be rigorously evaluated, and the responsibilities of both those who design these systems and those who enable their use—both test users and test designers—need to be defined and enforced. The sub-prime credit crisis at the turn of the current century provided ample examples of how flaws in accountability mechanisms can have catastrophic consequences for the systems over which they have been imposed.

## A ROLE FOR ETHICS

As is the case in the *Standards*, fairness has remained wedded to instrumental concerns in contemporary measurement theory. The concerns are explicitly evidenced in the 2010 issue of Language Testing in which Xi situates fairness within the framework of validity: "Fairness is characterized as comparable validity for relevant groups that can be identified. The fairness argument consists of a series of rebuttals that may challenge the comparability of score-based decisions and consequences for sub-groups" (p. 167). Likewise, The Standards' treatment of fairness remains rather cosmetic, essentially treating fairness as a subset of validity. For example, the current Standards limited their concern for subgroup difference to the issue of construct irrelevant variance and construct underrepresentation. Broader issues related to cultural bias—such as subgroup differences being related to undemonstrated assumptions about students rather than from reflective latent variable models validated under field-test conditions—are not taken up in the Standards. For reasons such as this, ethicists have made the point that technical competence is not synonymous with ethical use. While necessary, technical competence is an insufficient justification for use; simply because something is technically feasible does not make it morally or ethically justifiable. Indeed, focusing on the technical aspects alone holds the danger of technological determinism.

As is the case with bias, fairness in educational measurement has primarily been addressed through comparing items and test performance in different identifiable groups. Camilli (2006) referred to these techniques as the structural analysis of bias (including use of such models as differential item functioning) and external evidence of bias (including regression models to identify differential prediction). Our goal in this special issue was to interrogate fairness under equally rigorous philosophical frameworks, within paying special attention to current writing assessment frameworks that call for recognizing the social dimensions of assessment: local considerations, community-based assessment, and the effects of assessment. Yet this philosophical approach raises a critical question: How can we further an agenda for fairness if we cannot identify—and challenge—the philosophical tradition from which it arises?

Of the three guiding principles—validity, reliability, and fairness—fairness, with its attention to impacts of assessment practices on individuals, touches most closely on the need for new practices informed by moral philosophy. While definitions of ethical behavior date from antiquity, a contemporary definition of ethics by James Rachels (2012) in the Elements of Moral Philosophy affords an initial context to situate fairness within a broad philosophical realm: agentic. Rachels frames his definition in terms of the conscious moral agent as someone who is concerned impartially with the interests of everyone affected by what he or she does; who carefully sifts facts and examines their implications; who accepts principles of conduct only after scrutinizing them to make sure they are sound; who is willing to 'listen to reason' even when it means that his or her earlier convictions may have to be revised; and who, finally, is willing to act of the results of this deliberation (p. 11).

While we may argue that Rachel's definition is decidedly Western in its reliance on reason and careful sifting of facts as a path toward decision-making, our line of inquiry begins with this tradition because it a toehold into the steep cliff upon which measurement theories of fairness have been based. From Socrates to MacIntyre, a distinct set of qualities—emphasis on systematic reasoning, commitment to principled action, and concern for others—remains at the heart of Western orientations toward how we might best live. Indeed, for Rawls (1999, 2001) justice as fairness became central to his theory because it allowed both emphasis on obligations and attention to the individual.

Narrowing further, fairness (obligatory aims in pursuit equality of opportunity) is taken to be a distinct line of ethical inquiry (varied actions in pursuit of socially constructed concepts of the good). Because it is beyond the scope of this special issue to outline a comprehensive agenda common to each article, the special issue is best understood through identification of facets of fairness associated with writing assessment. By extension, articles in this special issue include attention to the following:

- *Sociocultural perspectives* on the origin of traditions, with attendant acknowledgment of the limits of practices redolent of colonialism and capitalism;
- *Access* to educational structures that are associated with literacy;
- *Opportunity to learn* as an often forgotten aim of assessment and a controlling factor in allocation of instructional resources;
- *Maximum construct representation* that is clearly articulated in advance of the assessment and neither implicit not derived through post-hoc methods;
- *Disaggregation of data* so that score interpretation and use can be clearly understood for all groups and each individual within those groups; and
- *Justice* as a principle of fairness so that opportunities do not merely exist but, rather, that so each individual has a fair chance to secure such opportunities.

While our authors define unique implications and applications of this definition, each holds firm belief in the following facets of the theory: the significance of the specific institutional site; the relevance of social sociocultural perspective; the importance of advancing opportunity to learn for both groups and individuals; the need for robust construct representation in terms of assessment advantage for all students; the relevance of refusing to fix pre-established definitions of the least advantaged; the need to secure resource allocation for those disadvantaged by the assessment; and the use of varied quantitative and qualitative techniques to ensure an actionable agenda for fairness.

Despite the comprehensive treatment of the authors of the special issue, each author agrees that significant questions remain for readers:

- Is fairness reactive or proactive?
- Where does fairness intersect with transformation and care?
- How can fairness account for what is unwitting or invisible in daily practice?
- How do we identify least advantaged when often such groups are not easily identifiable?
- Following identification, what is the role of agency when discussions of the least advantaged occur?
- What actions can or should lie within the reach of fairness?
- Because it is not solely a technical or measurement term, who ultimately owns fairness?
- What is to be done when the very cultural frame in which we work, one often associated with meritocracy, remorselessly denies working toward the benefit of the least advantaged?
- How can non-western traditions be brought to bear on fairness in writing assessment?

## ETHICS AND WRITING ASSESSMENT: NECESSITY AND SUFFICIENCY

Given both the necessity yet insufficiency of foundational design principles of fairness, validity, and reliability, in guiding ethical decision-making, a new unifying framework is needed; one that advances broader ethical concerns in the design, implementation, and use of tests. To this end, we are advancing by proposing a theory of ethics for the field of writing assessment, one that advances such a framework toward new conceptualizations that better serve students. Such a theory should assist all stakeholders in the assessment process in more thoroughly addressing questions regarding the moral aspects of assessment use. As such, we believe a theory of ethics for writing assessment must:

- Be the driving concern of educational stakeholders—the primary referential frame that conceptualizes instruction and assessment in terms of each other in ontological, epistemological, and axiological perspectives.
- Explore issues related to reliability and validity from multiple ontological and epistemic and axiological stakeholder perspectives concerned

with fairness, thereby offering an overall referential frame on what constitutes writing assessment that is robust enough to justify various uses of scores.
- Have an ecological orientation; one that pays attention to the role that assessment plays both within broader systems of education and within society as a whole. It needs to account for how assessments shape systems of education, and how they impact stakeholders within those systems.
- Provide a unifying function, one that draws together concerns for validity, reliability, and fairness, and it needs to provide an advancing function, one that ties these concerns to ethical decision-making. It must account for the perspectives and experiences of key stakeholders within the measurement process.
- Have value for a range of assessment contexts, both large scale, standardized testing and locally-developed, site-based assessments.
- Hold test-users to actionable standards of ethical practices, and it needs to require that assessment developers—whether site-specific or large scale—not allow themselves to become complicit in the unethical use of their tests (either by refusing to bid on RFPs that require they violate their standards, or by failing to publicly call attention to unethical uses of tests they have developed).

We offer this theory in the spirit that Gloria J. Jadson-Billings expressed in her lecture following her award receipt of the 2015 Social Justice in Education Award, when she stated that she wanted to "trouble" the term social justice. She asked her audience to participate in a fundamental rethinking of our past and our work as human beings. Social justice, she held, is not a concept expansive enough to confront the injustice that holds a deadly grip on our society. While we will surely differ in our concepts of moral philosophy, ethics, and fairness, our aim is at one with hers in the pursuit of justice for our students.

## REFERENCES

Alberta Education. (2015). Calgary Board of Education. http://schools.cbe.ab.ca/b870/Publications/CBE%20ELA%2030–1%20and%2030–2%20Diploma%20Exam%20Exemption%20FAQ%20Document.pdf.

American Educational Research Association, American Psychological Association & NCME. (2014). *Standards for educational and psychological measurement.* American Educational Research Association.

Camilli, G. (2006). Test fairness. In R. L. Brennan, (Ed.), *Educational measurement.* (4th edition, pp. 221–256). American Council on Education/Praeger.

Diaz-Bilello, E., Patelis, T., Marion, S., Hall, E., Betebenner, D. & Gong, B. (2014). Are the standards for educational and psychological testing relevant to state and local assessment programs? *Educational Measurement: Issues and Practice*, *33*(4), 16–18.

Hart, R., Casserly, M., Uzzell, R., Palacios, M., Corcoran, A. & Spurgeon, L. (2015). Student testing in America's great city schools: An inventory and preliminary analysis. *Council of Great City Schools*. http://www.cgcs.org/cms/lib/DC00001581/Centricity/Domain/87/Testing%20Report.pdf.

Huot, B. (2002). *(Re)Articulating writing assessment for teaching and learning*. Utah State University Press.

Mike, G. (2013). Towards an ethics of writing placement. *CEA critic*, *75*(1), 51–65.

Parkes, J. (2007). Reliability as argument. *Educational Measurement: Issues and Practice*, *4*, 2–10.

Plake, B. S. & Wise, L. L. (2014). What is the role and importance of the revised American Educational Research Association, American Psychological Association, NCME Standards for Educational and Psychological Testing? *Educational Measurement: Issues and Practice*, *33*(4), 4–12.

Rachels, J. (2012). *The elements of moral philosophy* (7th ed.). McGraw-Hill International Edition.

Rawls, J. (1999). *A theory of justice* (Rev. ed.). Cambridge University Press.

Rawls, J. (2001). *Justice as fairness: A restatement* (R. Kelly, Ed.). Harvard University Press.

Schendel, E. & O'Neill, P. (1999). Exploring the theories and consequences of self-assessment through ethical inquiry. *Assessing Writing*, *6*(2), 199–227.

Slomp, D., Corrigan, J., Sugimoto, T. (2014). A framework for using consequential validity evidence in evaluating large-scale writing assessments. *Research in the Teaching of English*, *48*(3), 276–302.

Spolsky, B. (2014). The Influence of ethics in language assessment. In A. J. Kunnan, (Ed.), *The companion to language assessment* (pp. 1571–1585). John Wiley and Sons.

# PART 5.
# STUDENTS' AND TEACHERS' LIVED EXPERIENCES

RETROSPECTIVE.

# TOWARD FAIRNESS IN WRITING ASSESSMENT

**Diane Kelly-Riley**
University of Idaho

**Ti Macklin**
Boise State University

**Carl Whithaus**
University of California, Davis

## SHIFTING AWAY FROM RELIABILITY AND VALIDITY TOWARDS FAIRNESS AND EQUITY

Looking back at the development of writing assessment over the last twenty years, we see the field increasingly attending to the importance of students' and teachers' lived experiences. The development of writing assessment instruments is still a prominent focus of the field, but the objective of accurately measuring the "true score" for a student's overall, generalized writing ability that would hold across contexts has diminished. It has been replaced by questions about contexts and the nuances around writers' backgrounds and the writing tasks they are being asked to engage in. Fairness has become a vital third consideration on par with validity and reliability. In fact, if we trace a forty-year historical arc from 1960 through 2000, writing assessments moved from indirect writing assessments to direct, timed writing assessments to portfolio-based writing assessments. Beyond 2000, they have continued to evolve. The interest in writing contexts that the use of portfolios promoted within the field has led researchers to ask more and more pointed questions about how situational elements may be included rather than excluded in writing assessment activities. This move has been expressed powerfully in Asao Inoue's (2015) emphasis on the importance of considering the entire ecology around a writing assessment and in Anne Ruggles Gere et al.'s emphasis on the importance of "communal justicing" (2021, p. 384). Within the pages of the *Journal of Writing Assessment*, we have seen these moves toward developing and studying situated forms of writing assessment such as directed self-placement or labor-based, contract grading. Overall, the field has shifted away from focusing on methods, such as inter-rater reliability and construct validity in large-scale writing assessments, and embraced questions about learning differences, working to create more just educational systems, and mitigating the impacts that present obstacles to equity, such as racism, ableism, and poverty. As a result, the role of fairness has increased and has become a major consideration informing the field's work.

Many of the writing assessment studies that have looked closely at the lived experiences of students and teachers have examined effects of racism. These studies have helped open the door to later work that includes a wider and more complex representation of fairness. Mya Poe and John Aloysius Cogan, Jr.'s "Civil Rights and Writing Assessment" as well as Wood's "Engaging in Resistant Genres as Antiracist Teacher Response" have been vital articles in the field's critique of racist assessment practices and the development of antiracist methods of writing assessment. Their work brought fairness into mainstream conversations about how writing program directors at community colleges, state colleges, and research universities should develop assessment practices to create the conditions for more equitable educational outcomes. At the same time that Poe, Cogan, and Wood have pushed forward the conversation about combating systemic racism within writing assessment systems, Leslie Henson and Katie Hern's "Let Them In: Increasing Access, Completion, and Equity in English Placement Policies at a Two-Year College in California" has utilized a disparate impact analysis to document how refinements to writing placement systems can be a powerful lever for reducing racial and ethnic gaps in terms of course completion outcomes. Their work takes a serious look at writing within the community college context and does so in a way that emphasizes how writing assessment may be reformed to increase equitable outcomes. Considerations of fairness also need to include the institutional context in which students and teachers work.

These local considerations should also include conversations about individuals' learning needs. In "Neurodivergence and Intersectionality in Labor-Based Grading Contracts," Kathleen Kryger and Griffin X. Zimmerman zero in on these questions around accessibility. They challenge racist and classist linguistic ideologies and ask how labor-based grading contracts may be used to honor neurodivergence and intersectional student identities. Their work digs into how student experiences and identities cannot be separated from a writing assessment and the way an assessment constructs and defines value (i.e., what is good writing). Kryger and Zimmerman's article embraces the possibilities for situated writing assessments, particularly labor-based grading contracts, to enhance fairness and make room for more nuanced readings and valuing of student writing. Shane Wood's "Engaging in Resistant Genres as Antiracist Teacher Response" provides a unique teacher perspective by focusing on the genre of teacher response to students' writing within a contract grading assessment ecology, something not frequently discussed in scholarship on the increasingly popular practice of contract grading. Wood challenges teachers to carefully consider how their response practices can—and do—reinforce White language supremacy, despite their best intentions, thus causing harm to students. By challenging scholars and practitioners to reconsider one of the most important and frequent sites of student-teacher interaction, Wood reframes and reconceptualizes the practice of teacher response to student writing. Like Kryger and Zimmerman's work, Wood's essay considers the intersections of antiracist praxis and teachers' assessment of student writing. These two works underscore the increased importance of fairness in relationship to writing assessment; they also ground writing assessment practices in students' and teachers' lived experiences rather than privileging the contexts of large-scale writing assessments.

Taken together Poe and Cogan's, Henson and Hern's, Kryger and Zimmerman's, and Wood's essays embody the field's shift away from studies that privilege reliability and validity without addressing questions of fairness and equity. Students' and teachers' contexts matter for these researchers as they embrace questions about learning differences, develop techniques for fairer writing assessment, and work to create more equitable educational outcomes for diverse student populations. These questions around fairness and equity are leading into more detailed discussions about how contract grading functions. For instance, Ellen Carillo's *The Hidden Inequities in Labor-Based Contract Grading* (2021) has taken up questions around labor-based grading contracts and how they make assumptions about normative achievements being tied to time spent working on a task. Her development of engagement-based grading contracts suggests ways in which situated assessment practices are being challenged and refined. That is, the development of questions about fairness and equity in writing assessment has not achieved a determined final form (i.e., the best practices are writing portfolios, or the best practices are labor-based grading contracts, or the best practices are engagement-based grading contracts). Rather the turn in writing assessment work to questions about fairness and equity is just beginning. Exploring the debates that run through Poe and Cogan's, Henson and Hern's, Kryger and Zimmerman's, and Wood's works help sketch out the contours on which further inquiries can be built. Studying these debates can also highlight the ways in which students' and teachers' lived experiences may become more central to research into writing assessment practices.

Considering questions about learning differences speaks not only to issues in contract grading but also to issues in writing assessment more broadly. Kryger and Zimmerman's work draws on a wealth of sources about neurodiversity, and engagement with these sources suggests the ways in which writing assessment scholarship may develop more nuanced and contextualized ways of considering the value of students' writing and the ways in which learning is represented in writing samples. These types of moves towards more situated understandings of how learning and knowledge are embedded within writing samples, reflective texts about writing processes and goals, and logs about labor or engagement may also mitigate the impacts of racism and discrimination as obstacles to student success. That is, the context-sensitive, situated forms of writing assessment championed by researchers considering neurodiversity may also prove beneficial when researchers, writing program administrators, and educational policymakers work to create more equitable educational systems. Poe and Cogan's, Wood's, and Henson and Hern's articles reflect how the field of writing assessment has confronted—and is working to address—inequitable learning outcomes driven by seemingly facially neutral, institutionalized forms of discrimination. Their works suggest that students' and instructors' lived experiences are valuable when designing writing assessment systems that range from the classroom-level to institutional-level and even to the state-level. Evaluating how writing assessments promote, or limit, access for diverse students is part of the work that writing assessment researchers need to engage in. The work becomes particularly meaningful when questions about students' and teachers' lived experiences are considered in detail and inform how writing assessments are designed or modified.

## FAIRNESS: CONSIDERING LIVED EXPERIENCES AS WAYS TO MITIGATE DISPARATE IMPACTS

In the *Journal of Writing Assessment's* Special Issue on a Theory of Ethics for Writing Assessment, Mya Poe and John Aloysius Cogan, Jr. detail the importance of a flexible, integrative framework to consider unintended consequences on demographic groups through writing assessment practices. This Special Issue was dedicated to the exploration of fairness more broadly and the fact that fairness had been underplayed in the research literature, in particular, on writing assessment. The group of authors aimed to extend the significant evolutions of educational measurement theory articulated in the 2014 revision of the *Standards for Educational and Psychological Testing* in which fairness was added as a foundational consideration. Poe and Cogan Jr. utilize and adapt the legal framework articulated in the Civil Rights Act of 1964—aimed to address intentional and unintentional discrimination—to writing assessment theory and practice.

In "Civil Rights and Writing Assessment: Using the Disparate Impact Approach as a Fairness Methodology to Evaluate Social Impact," Poe and Cogan highlight a model for considering the effects of assessment practices on discrete groups of students using concepts from the Civil Rights legislation. Writing assessment practices used by postsecondary programs, they argue, utilize seemingly facially neutral testing practices, but their inquiry demonstrated that there is no such thing as a neutral testing practice. Use of tests and the interpretation of their scores must be thoughtfully considered and if unintentional bias occurs, the program using the test must have a way to mitigate the disparate outcomes. By systematically reviewing student performance by disaggregated data, they were able to determine that their particular site indeed had an unintended, but still negative effect on a particular demographic group of students. That is, their testing practice—while on the surface appeared methodologically sound—actually disadvantaged the educational outcomes for a particular group of students. Their study provides a model grounded in empirical data to review the impacts of students and writing assessment tests within particular settings. As they note:

> In the end, if equitability is to be valued, it must be seen. Fairness in theory cannot be an afterthought to validity or reliability. Fairness in action demands local attention in which we repeatedly question how we can achieve equitable results with less adverse impact. . . . Test scores may reflect social inequality, but the use of test scores works to create that social inequality. Racial isolation and structural inequality are not merely reflective of such social mechanisms; social mechanisms work to sustain invisibility, racialized isolation, and structural inequality. The creation of opportunity structures through approaches such as disparate impact analysis holds the potential to provide visibility, community, and equity. (p. 151)

Poe and Cogan's work provides us with a concrete and practical way to situate the consideration of fairness. They acknowledge that tests and scores may result in disparate impacts on different demographic groups. That is not a reason to discard the test; rather, they advocate for a thoughtful way to mitigate the impact of the bias through other programmatic means. That is, no test will ever be perfect. We need to have programmatic ways to account for their limitations and to do so we must first know how the tests are operating.

In another *Journal of Writing Assessment* Special Issue on Two-Year College Placement, Leslie Henson and Katie Hern explore the ways in which disparate impact studies can be used to evaluate how legacy writing assessment systems have inequitable impacts on students' lives. Their project at Butte College in Northern California highlights how established writing assessment systems may have persistent, unintended consequences on particular demographic groups. Using a disparate impact analysis, Henson and Hern document how achievement gaps along racial and ethnic lines may be reinforced by the structure of a writing assessment and placement system. Henson and Hern contextualize their consideration of how writing assessment and placement systems work at Butte College within the larger data set of California's Community College System. They note that statewide most California community college students are considered "unprepared" with "more than 80% of incoming students [being required to] enroll in one or more developmental courses." Butte College's writing placement practices exist within this statewide system of placement and Henson and Hern show how the legacy of standardized tests has negatively affected practices at Butte. Their article critiques how "the standardized tests community colleges rely on to assess college readiness are a large contributor to the problem." But they also move beyond only a critique of current inequities based on the continued reliance on standardized, legacy forms of assessment and discuss how Butte College's new model of placements is leading to more equitable outcomes.

Based on multiple years of work, Henson and Hern trace the changes at Butte College through four different phases that include examining not only success in basic or first-year writing courses but also student success in later courses. Their work was part of a larger conversation within California about remediation at community colleges, and in particular, about concerns of the impacts of extensive levels of remediation being required for students of color. In 2018, the California legislature passed AB 705, a law that aligned with the writing assessment and placement practices Henson and Hern discuss. AB 705 requires community colleges to allow students to place into college-level (i.e., first-year composition rather than remedial English) as long as their writing assessments do not indicate that they are "highly unlikely to succeed." This state-wide policy shift addresses issues of fairness and highlights the ways in which debates around writing assessment systems can impact large numbers of students. It is indeed these relationships between writing assessment practices at particular colleges (e.g., Butte in this case) and larger assessment systems that provide a key area for considering the impact of fairness as an emerging concern for writing assessment scholars. These concerns are not only at play between the level of a single institution and state-wide policies. They may also be areas of investigation that connect individual classrooms and instructors' writing assessment practices with larger conversations in the field, such as neurodiversity.

Another *Journal of Writing Assessment* Special Issue, this one on contract grading, yielded two articles that focused specifically on teachers' lived experiences and issues of fairness that arise at the classroom level. Kathleen Kryger and Griffin X. Zimmerman's "Neurodivergence and Intersectionality in Labor-Based Grading Contracts" confront issues with the practice of contract grading while offering suggestions for more deliberately using grading contracts as a means of combating ableism experienced by students. Shane Wood's "Engaging in

Resistant Genres as Antiracist Teacher Response" draws on teachers' experiences to examine how response patterns may replicate White language supremacy. Moving beyond this observation, he identifies teacher response as a dynamic genre that can help build anti-racist forms of response. These studies remind us that it is important to interrogate contract grading as an assessment instrument. While contract grading shifts many pedagogical practices at the root, it makes those changes based around a new model of writing assessment. It is a conversation about what we value that connects assessment with pedagogical practices in ways that impact teachers' and students' lives.

Kryger and Zimmerman's chapter focuses on student experience. They confront issues of learning differences by challenging the notion that labor-based grading contracts are good for all, or even most, students by viewing this practice through the lens of neurodivergence. The authors remind us that both students and teachers represent a wide variety of learning experiences, styles, and preferences in writing classes and, although well-meaning, labor-based grading systems can and do result in the same unintentional discrimination that Poe and Cogan and Henson and Hern illustrate in their articles. The authors specifically address issues of fairness and equity by suggesting that the requirement of time logging in many labor-based grading systems is ableist and that this practice requires a more intersectional approach to classroom assessment. By complicating this increasingly popular grading system, like Wood, Kryger, and Zimmerman force readers to reconsider their understanding of a widely-accepted practice, focusing squarely on fairness as a priority in writing assessment practices. In this way, Kryger and Zimmerman set a foundation for continued work on labor-based grading to be a more inclusive and equitable approach to assessment while offering unique insight into the assessment experience for both neurodiverse students and teachers.

In his article, Shane Wood examines the ways in which both teacher and student response to student writing perpetuates White language supremacy. Wood calls for teachers and students to interrogate response to writing in order to disrupt the invisible reinforcement of linguistic racism. Specifically, the practice of response, one of the most common points of student-teacher interaction in writing classes, is taken to task for creating an inequitable learning environment, even in classes that practice seemingly antiracist writing assessment ecologies such as grading contracts. Like Poe and Cogan, Henson and Hern, and Kryger and Zimmerman, Wood identifies response to student writing as a site of (often unintentional) racist teaching practices. Wood's framework for this interrogation is situated on teacher and student lived experiences as a deeply reflective exercise, requiring students and teachers to identify the genre of response, consider the purpose and nature of response, analyze and identify how White language practices inform the response, and finally reflect on how response can resist the circulation of White language supremacy. This collaborative framework facilitates productive conversations surrounding language and power using the familiar genre of response as the site of study. This article illustrates how antiracist writing assessment work can and should be done at the class level as a partnership between teachers and students. All told, these four articles representing the lived experiences of teachers and students illustrate that, as Wood points out, "[g]ood intentions can still have violent consequences" (p. 233). Having a diversity of students and teaching practices at place in colleges across the United States requires us to have–and to interrogate–these new approaches. Examining them through the lens of teachers' and students' experiences may lead towards more fair and equitable learning outcomes.

## SHAPING THE FUTURE OF CONSIDERATIONS OF FAIRNESS

The future of writing assessment lies in evolving ways that we may consider and accommodate the complex identities of students, faculty, and the institutions in which work is assessed. These articles provide an important blueprint for the way forward. Gere et al.'s lens of "communal justicing" (2021, p. 384). demonstrates the importance of a thorough examination of disciplinary infrastructure. Gere et al. argue that "to change the disciplinary infrastructure that shapes assessment, justicing must be *communal*: we all need to participate in the revision of the pasts, policies, and publications on which writing assessment depends" (p. 385). This means that we need to consider the entire ecology, to use Asao Inoue's terminology, that surrounds the assessment of writing.

Such an effort has been underway for decades in educational measurement practices through the major revisions resulting in first the substantive philosophical reconceptualization of validity in 1998 and subsequently resulted in the 2014 revision to include consideration of fairness. These writing assessment practices have been evolving to be more expansive and inclusive in considering student performance and how we measure it. At this juncture—during a time of racial and cultural reckoning in the early 2020s—we argue that it is important to maintain the expansiveness in the consideration of fairness to protect this evolution in our practices. The approaches highlighted in this section point to an important path forward: one deeply committed to considering the lived experiences of students and faculty who inhabit the multiple institutional sites in which we teach, learn, and assess.

As these articles detail, we must consider the multiple and discrete ways in which students come to our institutions and demonstrate their writing abilities. Disciplinary identity is enacted through written communication, and that language-informed identity makes us rethink traditional views of instruction and assessment. The lens of fairness is the means through which writing assessment practices may continue to necessarily evolve. Fairness while it is variously defined can be unified under principles of equity and opportunity to learn. Such aims necessarily need to be contextualized within specific institutional sites, where attention is paid to the ability of admitted students to access knowledge, skills, and attitudes of their particular fields of study with special attention paid to the affordances and barriers that accompany intersectionality (of socioeconomic status, ability, gender, race, and other individual differences). Students move in and out of identities that may advantage or disadvantage them in particular contexts. Our writing assessment practices need to accommodate the complexities with which our students present themselves. No longer can we assume a monolithic identity that represents a "college student."

Likewise, we cannot and should not assume that a college student has the same experience at different institutional sites. Our practices need to reflect the particular missions of the postsecondary institutions and the faculty who teach at them should also be supported to assess students' writing in ways that are valuable and meaningful to the people in their courses. Writing assessment practices have been evolving parallel to educational measurement practices. We've moved from the emphasis on method (holistic scoring and an emphasis on reliability) to a more situationally-based writing assessment practice. Directed self-placement and contract grading underscore the adaptability and flexibility of writing assessment practices to be attentive to the diverse needs of students in postsecondary courses and to adjust to the situational needs of an institution.

The shift in writing assessment has been a move from a high focus on methodology questions towards a more expansive conversation about how assessment practices can benefit students. *The Journal of Writing Assessment* has helped the field advance that change. The field of writing assessment has pushed for moves away from indirect writing assessments to direct writing assessments, from direct writing assessments to portfolio-based writing assessment as a way of capturing how writers develop over time, and now towards more situated forms of writing assessment that consider social contexts, their complexities, and ultimately the impacts on students. Articles published in *JWA* have pushed for more complexity in how colleges placed students, for portfolio-based assessment, for student involvement in directed self-placement, and now for better representation in how students come to our classes.

As the final section of *Considering Students, Teachers and Writing Assessment*, these chapters look to the future and provide us with a path forward. For a moment, it's worth attending to, even meditating on, on what we want to see as writing assessment practices continue to develop. Even though the field has shifted the locus of where writing assessment happens, particularly in the development of contract grading practices–we're still obligated to interrogate them. Writing assessment practices are not intrinsically good because they are new. Changes to writing assessment systems address deficiencies in current practice. These changes to practice have been rooted in categories that are visible–race and gender, for example—but we need to continue moving towards ways in which to account for things 'unseen'—learning differences, economic background, sexual orientation, and other considerations and how they might play out in our assessment of students' writing.

What might we expect to see in terms of fairness and emerging research? Researchers might take a more community-based approach to their data collection and studies. These approaches could lead not only to more diverse student and teacher voices being included within writing assessment studies but could also increase the diversity among researchers. These shifts would require changes in methodologies and the guidelines for these types of studies. How, for instance, will studies of contract grading evolve so that they speak across institutions? Will researchers continue to work on alignment between shared empirical practices and the complexity of local contexts? Will researchers be able to develop studies that are replicated across contexts? What will be the dynamics among the categories of reliability, validity, and fairness? If, as we have argued in this collection, there has been a shift towards including fairness and looking at equitable outcomes, then what shifts will occur within large-scale writing assessment practices as well as local writing assessment practices? Will studies consider different scales and different scopes of writing assessment systems? That is, will questions about how writing assessment policies work at local, institutional, state, and national level develop in ways that continue to balance reliability, validity, and fairness?

## REFERENCES

American Educational Research Association, American Psychological Association & NCME. (2014). *Standards for educational and psychological testing*. American Educational Research Association.

Carillo, E. (2021). *The hidden inequities in labor-based contract grading*. Utah State University Press.

Gere, A. R., Curzan, A, Hammond, J. W., Hughes, S., Li, R. Moos, A., Smith, K., VanZanen, K., Wheeler, K. L. & Zanders, C. (2021). Communal justicing: Writing assessment, disciplinary infrastructure, and the case for critical language awareness. *College Composition and Communication, 72(3)*, 384–411.

Inoue, A. B. (2015). *Antiracist writing assessment ecologies: Teaching and assessing writing for a socially just future*. The WAC Clearinghouse; Parlor Press. https://doi.org/10.37514/PER-B.2015.0698.

# CHAPTER 15.
# CIVIL RIGHTS AND WRITING ASSESSMENT: USING THE DISPARATE IMPACT APPROACH AS A FAIRNESS METHODOLOGY TO EVALUATE SOCIAL IMPACT

**Mya Poe**
Northeastern University

**John Aloysius Cogan, Jr.**
University of Connecticut School of Law

*The Civil Rights Act of 1964 has served as an influential legal framework for addressing intentional (disparate treatment) and unintentional (disparate impact) discrimination. While philosophical and methodological discussions of Title VI and Title VII are well articulated in the legal scholarship, the disparate impact approach—a method for evaluating unintended racialized differences in outcomes resulting from facially neutral policies or practices—remains an underutilized conceptual and methodological framework in assessment literature. In this article, we argue that the burden-shifting heuristic used by entities such as the Office for Civil Rights to redress disparate impact is a valuable approach in evaluating fairness of writing assessment practices. In demonstrating an application of the burden-shifting approach at one university writing program, we discuss the value of the proposed integrative framework and point to remaining questions regarding sampling concerns—group identification, group stability, and intersectionality.*

On June 11, 1963, U.S. President John F. Kennedy delivered what has become known as the Civil Rights Address, a speech given the evening after Alabama National Guardsmen were sent to the University of Alabama to "carry out the final and unequivocal order of the United States District Court of the Northern District of Alabama" that required the university to admit "two clearly qualified young Alabama residents who happened to have been born Negro." (Kennedy, 1963) In Kennedy's address regarding the admission of Vivian Malone and James Hood to the University of Alabama, he invoked the ideals of human rights, tolerance, reciprocity, and color-blindness. He called the issue of equal rights a "moral issue," an issue that every American should embrace because of its connections to the founding principles of American democracy:

> I hope that every American, regardless of where he lives, will stop and examine his conscience about this and other related incidents. This Nation was founded by men of many nations and backgrounds. It was founded on the principle that all men are created equal, and that the rights of every man are diminished when the rights of one man are threatened.

Kennedy also invoked the notion of standards in his use of the phrase "clearly qualified." In doing so, he signaled that Malone and Hood were not being given special privileges because they were African American. By the university's admissions standards, they were qualified—"clearly qualified"—for admission.

Kennedy went on in his speech to trace the relationship between opportunity, talent, and motivation:

> As I've said before, not every child has an equal talent or an equal ability or equal motivation, but they should have the equal right to develop their talent and their ability and their motivation, to make something of themselves.

For Kennedy, access—the right to develop one's talent—was more important than the actual talent one possessed. Measurement of ability was secondary to equitability.

Kennedy's vision would become codified after his death in the Civil Rights Act of 1964. The Act would advance not just a moral dictum for eliminating discrimination but also a legal framework for actionable standards—a framework that outlawed barriers to access through intentional as well as unintentional discrimination. Specifically, in identifying unintentional discrimination, what would become known as "disparate impact"—"facially neutral policies that are not intended to discriminate based on race, color, or national origin, but do have an unjustified, adverse disparate impact on students based on race, color, or national origin" (Department of Education, 2014, p. 8)—the Civil Rights Act of 1964 has given us a framework for evaluating and remedying barriers to access that are not immediately visible.

Today, in higher education the barriers set through placement and proficiency testing can be enormous. The number of students whose lives are affected by our decisions to deny them access to first-year courses is startling. For example, in 2006 in the California higher education system, 30% of students in the university system, 60% in the state system, and 90% in the community college system required remediation (Murray, 2008). Nationally, approximately 20% of students entering four-year colleges and 50% of students entering community college require remediation (Complete College America, 2012). And the numbers for students of color are even more sobering. African American students are placed in remedial classes at rates of almost 40% for four-year colleges and 67% for two-year colleges. Hispanic students are placed at rates of 21% and 58% respectively while white students are placed at rates of 14% and 47% (Complete College America, 2012, p. 6).[1]

When it comes to course completion, again, the numbers for students of color are dismal. Almost 70% of African American students in four-year colleges and more than 85% of African American students in two-year colleges did not complete remedial and associated college-level courses within two years. Hispanic and white students faired only a bit better at approximately 64% and 76%, respectively (Complete College America, 2012, p. 8). And graduation rates? They are adversely affected as well. While nationally, the overall six-year graduation rate for students enrolled in four-year colleges is well over one-half (55.7%), the graduation rate falls by over one-third to 35.1% for students required to complete remedial and additional coursework. The same effect can be seen in the graduation rate at two-year colleges. The overall three-year graduation rate at those schools is 13.9%, but drops by nearly one-third to 9.5% for students required to complete remedial and additional coursework (Complete College, 2011, p. 14).

In identifying students who need additional help for writing, courses like basic writing have an important place in higher education. Approaches ranging from studio models (Grego & Thompson, 1995, 2007) to stretch programs (Glau, 1996) to accelerated instruction (Adams et al., 2009) have all been innovations to better support students enrolled in basic writing. Without such courses, many students would find themselves without the support they need to develop college-level writing practices. More importantly, corequisite classes like studio, stretch, and accelerated basic writing have been shown to work; students who enrolled in single-semester, corequisite English courses typically succeeded at "twice the rate of students [enrolled] in traditional prerequisite English courses" (Complete College America, 2015a, n.p.) Yet, corequisite options remain the exception at many institutions where basic writing typically

---

1  Recent research by Isaacs (2018) has shown that 82.3% of comprehensive colleges and universities that offer basic writing use the results of a purchased test, such as the SAT®, Accuplacer® or state test for placement decisions (p. 126).

does not carry college credit toward graduation and students must pass an exit exam to matriculate into first-year writing (Isaacs, 2018, p. 129).

Ultimately, students of color and multilingual students are the most likely to face the negative consequences of remediation (Sternglass, 1997; Soliday, 2002). Institutional writing assessment practices are often selected without regard to their effects on diverse student populations (Lioi & Merola, 2012; Elliot et al., 2012), human readers and machines alike can respond quite differently to identity markers in essays (Lindsay & Crusan, 2011; Marefat & Heydari, 2016; Shermis, Lottridge & Mayfield, 2015), and scoring procedures can yield quite different predictive results (Wilson et al., 2016). If test design and curriculum are so fraught with questions about equitability, are equitable outcomes simply comparable test scores, as has been the assumption behind legislation the recent reauthorization of the Elementary and Secondary Education Act of 1965 by the Every Student Succeeds Act (2015)? What if test scores reflect unequal opportunity to learn—i.e., the conditions that promote learning for students? And, finally, what is the relationship between fairness and equity?

Our argument in this article is a simple one: If fairness is to be a central tenet of assessment practice (or as Elliot argues in this special issue, the *first* aim of assessment[2]), it needs conceptual frameworks and empirical methodologies. As such, fairness methodologies should be tasked with questions regarding four lines of inquiry: access (cultural norms for participation throughout the assessment process—e.g., engagement through appeals process), response processes (individual learner differences), score interpretation (safeguards to accurate and meaningful test score interpretation) and social consequences (unintended adverse effects of assessment). Such methodologies, while resonant with validity, would also work independently so as to maximize their applicability.

It is beyond the scope of this article to discuss all four dimensions of fairness. Instead, our goal in this article is to advance a line of reasoning related to the disparate impact conceptual framework and methodology that grew out of the Civil Rights Act (Title VI and Title VII) to determine unintentional discrimination.[3] The framework, we argue, is valuable for linking inaccurate score use and

---

2   Elliot's point has also been articulated by Worrell, a member of the Joint Committee to revise the *Standards*: "The concept of fairness is something that anyone engaging in testing needs to think about from the beginning of the process" (F. Worrell, personal communication, March 17, 2012)

3   Measurement scholars have certainly not been remiss in engaging with legal scholarship, although discussions have often ignored shifting legal precedent (Sireci & Parker, 2006; Elul, 1998; Green, 1996), contained incorrect information (Sireci & Parker, 2006; Phillips & Camara, 2006), failed to address state and local laws (Sireci & Parker, 2006; Davis, 2006; Camilli, 2006; Pollock, 2005; Verdun, 2005; Ryan, 2003; Kidder & Rosner, 2002), or misused technical terms like disparate impact (Popham, 2012). Likewise, the legal community has been

its social consequences, which may result in a disparate impact for certain groups (see Elliot 2016, § 2.3.4).

In making this argument, we are extending the work previously published with our colleagues (Poe, Elliot, Cogan & Nurudeen, 2014) in which we demonstrated the use of the Department of Education Office for Civil Rights (OCR) methodology to demonstrate its viability for writing program self-study. Here, we deepen our previous work to discuss the conceptual value of disparate impact as part of an ethical framework for writing assessment. We begin with a discussion of fairness as currently found in the *Standards for Educational and Psychological Testing* (*Standards*) (AERA, APA & NCME, 2014) and in the measurement literature. We then discuss the various means by which discrimination has been addressed through the courts to frame our discussion of disparate impact. After a detailed discussion of the Civil Rights Act and Title VI, we then explain the disparate impact approach as applied through the OCR. Applying the OCR "burden-shifting approach" in a writing assessment case, we discuss the methodological questions that remain unaddressed through the disparate impact approach as well as identify its conceptual and methodological potential.

Two caveats here are important before proceeding: First, we are not advancing a legal argument for or against the use of disparate impact theory (Braceras, 2005). We are simply arguing that the disparate impact approach, which has been refined and has withstood numerous challenges for more than 50 years to determine when societal action was needed to reassess the interpretation of outputs and remedy the unequal distribution of inputs in a variety of institutional settings, can be a valuable tool to assess the differential effects of assessment practices. Furthermore, the Department of Education Office for Civil Rights' "burden-shifting approach" is a valuable heuristic—akin to a validation study—for remedying differential effects. Second, for the sake of simplicity, our discussion in this article is limited to claims of racialized differences. The disparate impact approach, however is flexible and has the capacity to identify disparate impact across other group identities (e.g., sexual orientation) (Department of Justice, 2015).

## SHIFTING CONCEPTIONS OF FAIRNESS

The measurement community, like the writing community, has long debated the responsibility of professionals in the community in ensuring equitable outcomes.

---

fickle in its uptake of the *Standards*, although, as Pullin (2014) pointed out, "the *Standards* have sometimes been an important influence in the outcomes of some high-visibility court cases in education and in employment" (p. 19) as well as "the more routine, ground-level decisions made in legal contexts" (p. 20).

However, as Slomp (2016) writes in the introduction to the *JWA* special issue on a theory of ethics for writing assessment, the *Standards for Educational and Psychological Testing* provides a "rather cosmetic" discussion of fairness. (Broad in the special issue, also, takes up the cosmetic features of fairness in ETS and Pearson standards, 2016.). This is surprising, given that the *Standards* (AERA, APA & NCME, 2014) is touted by the APA as "the gold standard in guidance on testing in the United States and in many other countries."

In lieu of a sustained coherent discussion about the history of fairness frameworks in measurement, the authors of the *Standards* attempted to provide a technical framework for fairness by linking it to validity:

> The validity of test score interpretations of intended use(s) for individuals from all relevant subgroups. A test that is fair minimizes the construct-irrelevant variance associated with individual characteristics and testing contexts that otherwise would compromise the validity of scores for some individuals. (AERA, APA & NCME, 2014, p. 219)

As is obvious here, the link to validity is a rather thin link, almost exclusively based on construct representation and testing context. (Ellen Cushman in the 2016 special issue has an excellent critique of the imperial history of validity: "Validity as an imperial concept was developed to justify what counts as claim, evidence, and warrant, defined as such, in support of the enunciation of empire in all realms of legal, moral, intellectual, and physical being."). Disaggregation of data by "relevant subgroups" is the primary means for assessing comparative fairness. The chapter goes on to offer a range of possible topics that might be encompassed in a discussion of fairness, including the following: equality of opportunity, technical properties of tests, the ways in which test results are reported and used, the factors that affect the validity of score interpretations, the consequences of test use, and "the regulations, statutes, and case law that govern test use and the remedies for harmful testing practices" (AERA, APA & NCME, 2014, p. 49). With the exception of accessibility concerns and universal design, these issues are not systematically taken up in the chapter.

What may be concluded from the current edition of the *Standards* is that the current view of fairness rests on access to constructs measured (e.g., how individuals respond in testing contexts and thus offering appropriate modifications or adjustments) and score interpretation (e.g., disaggregating scores to determine group differences). It is a view of fairness located in a moment in time—at a point of access or *in témpore* score interpretation, not as an ongoing decision-making process, which would be consistent with current views of validity. This view of fairness, also, does not locate it within a theory of action, such as found in through-course validity arguments (Bennett, Kane & Bridgeman, 2011). In the end, the authors of the *Standards* left the larger challenge for fairness—the relationship of "opportunity to learn" to social consequences—relatively untouched. Such omission is not unexpected given the measurement community's conventional views on opportunity to learn. As Haertl, Moss, Pullin & Gee (2008) argued, prevailing psychometric conceptions of opportunity to learn locate knowledge "inside the heads of individual learners, privileging symbolic representation over embodied experience, and relegating the social dimensions of learning . . . to the role of background or context in the business of measuring learning outcomes" (p. 3).

This is not to say, however, that the measurement community has always been limited by an epistemological separation of innate ability and social context or has not seriously engaged with issues related to ethics and fairness. For example, in the late 1960s the American Psychological Association established the Task Force on Employment Testing of Minority Groups. The task force was comprised of measurement researchers like Samuel Messick, who would go on to champion consequential validity, and led by Brent Baxter, an industrial psychologist who worked for Prudential Insurance Company and would later become Vice President of the American Institutes for Research. The committee published its findings in "Job testing and the disadvantaged" (APA, 1969)—a report framed in a way that is consistent with Kennedy's vision of equality of opportunity:

> In an ideal world . . . Each person would use his capabilities in the most productive and self-enhancing fashion, and his society thereby would make the wisest and most humane use of its manpower resources. Such a goal is not easily realized. Its attainment may be blocked sometimes by the personal maladaptive tendencies of the individual. More generally, however, it is society that often thwarts the matching between an individual's capabilities and his vocational role. (APA, 1969, p. 637)

The report examined "the chain of events that can lead to the inappropriate use of manpower and unfair and self defeating personnel practices" (p. 637). While the authors argued that knowledge-based tests are "free of bias," they also argued that aptitude testing is "a more subtle and complex issue" (p. 640) because of "cultural deprivation" (an unfortunate choice of wording), "test-induced anxiety," "unfairness of test content," "improper interpretation of test scores," and "lack of content relevance" (pp. 640-642). Thus, in outlining the various dimensions by which aptitude tests may misrepresent an examinee's actual abilities, the authors of the Baxter report pointed to the flawed logic of standardization—that consistency is equivalent to fairness.

In 1976 a special issue of the *Journal of Educational Measurement* (*JEM*) was devoted to the topic of bias. As Jaeger (1976) wrote in the introduction, "Attempts to advise the U.S. Department of Justice on an appropriate definition of 'fair' selection have resulted in 'an agreement to disagree'" (p. 1), resulting in a tenuous statement in the 1974 edition of the *Standards* regarding the definition of fairness: "It is important to recognize that there are different definitions of fairness, and whether a given procedure is or is not fair may depend upon the definition accepted" (AERA, APA & NCME, 1974, p. 44). The goal of 1976 *JEM* issue, then, seemed to provide some guidance to subsequent editions of the *Standards* and educate the practitioner community that fairness was no longer simply "selection . . . based on the predicted criterion" (Sawyer, Cole & Cole, 1976, p. 59). This goal was achieved under the guise of giving authors who had contributed to earlier fairness models "an opportunity to bring their ideas up to date, and to comment on the [new fairness] model proposed [in the lead article to the special issue] by Petersen and Novick" (Jaeger, 1976, p. 1).

In their article, Petersen and Novick attempted to correct for faulty judgments in "culture-free selection" and group parity models, such as the regression model that equates optimal prediction for lack of bias, that end up sanctioning "the very discrimination they seek to rectify" (1976, p. 5, p. 28). The article received mixed reviews. While Cronbach in the same *JEM* special issue praised Petersen and Novick, he also noted, "most of the attention has been given to the simplest of payoff matrices, uniform for all groups, and to single-stage selection. In time, it will be necessary to derive indices of fairness that reflect more complex matrices" (1976, p. 40). In another article in the *JEM* special issue, Linn advocated for a "decision-theoretic" approach. The decision-theoretic approach, he argued, allowed for public scrutiny and debate about value judgments. Linn went on to argue that such an approach, one that is "a way of formalizing the judgments and observing the consequences," "makes the process of attaching values to different outcomes a political one [rather than purely a technical one], which is what it should be" (1976, p. 56). In the end, the authors of the 1976 *JEM* special issue seemed resigned, as Breland and Ironson concluded, that "the solution to the broad social dilemma [of inequality] is not to be found in psychometric models" (1976, p. 98).

By the 1980s, Cronbach and Messick were both arguing that social consequences were related to validity. For example, in his 1989 article, "Meaning and Values in Test Validation: The Science and Ethics of Assessment," Messick wrote that social consequence was integral to a unified theory of validity: "The key issues of validity are the meaning, relevance, and utility of scores, the import or value implications of scores as a basis for action, and the functional worth of scores in terms of the social consequences of their use" (p. 5). Yet, Cronbach and Messick disagreed as to the reach of social consequences. While Cronbach (1988) argued that "tests that impinge on the rights and life chances of individuals are inherently disputable" (p. 6), Messick argued:

> If the adverse social consequences are empirically traceable to sources of test invalidity, then the validity of the test use is jeopardized. If the social consequences cannot be so traced—or if the validation process can discount sources of test invalidity as the likely determinants, or at least render them less plausible—then the validity of the test use is not overturned. (1989a, pp. 88–89)

In short, Messick was worried about consequences that strayed too far from a test's construct meaning.

Through the 1990s and into the 2000s, various articles appeared that wrestled with the degree of social consequences in relation to validity and fairness (e.g., Cole & Zieky, 2001; Gallagher, Bridgeman & Cahalan, 2002; Kane, 2012; Langenfeld, 2005; Lu & Suen, 1995). In addition to the collection *Fairness and validation in language assessment* from the 19th Language Testing Research Colloquium (Kunnan, 2000), one of the notable publications on the subject was the Moss et al. (2008) collection *Assessment, equity, and opportunity to learn*, both of which squarely took on the issue of social justice. For example, in her contribution to the Moss et al. collection, Pullin wrote:

> Equally significant [to measuring outcomes] are the implications of assessment for equity and social justice, insuring that *all* students, particularly those most at risk of educational failure, are the beneficiaries of an effective *opportunity to learn* (OTL) meaningful content. . . . This leads to a dramatically new perspective on OTL, not in terms of content covered and scores attained, but instead based on a more complex view centered on aspects of learning activities and the role of assessment as part of the learning environment. (p. 334)

Recent research that wrestles with the question of whether fairness should be subsumed under validity or strive for broader social justice goals includes Xi (2010) on comparable validity, Mislevy et al. (2013) on universal design, Solano-Flores (2002) on cultural validity, and Steele and Aronson (1995) on stereotype threat. Following Kane (2006), Xi has advanced an argument of fairness as "as comparable validity for all *relevant* groups" (p. 147). Working in the field of language testing, Xi's approach includes adding a corresponding fairness claim to each validity claim: "the fairness argument consists of a series of rebuttals that may challenge the comparability of scores, score interpretations, score-based decisions and consequences for sub-groups" (Xi, 2010, p. 157). Such an approach has also been used by Slomp, Corrigan, and Sugimoto (2014) to evaluate consequences.

One concern about the marriage of fairness and validity is whether an argument-based approach to fairness via validity is too unwieldy. As Borsboom (2005) has pointed out, the expansion of validity theory in-and-of itself has resulted in an unwieldiness in practice (see Chapelle, Enright & Jamieson, 2010):

> In the past century, the question of validity has evolved from the question whether one measures what one intends to measure from the question whether the empirical relations between test scores match theoretical relation in a nomological network (Cronbach and Meehl, 1955), to the question whether interpretations and actions based on test scores are justified—not only in the light of scientific evidence, but with respect to social and ethical consequences of test use (Messick, 1989). Thus, validity theory has gradually come to treat every important test-related issue as relevant to the validity concept, and aims to integrate all these issues under a single header. In doing so, however, the theory fails to serve either the theoretically oriented psychologist or the practically inclined tester. (Borsboom, 2005, pp. 149–150)

We take Borsboom's point to heart. If fairness in writing assessment design is to be achievable, it must appeal to both the theoretically-oriented writing researcher and the writing program administrator who needs to easily gather and present data to a wide range of stakeholders, often under very limited time constraints.

Another recent approach to fairness has been through universal design (i.e., access). Universal design is based on the premise that careful definitions of the construct to be measured can minimize test taker characteristics that interfere with score interpretation, or as Mislevy et al. (2013) explained, "deliberately varying aspects of an assessment for students to enable each student to access, interact with, and provide responses to tasks in ways that present minimal difficulty" (p. 122). Universal design is important because it challenges existing approaches that attempt to "retrofit" assessment to diverse student population—i.e., design a "color-blind" test and then account for diverse response processes (Mislevy et al., 2013, p. 137). Yet, while universal design acknowledges differences among test takers that may result in the misinterpretation of scores, thus aligning it more closely with socio-cultural perspectives (Behizadeh, 2014), it remains focused on access to construct representation for the purposes of score interpretation. Moreover, it assumes that we can know enough about latent responses to validate claims (i.e., latent variables are identifiable), that latent variables are stable within groups and for individuals (i.e., individual learning and development is ignored)[4], and that there is homogeneity within groups (i.e., that racial/ethnic groups are sufficiently homogeneous in cognitive and social profiles). In the end, while latent variable analysis may be useful for identification of genre features (e.g., what are common features of proposals), it can be very easily abused in essentializing writing performances of identity groups.

Cultural validity, likewise, is interested in "the socio-cultural influences that shape student thinking and the ways in which students make sense of . . . items and respond to them" (Solanes-Flores & Nelson-Barber, 2001, p. 555). [5] While the roots of universal design research stem from test accommodations for disabled students (Americans with Disability Act), cultural validity research stems from studies of linguistically diverse students. Like universal design, it neither accounts for historical conditions nor the unintended discrimination that arises from those conditions. It also inadvertently ties linguistic identity to racial/ethnic identity, assuming that latent variables are universal (or universal enough) across a group as to be meaningful for the purposes of designing fair assessment practices.

Stereotype threat theory, which is not the same as test anxiety, was developed to account for the lasting effects of discrimination. Stereotype threat postulates that students who identify with a particular domain (e.g., math) falter in performance when they struggle to overcome misconceptions about their abilities in that domain (e.g., women are bad at math). Stereotype threat research has been extended to a number of conditions (e.g., race, socioeconomic status, gender) (Nguyen & Ryan, 2008) and has been usefully applied in classroom conditions

---

4   Any model that rests on the assumed stability of latent variables is suspect. The stability of latent variables overlooks not merely that students change in their knowledge, motivation, and identification with academic performance but also that their identities change over time and that those shifting identity affiliations potentially have effects on the salient latent variables (Worrell, 2014).

5   The Center for Culturally Relevant Evaluation and Assessment at the University of Illinois has been a particularly active in the area of "culturally responsive assessment" (About CREA, n.d.). Culturally responsive assessment is a sister term to culturally responsive pedagogy, and recognizes the relevance of cultural identity in all aspects of a student's educational experience (Ladson-Billings, 1994; Nieto, 2013).

(Aronson, Fried & Good, 2002; Cohen, Steele & Ross, 1999). Its applicability to test design has been limited because it is not clear what methodologies are to be developed from it for the purposes of assessment (Good, Aronson & Inzlicht, 2003; Stricker, 2008; Stricker & Ward, 2004; Walker & Bridgeman, 2008; Yaeger & Walton, 2011). Nonetheless, its implications for assessment are on the horizon. For example, research by Walton and Spencer (2009) has pointed out that the ability of stereotyped students is latent, thus "underestimated by their level of prior performance" (p. 1133) and that "threat" may actually increase "at each rung of the educational ladder" (p. 1133). In a series of studies, they found that underestimation of intellectual ability was the result of psychological threat, but that "psychological treatments can recover much of this otherwise lost human potential" (Walton & Spencer, 2009, p. 1137). Walton and Spencer (2009) argued, "To close achievement gaps, it is necessary both to eradicate psychological threats embedded in academic environments and to remove other barriers to achievement including objective biases, the effects of poverty, and so forth" (p. 1137).

In the end, although the current issue of the *Standards* suggests otherwise, the assessment community has long wrestled with questions of fairness in testing. In what follows, we seek to add to that conversation by drawing on the disparate impact analysis framework. Before continuing with our discussion, we explain the legal context from which the method was derived and how the method has been used. In the following section, we begin by setting forth the various legal standards—constitutional, statutory, and regulatory—through which racial discrimination has been addressed. This contextualization is critical in understanding the impediments faced by claimants alleging unintentional discrimination and theorization difficulties faced by courts addressing such claims. This background also situates the disparate impact approach and its burden-shifting methodology among the field of legal approaches to racial discrimination. We then discuss the history of the Civil Rights Acts, including Title VI: Nondiscrimination in Federally Assisted Programs before concluding with a discussion of the OCR process—the process used at all federal agencies—to address complaints.

## LEGAL PURSUIT OF DISCRIMINATION CLAIMS

While federal laws prohibiting racial discrimination date back to the post Civil War era, the century that followed the Civil War saw only limited progress in ending racial discrimination. In attempting to address continued and pervasive racial discrimination, Presidents Kennedy and Johnson sought to lay out legal frameworks that complemented constitutional rights and augmented gaps in existing state and federal statutes and regulations.[6] For example, in addition to the Civil Rights Act, the Voting Rights Act of 1965, was enacted to prevent and remedy racial discrimination in voting, and the Fair Housing Act (1968), was enacted to prohibit discrimination in real estate sales, rental, lending, insurance, and other related services based on race, color, sex, religion, and national origin (with familial status and handicap added later).

Specifically, in an educational context, discrimination can be challenged through various avenues, including constitutional, statutory, and regulatory paths: (1) under the Equal Protection Clause of the Fourteenth Amendment to the United States Constitution, (2) under Title VI of the Civil Rights Act of 1964 (or with complaint to the U.S. Department of Education based on Title VI regulations), (3) under 42 U.S.C. § 1983, (4) under state constitutional provisions, and (5) under state constitutional and statutory/regulatory anti-discrimination laws. Table 4.1 summarizes these avenues with a state example taken from a single state, New Jersey.

New Jersey's laws are used for illustrative purposes only. Each approach has non-obvious limitations with respect to disparate impact claims. For example, a practitioner might assume that the most obvious legal avenue for a discrimination claim would be the Equal Protection Clause of the Fourteenth Amendment to the U.S. Constitution. The Equal Protection Clause states, "no State shall . . . deny any person within its jurisdiction the equal protection of the laws" (U.S. Const. amend. XIV, § 1). But the Equal Protection clause is subject to two significant limitations. First, it is only applicable to state, not private, action. Thus, while a public university's policy that expressly discriminates based on race would fall within the ambit of the Equal Protection Clause, the same blatantly discriminatory behavior undertaken by a private university would not involve state action and therefore would not violate the Equal Protection Clause (*Powe v. Miles*, 1968). Moreover, the fact that a private school receives government funding and is heavily regulated by public authorities does not render the school a state actor for the purposes of the Equal Protection clause (*Rendell-Baker v. Kohn*, 1982). Second, the Equal Protection clause does not apply to disparate impact claims. The Supreme Court has made clear that the Equal Protection Clause only prohibits actions that can be shown to constitute intentional discrimination (*Washington v. Davis*, 1976).

---

6   Statutes and regulations are different. Statutes are bills passed by legislative bodies, such as the U.S. Congress or the New Jersey General Assembly. Regulations are detailed rules promulgated by an administrative agency, such as the U.S. Department of Education, under authority granted to the agency by a statute. Regulations outline how statutes will be interpreted and applied by an administrative agency. Both statutes and regulations have the force and effect of law.

Table 4.1. Comparison of Federal and State of Laws Against Discrimination: Comparison of Federal and State of Laws Against Discrimination

|  | Federal | | | State (NJ) | |
| --- | --- | --- | --- | --- | --- |
|  | Constitutional | Statutory/ Regulatory Claims | | Constitutional | Statutory/ Regulatory Claims |
|  | Equal Protection Clause of the 14th Amend. | Title VI of the Civil Rights Act of 1964[a] | 42 U.S.C. § 1983 | Equal Protection under NJ state constitution | NJ Law Against Discrimination |
| **Institution Type** | | | | | |
| Applicable Against Public Institutions | Yes | Yes | No | Yes | Yes |
| Applicable Against Private Institutions | No | Yes | No | No | Yes[b] |
| **Private Claim Available** | | | | | |
| Intentional Discrimination | Yes | Yes | No | Yes | Yes |
| Disparate Impact | No | Yes, but may only be enforced by OCR. | Not likely | No | Yes |

a Applies only to recipients of federal funds.
b The N.J. Law Against Discrimination does not apply to private religious educational institutions.
c A version of this table appeared in our previous article (Poe, Elliot, Cogan & Nurudeen, 2014). It is given here with permission in order to provide a fuller expansion of the laws than was possible in our previous publication due to space limitations.
d State laws differ, sometimes significantly.

Some commentators have suggested that it might be possible to bring a private discrimination lawsuit based on one federal statute (Section 1983 of Title 42 of the U.S. Code) to make a disparate impact claim under another federal statute (Section 602 claim under Title VI of the Civil Rights Act of 1964) (Kidder & Rosner, 2002). Section 1983 does not create rights. Instead, as part of the Civil Rights Act of 1871, it was designed as a vehicle to redress violations of federal Constitutional and statutory rights to combat Reconstruction Era racial violence by the Ku Klux Klan and other White supremacists in the Southern states. In theory, a plaintiff could sue under Section 1983 to redress a violation of his or her federal civil rights by a government official. However, the Supreme Court has never squarely addressed this issue, although federal circuit courts have. Those decisions are split as to whether Section 1983 may be used for disparate impact claims. For example, the Third Circuit (covering Delaware, New Jersey, and Pennsylvania) has ruled that Section 1983 may not be used to enforce disparate impact regulations promulgated under Title VI (*South Camden Citizens in Action v. New Jersey Department of Environmental Protection*, 2001). Likewise, the Sixth Circuit (covering Tennessee, Ohio, Michigan, and Kentucky) and the Ninth Circuit (covering California, Oregon, Washington, Nevada, Montana, Idaho, Arizona, Alaska, and Hawaii) have also ruled that Section 1983 may not be used to enforce disparate impact regulations promulgated under Title VI (*Wilson v. Collins*, 2008; *Save Our Valley v. Sound Transit*, 2003). However, the Tenth Circuit (covering Colorado, Kansas, New Mexico, Oklahoma, Utah, and Wyoming), has indicated that Section 1983 may be used to enforce disparate impact regulations promulgated under Title VI (*Robinson v. Kansas*, 2002). Yet, even in those areas where a circuit court has not explicitly ruled out the use of Section 1983 to enforce disparate impact regulations, the likelihood of a court allowing such a claim is slim (Daly, 2006; Black, 2002). The bottom line regarding the use of Section 1983 to enforce a disparate impact claim under disparate impact regulations is that the standard is applied inconsistently by intermediate-level appellate courts and may not withstand a Supreme Court challenge, thus leaving no national standard.

Finally, in addition to federal laws, some states provide a remedy for disparate impact discrimination (e.g., Or. Rev. Stat. § 659.850 [West Supp. 2015]; 740 Ill. Comp. Stat. § 23/5 [2004]; Cal. Gov't Code § 11135 [West Supp. 2015]; Cal. Gov't Code § 11139 [West Supp. 2015]). However, state constitutions and laws vary as to whether disparate impact is available and if so, how it is applied.

As explained below, Title VI of the Civil Rights Act of 1964 remains the primary legal avenue for addressing claims of disparate impact for federally-funded programs and facilities and the OCR burden-shifting approach remains the most viable conceptual and methodological guidance from which an approach to fairness in assessment may be developed.[7]

---

7   Since the Baxter report, much has been written about Title VII: Equal Employment Opportunity in the measurement literature (Pullin, 2013, 2014; Smith & Hambleton, 1990; Sireci & Green, 2005). Title VII makes it "unlawful to discriminate in any aspect of employment." The legal precedent for Title VII was established in the Griggs v. Duke Power Company case (1971) in which the Supreme Court ruled "unvalidated tests were equated with intentional discrimination" (Selmi, 2006, p. 723). In 2009 there was a twist to Title VII cases in the Ricci v. DeStefano case, when the city of New Haven threw out promotion test results that showed differential performance for African American candidates. White and Hispanic firefighters in New Haven challenged the city's action to throw out test results, citing disparate treatment based on race. In other words, the

# THE CIVIL RIGHTS ACT OF 1964 AND DISPARATE IMPACT

Signed by President Lyndon B. Johnson, the Civil Rights Act of 1964 was landmark legislation prohibiting discrimination in housing, employment, and education. The preamble to the Act states that its purpose is:

> To enforce the constitutional right to vote, to confer jurisdiction upon the district courts of the United States to provide injunctive relief against discrimination in public accommodations, to authorize the Attorney General to institute suits to protect constitutional rights in public facilities and public education, to extend the Commission on Civil Rights, to prevent discrimination in federally assisted programs, to establish a Commission on Equal Employment Opportunity, and for other purposes.

The Act extends the protections granted in the Fourteenth Amendment of the Constitution. Through eleven titles or sections, the Act addresses discrimination in the use of public facilities and accommodations, access to educational facilities, employment hiring and promotion, and voting rights. The Act also establishes various mechanisms for addressing social inequality, including paying for training institutes for teachers, conducting empirical studies to assess ongoing discrimination in educational settings and voter registration, and permitting the Attorney General to initiate legal proceedings in discrimination cases. Finally, the Act sets rules for hearings conducted by the Commission on Civil Rights, which had been established under the Civil Rights Act of 1957, and establishes the Community Relations Service through the Department of Commerce.

The Act addresses discrimination along multiple axes: location, funding, and types of discrimination. On one axis, the Act targets locations of discrimination, ranging from such social institution as schools and hotels. For example, Title II: Injunctive Relief Against Discrimination in Places of Public Accommodation states individuals should have "full and equal enjoyment of the goods, services, facilities, and privileges, advantages, and accommodations of any place of public accommodation . . . without discrimination or segregation on the ground of race, color, religion, or national origin" (1964, §201).

---

plaintiffs accused the city of using intentional discrimination to alleviate unintentional discrimination. The Court held that the City incorrectly discarded the test because it had not "demonstrate[d] a strong basis in evidence that, had it not taken the action, it would have been liable under the disparate-impact statute." The Ricci case is a good example of how test results alone, devoid of contextual factors and analysis, are insufficient to prove disparate impact.

On another axis, the Act targets funding mechanisms, specifically recipients that receive federal funds. Title VI: Nondiscrimination in Federally Assisted Programs, §601, for example, provides:[8]

> No person in the United States shall, in the ground of race, color, or national origin, be excluded from participation in, be denied the benefits of, or be subjected to discrimination under any program or activity receiving Federal financial assistance. (Prohibition against exclusion, 2012)

From a theoretical point of view, what is striking about the Act is the way it captures discrimination (See Perry, 1991 for a useful review of discriminatory purpose theories). The Act acknowledges that both intent ("disparate treatment") and lack of attention ("disparate impact") can result in discrimination. This conceptual framework has been instrumental in the shaping the uptake of the Act in Supreme Court decisions. For example, as Chief Justice Berger wrote in the decision for *Griggs v. Duke Power Company* (1971) case:

> [Although] the Company had adopted the diploma and test requirements without any "intention to discriminate against Negro employees" (420 F.2d at 1232). . . . good intent or absence of discriminatory intent does not redeem employment procedures or testing mechanisms that operate as "built-in headwinds" for minority groups and are unrelated to measuring job capability.

In this way, the Act's architects saw discrimination as located not only in individual action but also in institutional and social practices. Past discrimination was linked to current effects ("built-in headwinds"), thus acknowledging the temporal aspects of discrimination. In other words, the effects of racist policies and actions—including assessment policies and practices—may not be known until after their effects have occurred.

## TITLE VI: NONDISCRIMINATION IN FEDERALLY ASSISTED PROGRAMS

Title VI of the Civil Rights Act of 1964 provides: "No person in the United States shall, on the ground of race, color, or national origin . . . be denied the

---

[8] § 602 states, "each Federal department and agency which is empowered to extend Federal financial assistance to any program or activity, by way of grant, loan, or contract other than a contract of insurance or guaranty" is required to ensure that recipients are not discriminated against (1964).

benefits of, or be subjected to discrimination under any program . . . receiving Federal financial assistance" ( Prohibition against exclusion, 2012). Title VI regulations thus prohibit recipients of federal funds from engaging in practices that "utilize criteria or methods of administration which have the effect of subjecting individuals to discrimination because of their race, color, or national origin" (Discrimination prohibited, 2015). The statute allows for the possibility that federal funds can be denied to a federal grantee—private and public universities—that discriminates (Federal authority and financial assistance, 2012).

Title VI was the most controversial provision in the Act because its vast regulation of the use of public funds. In calling for the enactment of Title VI, Kennedy (1963) stated:

> Simple justice requires that public funds, to which all taxpayers of all races contribute, not be spent in any fashion which encourages, entrenches, subsidizes, or results in racial discrimination. *Direct discrimination by Federal, State, or local governments is prohibited by the Constitution. But indirect discrimination, through the use of Federal funds, is just as invidious; and it should not be necessary to resort to the courts to prevent each individual violation.* [emphasis added]

By targeting discrimination through the federal government's spending powers (Watson, 1990), Kennedy was prescient in understanding that it was insufficient to address discrimination only in existing social institutions.

Unlike the Equal Protection clause of the U.S. Constitution, which only prohibits intentional discrimination by a state actor, Title VI of the Civil Rights Act of 1964 applies to intentional and non-intentional discrimination by state and private actors. However, Title VI does not define what constitutes "discrimination" and does not specify whether the statute includes only intentional discrimination or whether it also reaches more subtle forms of discrimination, such as those that produce racialized disparate effects (Abernathy, 1981; Watson, 1990). Although Congress debated the issue of whether Title VI banned only segregation or extended to de jure discrimination, it never resolved the question. In 2001, however, the Supreme Court, in its *Alexander v. Sandoval* decision, provided some guidance, and in doing so severely restricted disparate impact claims under Title VI.

While the Supreme Court upheld disparate impact in the *Sandoval* case, it foreclosed the ability of private litigants to initiate Title VI disparate impact suits in federal court as it determined Title VI does not create a private right of action (that is, an ability for private, non-governmental actors to initiation legal action) for disparate impact claims. The Court did, however, leave open the possibility of enforcement through agency proceedings (Abernathy, 2006). This means that private parties may file disparate impact complaints with federal agencies, such as the Department of Education, which have the power to investigate, review, and revoke federal funds pursuant to Title VI (Judicial review, 2012). Thus, while the *Sandoval* decision precluded a private lawsuit to enforce a disparate impact claim under Title VI, someone aggrieved by the discriminatory impact of a test can still file a complaint with the U.S. Department of Education alleging disparate impact.

The *Sandoval* decision held that proof of discriminatory impact was sufficient to demonstrate a violation of the Title VI regulations (532 U.S. 275, 2001, pp. 281–282) ("[R]egulations promulgated under § 602 of Title VI may validly proscribe activities that have a disparate impact on racial groups. . . .") In the absence of direct proof of discriminatory motive, claims of intentional discrimination under Title VI may be analyzed using a so-called "burden shifting" approach (United States, Department of Justice, Title VI Manual, 2002, pp. 44–45). (See § 3.0 below.) Under this approach, if statistical data raise a prima facie case of discrimination (i.e., the data demonstrates that the challenged practice or policy results in significant disparities between groups based on race), the burden shifts to the defendant. The defendant must then articulate a non-discriminatory reason for the apparently discriminatory outcome. If the defendant fails to articulate a non-discriminatory reason, the plaintiff prevails. If the defendant can articulate a non-discriminatory reason, the burden shifts back to the plaintiff to demonstrate either existence of a less discriminatory approach or that the articulated non-discriminatory reason is simply a pretext for discrimination. In the end, the burden-shifting approach links statistical evidence with contextual analysis. As we explain in the next section and then demonstrate in §3.0, disparate impact analysis is not simply a numbers game. Context matters and is the heart of the analysis.

## INVESTIGATION OF DISPARATE IMPACT CLAIMS VIA U.S. DEPARTMENT OF EDUCATION OFFICE OF CIVIL RIGHTS

In a 2014 letter, the Department of Education noted:

> School districts that receive Federal funds must not intentionally discriminate on the basis of race, color, or national origin, and must not implement facially neutral policies that have the unjustified effect of discriminating against students on the basis of race, color, or national origin. (Department of Education, p. 5)

Individuals can file complaints with the OCR alleging that an institution's assessment practices have a Title VI discriminatory effect on the basis of race (Department of Justice, 2001; Department of Education, 2012).

When investigating complaints of disparate impact, the OCR will undertake a three-step inquiry as outlined in Table 4.2.

**Table 4.2. OCR's Process for Complaint Inquiry**

| Step | Question |
|---|---|
| 1 | Does the school district have a facially neutral policy or practice that produces an adverse impact on students of a particular race, color, or national origin when compared to other students? |
| 2 | Can the school district demonstrate that the policy or practice is necessary to meet an important educational goal? If the policy or practice is necessary to serve an important educational goal, then OCR would continue to Step 3. |
| 3 | Are there comparably effective alternative policies or practices that would meet the school district's stated educational goal with less of a discriminatory effect on the disproportionately affected racial group; or, is the identified justification a pretext for discrimination? (Department of Education, 2014, p. 8) |

## STEP 1—DOES THE SCHOOL DISTRICT HAVE A FACIALLY NEUTRAL POLICY OR PRACTICE THAT PRODUCES AN ADVERSE IMPACT ON STUDENTS OF A PARTICULAR RACE, COLOR, OR NATIONAL ORIGIN WHEN COMPARED TO OTHER STUDENTS?

The first requirement for making a Title VI disparate impact claim is evidence of a discriminatory effect on minority applicants. As the Department of Education letter (2014) makes clear, "Applying this disparate impact framework, OCR would not find unlawful discrimination based solely upon the existence of a quantitative or qualitative racial disparity resulting from a facially neutral policy" (p. 8). The effect or impact of such policies must be demonstrated through a multi-phase inquiry.

Courts have traditionally relied on a four-step process method to assess impact: (a) calculate the pass rate for each group, (b) observe which group has the highest pass rate, (c) calculate measures of impact by comparing the pass rate for each group with that of the highest group, (d) and observe whether the difference in pass rates is substantial (Fassold, 2000, pp. 460–461).

In other words, test score difference alone does not constitute a case of disparate impact. There must be evidence of impact, as well. The courts have not relied on a single measure to assess "impact," but four common methods include the Hazelwood rule, Shoben rule, a rule of practical significance, and the four-fifths rule.

As Fassold (2000) explained, "The Hazelwood rule is based on the binomial distribution taking into account the standard deviation of a binomial event" (p. 42). Used in cases such as *Castañeda v. Partida* (1977), the Hazelwood rule is appropriate where (1) there are only two possible outcomes—e.g., the selection of an African American candidate or a white candidate from a pool of applicants—and (2) where the observed number is greater than two to three times the standard deviation of the expected value.

The Shoben rule is similar to the Hazelwood rule in that it relies on statistical significance. Under the Shoben rule, independence is assumed in that the performance of one individual is not dependent on the performance of another individual. The rule also assumes that sample size is sufficiently large and representative of the population. If these three conditions are met with a 95% confidence interval, "A difference or '$Z$' value greater than 1.96 standard deviations is ordinarily sufficient to support a finding of adverse [racial] impact" (*Richardson v. Lamar County Board of Education*, 1989, p. 816).

The four-fifths rule and the rule of practical significance are complementary approaches. Under the four-fifths rule, disparate impact is found when the effects of a policy or practice have a pass rate of less than 80%, or four-fifths, on a particular race versus the rate of effects on the reference group (West-Faulcon, 2009). Because the four-fifths rule does not take sample size into consideration, it is sometimes complemented with the rule of practical significance. The rule of practical significance is a measure of magnitude of difference where statistical significance can be determined because of sample size (Fassold, 2000, p. 464).

As obvious from the discussion above, impact is a statistical argument—observed value two to three times the standard deviation of the expected value, a $Z$ value greater than 1.96 standard deviations, or pass rates of less than 80%. More importantly, while the statistical determination of disparate impact is valuable, statistical analysis alone does not probe the underlying arguments for differential outcomes. It also does not suggest what remedies should be put into place to address adverse impact or how that process might unfold.

### Step 2—Can the school district demonstrate that the policy or practice is necessary to meet an important educational goal?

In conducting the second step of this inquiry, the university is given the opportunity to rebut the evidence of discriminatory effect by demonstrating that the criterion that resulted in the impact is required by educational necessity. OCR would consider both the importance of the educational goal and the tightness of the fit between the goal and the policy or practice employed to achieve it. If the policy or practice is not necessary to serve an important educational goal, OCR would find that the school district has engaged in discrimination. If the policy or practice is necessary to serve an important educational goal, then OCR would continue to Step 3.

### STEP 3—ARE THERE COMPARABLY EFFECTIVE ALTERNATIVE POLICIES OR PRACTICES THAT WOULD MEET THE SCHOOL DISTRICT'S STATED EDUCATIONAL GOAL WITH LESS OF A DISCRIMINATORY EFFECT ON THE DISPROPORTIONATELY AFFECTED RACIAL GROUP; OR, IS THE IDENTIFIED JUSTIFICATION A PRETEXT FOR DISCRIMINATION?

If the answer to either question is "yes," then OCR would find that the school district had engaged in discrimination. In other words, if the defendant university successfully demonstrates that the racialized disparate impact of its policy is educationally justified, the institution is still liable for violating Title VI if there is evidence that a less discriminatory alternative exists to the challenged criterion. If no, then OCR would likely not find sufficient evidence to determine that the school district had engaged in discrimination (Department of Education, 2014, p. 8).

Upon conclusion of the process, OCR process begins with efforts at voluntary compliance first. When such cases fail, the OCR can initiate an enforcement action, either referring the case to the Department of Justice for federal court action or proceeding to an administrative hearing to terminate federal funding to the school. Even in the absence of a complaint, DOJ and OCR have the authority to investigate colleges and universities suspected of failing to comply with Title VI (West-Faulcon, 2009; Department of Education, 2012; Department of Justice, 2001).

From an assessment point of view, the OCR burden-shifting approach is particularly appealing; it takes the formalistic framework of the disparate impact approach—an approach that relies on statistical evidence—and extends it by interrogating how we might achieve educational goals through alternative means with less of a discriminatory effect on the disproportionately affected racialized group. This socio-contextual view of assessment is powerful as its interrogates how local decisions about test score interpretation can be put in conversation with larger social goals toward fairness and OTL. In the following example, we illustrate the benefits of the OCR burden-shifting approach to disparate impact in a writing assessment case while also detailing its limitations.

## A FINAL NOTE ABOUT DISPARATE IMPACT TODAY

Before continuing to an illustration of disparate impact analysis, it is important to note the recent Supreme Court decision handed down in June 2015.

Much to the surprise of critics, the Court, again, upheld the viability of disparate impact theory in *Texas Department of Housing and Community Affairs v. The Inclusive Communities Project*. In its decision regarding disparate impact theory under the Fair Housing Act (FHA), however, the Court placed various restrictions on disparate impact claims. Writing the majority opinion, Justice Kennedy stated, "Recognition of disparate-impact liability under the FHA . . . plays a role in uncovering discriminatory intent: It permits plaintiffs to counteract unconscious prejudices and disguised animus that escape easy classification as disparate treatment" (*Texas Department of Housing and Community Affairs v. The Inclusive Communities Project*, 2015, p. 17). Yet, the Court also ruled that racial imbalance alone cannot substantiate disparate impact claims and that lower courts should:

> Examine with care whether a plaintiff has made out a prima facie case of disparate impact[,] and prompt resolution of these cases is important. A plaintiff who fails to allege facts at the pleading stage or produce statistical evidence demonstrating a causal connection cannot make out a prima facie case of disparate impact. (*Texas Department of Housing and Community Affairs v. The Inclusive Communities Project*, 2015, p. 21)

Among other limitations, the Court also ruled that "even when courts do find liability under a disparate-impact theory, their remedial orders must be consistent with the Constitution," "should concentrate on the elimination of the offending practice that 'arbitrar[ily] . . . operate[s] invidiously to discriminate on the basis of rac[e]'" and "should strive to design them to eliminate racial disparities through race-neutral means" (p. 22).

In the end, despite critics' predictions that disparate impact would be struck down by the current Supreme Court, the precedent remains in place. Nevertheless, methodological connections between statistical data, consequence, and remedy remain in flux. This trajectory from statistical evidence to consequence to remedy is a powerful, distinct approach for advancing fairness—an approach that we demonstrate in the remainder of this article, using the burden-shifting approach outlined by the U.S. Department of Education.

## DEMONSTRATION OF THE OCR APPROACH IN A WRITING ASSESSMENT CASE

In previous work (Poe, Elliot, Cogan & Nurudeen, 2014), we demonstrated the application of the OCR burden-shifting approach in a writing program. As we argued in our case drawn from an institutional dataset at a college we called Brick City University, the disparate impact approach is a valuable tool for self-study and is particularly relevant in the use of writing program assessment data, such as placement exams, portfolio assessment, and other kinds of proficiency testing.

Brick City University is a public four-year, doctorate-granting institution in Newark, New Jersey. Brick City has an acceptance rate of 65% and most students come to Brick City with a 3.1–3.5 high school GPA. Demographic percentages and SAT score comparisons are shown in Table 4.3 (College Board, *State Profile Report: New Jersey,* 2012; College Board, *Total Group,* 2013).

As Table 4.3 shows, African American, Native American, Hispanic, and white students admitted to Brick City have higher SAT scores than both the state and national averages. Asian students have slightly lower scores. However, through the writing placement exam—a locally developed timed, impromptu exam (see Poe, Elliot, Cogan & Nurudeen, 2014 for more information)—47% of African American students, 22% of Native American students, 28% of Hispanic students, 10% of white students, and 15% of Asian students place into basic writing. Regarding six-year graduation rates of all students, 59% of Asian and 54% of white students at Brick City University graduate within six years. Only about 40% of African American students and about 47% of Hispanic and Native American students graduate within six years.

Since Brick City graduation rates are similarly low for all students placed in basic writing,[9] the fairness issue for Brick City was not whether some students were required to take basic writing, rather whether that requirement was doing harm to some groups more than others. Let us emphasize here that differences in test scores alone do not constitute disparate impact; students come to college with different writing proficiencies. Rather, disparate impact occurs when a facially-neutral test places an unfair disadvantage on one group versus another. In the Brick City case, the test meant that certain groups of students were placed into a course—basic writing—that seemed to have a disproportionately negative effect on those students' educational outcomes, i.e.,

---

9   Differential graduation rates are often disguised in overall graduation data. Disaggregated graduation rates for students placed into remedial classes versus traditional or honors classes are rarely presented publicly but are important points of data for researchers interested in civil rights claims. For example, if graduation rates are low for students placed in basic writing (e.g., 18% in basic writing versus 40% in traditional courses), the effect of those low graduation rates are not obvious in overall graduation rates (e.g., 35%), especially if only a small number of students are required to take remedial courses versus the overall cohort. In turn, this effect is also found when data are disaggregated by race. As more students of one race are funneled into basic writing, with its lower graduation rate, the overall graduation rate for that race declines.

graduation rates.[10] If the students placed into basic writing were graduating at the same rate as other students, it would be difficult to show disparate impact because the course would seem to have no effect on educational outcomes. The question at Brick City, thus, was whether the high remediation rates for African American and Hispanic students into basic writing might be causing a disproportionate impact on those students' graduation rates.

To conduct their fairness assessment of the consequences of basic writing, the Brick City writing program provided a three-phase inquiry using the OCR burden-shifting approach.

**Table 4.3. Descriptive Statistics for Brick City University Admitted Students (n = 844)**

| Group | Number and Percent | Mean SAT Writing Scores | | | Writing Placement | | Graduation |
|---|---|---|---|---|---|---|---|
| | | Brick City Admitted | New Jersey | National | Basic Writing Number and Percent | First Year Writing Number and Percent | Within six years of admission |
| Overall | N/A | 519 (SD = 84) | 499 (SD = 116) | 488 (SD = 114) | 173 (24%) | 671 (76%) | 49% |
| African American | 107 (13%) | 493 (SD = 68) | 417 (SD = 97) | 417 (SD = 94) | 50 (47%) | 57 (53%) | 40% |
| Native American | 9 (1%) | 504 (SD = 76) | 458 (SD = 112) | 462 (SD = 103) | 2 (22%) | 7 (78%) | 47% |
| Asian | 191 (23%) | 526 (SD = 92) | 566 (SD = 131) | 528 (SD = 129) | 29 (15%) | 162 (85%) | 59% |
| Hispanic | 200 (24%) | 491 (SD = 76) | 440 (SD = 102) | 443 (SD = 92) | 57 (28%) | 143 (72%) | 47% |
| White | 337 (39%) | 538 (SD = 83) | 522 (SD = 103) | 515 (SD = 103) | 35 (10%) | 302 (90%) | 54% |

---

10   This analysis only measures the effects of remediation in a single subject area. The cumulative effect of students placed into remediation in multiple subjects (e.g., English and Mathematics) can be even more pronounced.

## STEP 1—DOES THE SCHOOL DISTRICT HAVE A FACIALLY NEUTRAL POLICY OR PRACTICE THAT PRODUCES AN ADVERSE IMPACT ON STUDENTS OF A PARTICULAR RACE, COLOR, OR NATIONAL ORIGIN WHEN COMPARED TO OTHER STUDENTS?

Using the placement exam data, we applied the four-fifths rule. As shown in Table 4.4, using white students as the benchmark group, the four-fifths rule was not violated for Asian, Native American, or Hispanic students. The rule, however, was violated for African American students.

Table 4.4. Four-fifths Analysis of Brick City University's Writing Placement Results: Four-fifths Analysis of Brick City University's Writing Placement Results

|  | Total Students | White Students | Asian Students | Hispanic Students | Native American | African American |
|---|---|---|---|---|---|---|
| Total Population | 844 | 337 | 191 | 200 | 9 | 107 |
| Number of Students in Group Tracked to First Year Writing | 671 | 302 | 162 | 143 | 7 | 57 |
| Percent of Students in Group Tracked to First Year Writing | 80% | 90% | 85% | 72% | 78% | 53% |
| Four-Fifths Threshold (.8 x Percentage of White Students Tracked to First Year Writing) | 72% (.8*.9=.72) | | | | | |
| Four-Fifths Rule Violated? | — | N/A | No | No | No | Yes |

## STEP 2—CAN THE SCHOOL DISTRICT DEMONSTRATE THAT THE POLICY OR PRACTICE IS NECESSARY TO MEET AN IMPORTANT EDUCATIONAL GOAL?

After statistical analysis revealed that Brick City placement testing had an adverse impact on African American students, Brick City would then need to articulate how the placement exam supports an educational goal. This empirical inquiry could include evaluating whether the construct representation of writing that the placement exam measures is accurate for college-level writing; ensuring that the placement exam assesses those traits that are most likely to result in difficulties in college-level writing; documenting that the basic writing curriculum addresses those traits; and demonstrating that the placement exam is significantly correlated with students' performance in subsequent first-year writing courses. Note here that the writing program may not be able to identify the impact of basic writing on graduation rates, but it can make a connection between remediation and persistence into first year courses, which has been shown to be predictive of continued success in college (Complete College America, 2015b).

### STEP 3—ARE THERE COMPARABLY EFFECTIVE ALTERNATIVE POLICIES OR PRACTICES THAT WOULD MEET THE SCHOOL DISTRICT'S STATED EDUCATIONAL GOAL WITH LESS OF A DISCRIMINATORY EFFECT ON THE DISPROPORTIONATELY AFFECTED RACIAL GROUP; OR, IS THE IDENTIFIED JUSTIFICATION A PRETEXT FOR DISCRIMINATION? (DEPARTMENT OF EDUCATION, 2014, P. 8)

In the final step of the OCR burden-shifting approach, Brick City would then explore alternatives available that met the school's stated educational goal with less of a burden on African American students. At this stage, the discourse and processes of assessment change dramatically. Rather than looking solely to test scores, this final phase of the OCR method invites stakeholders to participate in curricular reform while maintaining the educational goals for writing instruction. In the Brick City case, a corequisite option was selected.

In making this selection, Brick City test designers followed the guidance of Standard 3.20:

> When a construct can be measured in different ways that are equal in their degree of construct representation and validity (including freedom from construct-irrelevant variance), test users should consider, among other factors, evidence of subgroup differences in mean scores or percentages of examinees whose scores exceed the cut scores, in deciding which test and/or cut scores to use. (AERA, APA & NCME, 2014, p. 72)

## GROUP CLASSIFICATION CONSIDERATIONS USING THE DISPARATE IMPACT APPROACH

The Brick City case provides much optimism; it relies on established empirical methods for evaluating disparate impact, demands the articulation of curricular goals, and invites curriculum innovation while maintaining consistent educational goals. Yet, the burden-shifting approach is not without problems. Legal critics have argued, for example, that disparate impact analysis is reactive rather than proactive, thus making it out-of-step with international human rights standards (Hunter & Shoben, 2014), that there are not comparable methods or standards for evaluating intentional discrimination (Selmi, 2006; Willborn, 1985), and that the statistical measures suggestive of adverse impact, such as the $Z$ value greater than 1.96 standard deviations and four-fifths rule are arbitrary.

From a measurement perspective, the burden-shifting approach has another challenge—strength of sampling plan. Strength of sampling plan is a problem that has long vexed the measurement communities, especially with regard to small populations (Kane, 1982, 2011; Linn, 1989). Thus, when Standard 3.2 makes the seemingly straightforward recommendation that "those responsible for test development should include relevant subgroups in validity, reliability/precision, and other preliminary studies used when constructing the test," researchers should take to heart that this is not a straightforward process (AERA, APA & NCME, 2014, p. 64). Because of the challenges of statistical analysis using small populations, new techniques such as resampling (Yu, 2003), including Monte Carlo sampling (Yu, 2003), have been tools to ensure robust group sizes for statistical analysis even for small populations. This, however, is not the case in local writing assessment, where resampling may not be a viable technique for reporting purposes or data on group performances may not be collected. Ultimately, many writing program administrators are faced with the reality of having insufficiently large sample sizes from which to conduct comparative group analysis.[11]

Adoption of the burden-shifting approach, thus, requires some caution, as the issues identified in the legal and measurement literature are worthy of further discussion. For our purposes here—and to keep this article relatively brief—we want to address one concern that has been overlooked by both legal and assessment scholars—characterization of groups. By characterization of groups we mean how group populations are defined and identified. As we think of it, there are three questions that can be used to guide this inquiry: (1) Do the group identifications describe meaningful traits for the group that encompass social equity concerns? (2) Are the inferences drawn from the group identifications sufficiently grounded in the contextual conditions for that group? And (3)

---

11   The current edition of the *Standards* states that when quantitative evidence is not available, qualitative evidence may be used. But precedent tell us qualitative evidence is not viewed with the same level confidence as quantitative evidence, and, in fact, legislation such as No Child Left Behind (NCLB) dictated that only "scientifically-based evidence"—i.e., statistical evidence—could be used for reporting purposes. The authors of the *Standards*, in fact, acknowledged the demand for quantitative score-based data for the purposes of external reporting (p. 140). Given the lack of support typically found in measurement scholarship, legal cases, and administrative decision-making for qualitative evidence, we would be remiss to suggest that qualitative and quantitative evidence stand on equal footing.

Are there combinations of variables that suggest different inferences are salient for focal groups? To answer these questions, we discuss three issues: group specification, demographic shifts, and intersectionality.

It should be noted that in the following discussion, we use the term "group identity" here rather than subgroup, as it more accurately reflects today's demographic realities; subgroup may be statistically useful but socially demeaning. There are no longer groups and subgroups, simply groups.

## GROUP SPECIFICATION

The issue for population specification in regard to fairness is two-fold. First, we cannot assume that the group specification today is without its flaws—a complexity that is evidenced nationally in the shifting categories used on census records and in legal decisions (Lopez, 1997). Second, there must be a commitment to ensuring that the criteria used to define groups is meaningful across groups in order to provide the kinds of evidence needed to make fairness claims. Thus, population specification—"the ways in which cultural groups are defined and, therefore, the criteria used to determine when an individual belongs to a certain cultural group" (Basterra, Trumbull & Solano-Flores, 2011, p. 9)—is complex and should be treated as such.

A lesson from history is instructive here: In Cleary's classic 1966 study in which she argued a test is biased "if too high or too low a criterion score is consistently predicted for members of the subgroup when the common regression line is used" (p. 1), she engaged with two problems of sampling: group identification and sample size. First, as she explained, "the scarcity of Negro students in the integrated colleges is disturbing," thus leaving her a small number of schools for the study (p. 5). In regard to group identification, she explained, "Most schools had no record of the race of their individual students" (p. 5). In such cases, Cleary relied on the judgments of two "persons" who "examine[d] independently the standard identification pictures in the school files" (p. 6). Based upon the judges' assessment, the students were assigned a racialized identity. In instances where the judges could not agree, "the student was classified as white" (p. 6). She used NAACP records to corroborate judges' ratings.

As cultural critics would expect, Cleary's "look test" method of racial identification—a method also used by Pfeifer and Sedlacek (1971)—was less than perfect, a point she acknowledged in noting how she addressed outliers:

> Five students not on the NAACP list had been classified as Negro, and one student on the NAACP list had been classified as white. The five students not on the NAACP list were

> retained as Negroes after further examination of the identification pictures. The race code of the one student who was on the NAACP list but who had not been classified as Negro was changed to Negro. (p. 6)

In other words, students who "looked black" stayed in the Negro sample for the study, and the student who phenotypically passed for white but was listed on the NAACP record was replaced into the Negro sample. We would argue that such methodological choices are reflective of U.S. historical norms regarding the one-drop rule, not scientific method.

Today, most studies such as our Brick City example rely on student's self-reported racialized identity using the Office of Management and Budget categories (Office of Management and Budget, 1995).[12] While racialized identity may be tied to federal census categories set by the Office of Management and Budget, other group identifications such as socioeconomic status and linguistic identity are even more complicated. Family income and educational levels, for example, have conventionally been used as proxies for socioeconomics status (SES) (ACT, 2014; Sacket et al., 2009). In K-12 studies, researchers may also use qualification for free or reduced meals as an indicator of socioeconomic status.[13] And the National Center for Educational Statistics (2012) has recommended:

> Family income and other indicators of home possessions and resources, parental educational attainment, and parental occupational status should be considered components of a core SES measure . . . Neighborhood and school SES could be used to construct an expanded SES measure. (2012, p. 5)

Among the many criticisms of self-economic status indicators as meaningful markers of group identity are that income (e.g., annual salary) and education are not what separate racialized groups. Instead, it is wealth (e.g., investments, home ownership, etc.). In 2006, the median net worth of a white family was $120,900; for people of color, it was $17,100 (Liu et al., 2006, p. 3). In 2009, the median wealth of white families was $113,149; for Latino families it was $6,325 and for black families it was $5,677 (Kochar, Fry & Taylor, 2011). In a study conducted

---

12   Self-report racial/ethnic identity can also present challenges. Likely, the most well-known challenge is the category "mixed race," which includes many Native American students. Native American self-reporting can also be challenging because self-reporting may or may not include members who are officially enrolled in an indigenous nation—for example, there are 819,000 self-identified Cherokee on the U.S. Census but only 314,000 officially enrolled Cherokee citizens.

13   Currently, recipients qualify for reduced meals at 185% the federal poverty level and free meals at 130% the federal poverty level (Department of Education, 2015).

by the Institute for Assets and Social Policy at Brandeis University, researchers traced the same households over 25 years. During that time, the total wealth gap between white and African-American families increased from $85,000 in 1984 to $236,500 in 2009 (Shapiro, Meschede & Osoro, 2013, p. 1). Home ownership, income, unemployment, education, and inheritance were the main drivers of wealth inequality with home ownership being the largest predictor for wealth gap (p. 3). Moreover, additional income gains, inheritance, other financial supports, and marriage yielded different rates of return—for example, a $1 increase in income for a white family converted to $5.19 of wealth. That same dollar increase for Black families yielded 69 cents in wealth. Finally, a criticism of conventional socioeconomic indicators is that they do not reflect historical legacy. Rubin et al. (2014) have argued that SES is different than social class with SES referring to one's current social and economic situation and social class referring to one's sociocultural background (p. 196). SES, they argued, may be quite variable while social class tends to remain more fixed.

Linguistic identity is also illustrative here. Much has been written in the field of second language writing regarding how researchers might best capture the nuances of contemporary multilingual identity (e.g., Shohamy, 2011). This attention to evolving definitions of World Englishes and "languaging" is often not found in the assessment literature (Dryer, 2016). For example, in a recent study conducted by Sinharay, Dorans, and Liang (2011) regarding fairness procedures for test-takers whose first language is not English, they used a rather thin definition to determine group specification:

> For illustrative purposes, we use the first-language status of a test taker as a surrogate for language proficiency and describe an approach to examining how the results of fairness procedures are affected by inclusion or exclusion of those who report that English is not their first language in the fairness analyses. (p. 25)

## SHIFTING DEMOGRAPHICS

Demographic shifts are the largest challenges to making longitudinal claims about fairness for two reasons (Aud, Fox & Kewal Ramani, 2010). First, traditional categories used to describe racial/ethnic groups may belie fundamental changes within those groups. Second, the use of white students as the reference group may no longer be appropriate if they are no longer the majority population—or even the population that reports back the highest scores on tests and other assessments. In such cases where group identification is shifting, researchers must proceed with extra caution in making inferences. This point cannot be understated. If the gold standard of validity is to be prediction, then longitudinal claims must be interrogated carefully.

Again, history is illustrative here: The 1966 Equality of Educational Opportunity report, also known as the Coleman report for its lead author, sociologist James Coleman, was submitted in response to the Civil Rights Act of 1964, which ordered a survey and a report to the President and the Congress

> concerning the lack of availability of equal educational opportunities for individuals by race, color, religion, or national origin in educational institutions at all levels in the United States, in territories and possessions, and the District of Columbia. (§402)

The Coleman report researchers were tasked with determining the extent of racial segregation in U.S. schools and "whether the schools offer equal educational opportunities in terms of a number of other criteria which are regarded as good indicators of educational quality" (Coleman et al., 1966, p. iii). The researchers did not review differences by religion or country of origin, and instead relied on six racial categories: Negroes, American Indians, Oriental Americans, Puerto Ricans living in the continental United States, Mexican Americans, whites other than Mexican Americans and Puerto Ricans (Coleman et al., 1966, p. iii).

With respect to demographics, there are two lessons from the Coleman report. First, the racial designations used by the Coleman researchers 50 years ago are out-of-sync with today's terminology. Moreover, in contrast to the Civil Rights era, today most immigrants are classified under Asian or Hispanic group designations (Migration Policy Institute; Census, 1999).[14] As previously demonstrated (Inoue & Poe, 2012), longitudinal claims about group performances can lead to inaccurate conclusions when group ethnic formations are not compared. In the Inoue & Poe study, results of the California State University English Placement Test were traced over 25 years, noting that the results suggested a decline in the performance Asian students. Upon closer investigation, it was determined that the ethnic groups that comprised the Asian group had shifted dramatically during the time period under study. While previously students had been of Chinese background, more recent students were Hmong, a group that has strong agrarian ties and, given their refugee status across multiple countries, often does not have a history of formal education within families.

---

14  Hispanic, of course, was not an identity designation until 1970 and even now is not considered a racial category on the U.S. Census. Instead, Hispanic origin is defined a "the heritage, nationality, lineage, or country of birth of the person or the person's parents or ancestors before arriving in the United States. People who identify as Hispanic, Latino, or Spanish may be any race" (Census, n.d.).

Second, the architects of the Coleman report—following the history of U.S. legal and social precedent—constructed a narrative of the U.S. that is based on distinct racialized categories and north/south geographic comparisons. White students were always the demographic group to which African American students were compared. In today's shifting U.S. demographics—a demographic change that has been called "stunning" (Teixeira, Frey & Griffin, 2015, p. 2)—white students may no longer be the appropriate reference group, thus shifting the entire referential frame by which group comparisons are made.

In Brick City's case, Hispanic students now make up the second largest group of admitted students (200 Hispanic students versus 337 white students). In the last 10 years, while the number of Asian American students and African American students has remained consistent, the number of Hispanic students admitted to Brick City has doubled, reflecting the changing demographic patterns of its regionally-serving identity. If such a trend continues, within the next decade Hispanic students will become the reference group against which all others will be compared.

## INTERSECTIONALITY

Likely the most methodologically challenging aspect of disparate impact analysis is intersectionality—the multidimensionality of identity that reveals intergroup differences. Crenshaw's scholarship in legal journals (1989, 1991) is widely cited on intersectionality. For Crenshaw, discrimination challenges often are imbued with a flawed logic that separates race from gender: " . . . in race discrimination cases, discrimination tends to be viewed in terms of sex- or class-privileged Blacks; in sex discrimination cases, the focus is on race- and class- privileged women" (1989, p. 140). As a result, those who are "multiply-burdened" are marginalized and claims are obscured "that cannot be understood as resulting from discrete sources of discrimination" (Crenshaw, 1989, p. 140). What Crenshaw posits then is, for example, that the effects of race/gender/class are more subtle and perhaps greater than race plus gender plus class. Further disaggregating columns in a spreadsheet or conducting a multiple regression analysis will not reveal the cascading effects of a legacy of brutality. Interestingly, it is a subtlety that Johnson, too, pointed out in his 1965 commencement speech at Howard University:

> For Negro poverty is not white poverty. Many of its causes and many of its cures are the same. But there are differences—deep, corrosive, obstinate differences—radiating painful roots into the community, and into the family, and the nature of the individual. These differences are not racial differences.

> They are solely and simply the consequence of ancient brutality, past injustice, and present prejudice. (Johnson, 1965)

In reviewing decades of assessment literature, it is striking how traditionally few researchers looked at combinations of variables. Today, researchers like Zwick and Green (2007) and Zwick and Himelfarb (2011) provide some useful direction in that they revisit existing wisdom about prediction of SAT scores and high school grades through the lens of school resources and within versus across school comparisons. Yet, more is to be done in the development of fairness methods. Specifically, further advancement is needed to understand the cascading effects of multiple variables as well as to understand intergroup differences. (For example, if we start out to look at differences between Asian and White students, we are likely to find them without attending to the differences within the performance of Asian students.) These "indices of fairness that reflect more complex matrices," as Petersen and Novick called them 40 years ago, should look at identity clusters within groups (e.g., African American women from middle class backgrounds) to help researchers make more nuanced claims about fairness and ensure that researchers do not assume homogeneity within groups. Bottom line: Without nuance, meaningful change is unlikely.

## THE POSSIBILITY OF FAIRNESS

At the 1965 Howard University commencement address, Lyndon B. Johnson declared:

> You do not take a person who, for years, has been hobbled by chains and liberate him, bring him up to the starting line of a race and then say, "you are free to compete with all the others," and still justly believe that you have been completely fair. Thus it is not enough just to open the gates of opportunity. All our citizens must have the ability to walk through those gates.

Our goal in writing this article was to advance disparate impact theory, and more specifically the burden-shifting approach, as a conceptual and methodological framework for fairness. Like Kane, we are inclined to define fairness and validity broadly (2010), but our fear is that collapsing fairness into validity will result in the inattention to fairness. As we have suggested, methodological advancements such as those by Zwick and Green (2007), Zwick and Himelfarb (2011), and Xi (2010) are useful, important, and insufficient if they are not viewed as part of the process of developing a rigorous conceptual and methodological framework for fairness. Such a framework must include questions of access, response processes, test score interpretation, and social consequence.

Disparate impact theory and the burden-shifting approach as outlined by the OCR provides a theory and a method by which we can recognize that past inequality has consequences today. The approach combines empiricism and contextualization—i.e., data do not speak to themselves without the force of history and social action. In doing so, the OCR process invites reflection; it encourages us to think expansively, beyond comfortable, known strictures. Finally, the disparate impact approach has been sustainable, weathering the political shifts of the Supreme Court and the shifting social and demographic changes of the U.S. over the last 50 years.

Of course, there remain questions. Disparate impact analysis, for example, has not been evaluated using intersectional identities: Are the effects of unintentional discrimination different for African American women, for example, than for African Americans as a group? Likewise, under what time scales can disparate impact analysis be meaningful when racialized group identifications can shift dramatically in a few generations? And without interrogation of group identification during step 1 of the disparate impact analysis, arguments made about fairness could be made only of gossamer. Such questions should not arouse suspicions about the viability of disparate impact. Instead, through the pursuit of these questions and others, disparate impact theory and the burden-shifting approach can be enriched and deepened for the purpose of fairness studies.

In the end, if equitability is to be valued, it must be seen. Fairness in theory cannot be an afterthought to validity or reliability. Fairness in action demands local attention in which we repeatedly question how we can achieve equitable results with less adverse impact—in which "the rights of every man are diminished when the rights of one man are threatened" (Kennedy, 1963). Test scores may reflect social inequality, but the *use* of test scores works to create that social inequality. Racial isolation and structural inequality are not merely reflective of such social mechanisms; social mechanisms work to sustain invisibility, racialized isolation, and structural inequality. The creation of opportunity structures through approaches such as disparate impact analysis holds the potential to provide visibility, community, and equity.

# REFERENCES

Abernathy, C. (1981). Title VI and the constitution: A regulatory model for defining "discrimination." *Georgetown Law Journal, 70*, 1–49.

Abernathy, C. (2006). Legal realism and the failure of the "effects" test for discrimination. *Georgetown Law Journal, 94*(2), 267–319.

Center for Culturally Responsive Evaluation and Assessment. (n.d.) About CREA. http://education.illinois.edu/CREA/about-crea.

ACT. (2014). *The condition of college & career readiness 2014: Students from low-income families.* https://www.act.org/readiness/2014.

American Educational Research Association, American Psychological Association & NCME. (1974). *Standards for educational and psychological testing.* American Educational Research Association.

American Educational Research Association, American Psychological Association & NCME. (2014). *Standards for educational and psychological testing.* American Educational Research Association.

American Psychological Association Task Force on Employment Testing of Minority groups. (1969). Job testing and the disadvantaged, *American Psychologist, 24,* 637–650.

Adams, P., Gearhart, S., Miller, R. & Roberts, A. (2009). The accelerated learning program: Throwing open the gates. *Journal of Basic Writing, 28*(2), 50–69.

Alexander v. Sandoval, 532 U.S. 275 (2001).

Aronson, J., Fried, C. & Good, C. (2002). Reducing the effects of stereotype threat on African American college students by shaping theories of intelligence. *Journal of Experimental Social Psychology, 38*(2), 113–125.

Aud, S., Fox, M. & Kewal Ramani, A. (2010). *Status and Trends in the Education of Racial and Ethnic Groups. National Center for Educational Statistics Report* (NCES 2010–015). U. S. Department of Education.

Basterra, M. R., Trumbull, E. & Solano-Flores, G. (Eds.). (2011). *Cultural validity in assessment: Addressing linguistic and cultural diversity.* Routledge.

Behizadeh, N. (2014). Mitigating the dangers of a single story: Creating large-scale writing assessments aligned with sociocultural theory. *Educational Researcher, 43*(3), 125–136.

Bennett, R., Kane, M. & Bridgeman, B. (2011). *Theory of action and validity argument in the content of through-course summative assessment.* Educational Testing Service.

Black, D. (2002). Picking up the pieces after Alexander v. Sandoval: Resurrecting a private cause of action for disparate impact. *North Carolina Central Law Review, 81*(1), 56–391.

Borsboom, D. (2005). *Measuring the mind: Conceptual issues in contemporary psychometrics.* Cambridge University Press.

Braceras, J. (2002). Killing the messenger: The misuse of disparate impact theory to challenge high-stakes educational tests. *Vanderbilt Law Review, 55,* 1111–1203.

Breland, H. & Ironson, G. (1976). DeFunis Reconsidered: A Comparative Analysis of Alternative Admissions Strategies. *Journal of Educational Measurement, 13*(1), 89–99.

Broad, B. (2016). This is not only a test: Exploring structured ethical blindness in the testing industry. *The Journal of Writing Assessment, 9*(1). https://escholarship.org/uc/item/2bt3m3nf.

Cal. Government Code § 11135 (West Supp. 2015). 16/24.

Cal. Government Code § 11139 (West Supp. 2015).

Camilli, G. (2006). Test fairness. In R. Brennan (Ed.), *Educational measurement* (4th edition, pp. 221–256). Rowman & Littlefield Publishers.

Castañeda v. Partida, 430 U.S. 482 (1977). Census Bureau (n.d.). Hispanic origin. http://www.census.gov/topics/population/hispanic-origin.html.

Census Bureau (1999). Race and Hispanic origin of the population by nativity: 1850 to 1990. http://www.census.gov/population/www/documentation/twps0029/tab08.html.

Chapelle, C., Enright, M. & Jamieson, J. (2010). Does an argument-based approach to validity make a difference? *Educational Measurement: Issues and Practice, 29*(1), 3–13.

Civil action for deprivation of rights. 42 U.S.C. § 1983 (2012).

Civil Rights Act. 42 U.S.C. § 2000e (2012).

Cleary, T. (1966). *Test bias: Validity of the scholastic aptitude test for Negro and white students in integrated colleges.* (College Entrance Examination Board RDR-65-6, No. 18). Educational Testing Service.

Cohen, G., Steele, C., Ross, L. (1999). The mentor's dilemma: Providing critical feedback across the racial divide. *Personality and Social Psychology Bulletin, 25*(10), 1302–1318.

Cole, N. & Zieky, M. (2001). The new faces of fairness. *Journal of Educational Measurement, 38*(4), 369–382.

Coleman, J., Campbell, E., Hobson, C., McPartland, J., Mood, A., Weinfeld, F. & York, R. (1966). *Equality of educational opportunity.* National Center for Educational Statistics.

College Board. (2012). *State Profile Report: New Jersey.* College Board.

College Board. (2013). *Total Group Profile Report.* College Board.

Complete College America. (2011). *Time is the enemy: The surprising truth about why today's college students aren't graduating . . . and what needs to change.* Complete College America.

Complete College America. (2012). *Remediation: Higher education's bridge to nowhere.* Complete College America.

Complete College America. (2015a). *The results are in. Corequisite remediation works.* http://completecollege.org/the-results-are-in-corequisite-remediation-works.

Complete College America. (2015b). *Corequisite Remediation: Spanning the Completion Divide.* Complete College America. http://completecollege.org/spanningthedivide/wp-content/uploads/2016/01/CCA-SpanningTheDivide-ExecutiveSummary.pdf.

Crenshaw, K. (1989). Demarginalizing the intersection of race and sex: A black feminist critique of antidiscrimination doctrine, feminist theory and antiracist politics. *The University of Chicago Legal Forum, 140,* 139–167.

Crenshaw, K. (1991). Mapping the margins: Intersectionality, identity politics, and violence against women of color. *Stanford Law Review, 43*(6), 1241–1299.

Cronbach, L. (1976). Equity in selection: Where psychometrics and political philosophy meet. *Journal of Educational Measurement, 13*(1), 31–42.

Cronbach, L. J. (1988). Five perspectives on validity argument. In H. Wainer (Ed.), *Test validity* (pp. 3–17). Erlbaum.

Cushman E. (2016). Decolonizing validity. *The Journal of Writing Assessment, 9*(1). https://escholarship.org/uc/item/0xh7v6fb.

Daly, A. (2006). How to speak American: In search of the real meaning of "meaningful access" to government services for language minorities. *Penn State Law Review*, *110*(4), 1005–1046.

Davis, E. (2006). Unhappy parents of limited English proficiency students: What can they really do. *Journal of Law and Education*, *35*(2), 277–288.

Department of Education. (2012, December 5). Compliance review letter metropolitan school district of Pike Township [Letter to Nathaniel Jones]. Office for Civil Rights. https://www2.ed.gov/about/offices/list/ocr/docs/investigations/05085002-a.pdf.

Department of Education. (2014). Dear colleague letter: Resource compatibility [Letter on educational opportunity]. Office for Civil Rights. http://www2.ed.gov/about/offices/list/ocr/letters/colleague-resourcecomp-201410.pdf.

Department of Housing and Urban Development. (2013). Implementation of the Fair Housing Act's Discriminatory Effects, *78*(32). http://portal.hud.gov/hudportal/documents/huddoc?id=discriminatoryeffectrule.pdf.

Department of Justice. (2002). *Guidance to federal financial assistance recipients regarding Title VI prohibition against national origin discrimination affecting limited English proficient person*s. U.S. Department of Justice. https://tinyurl.com/b5tasfdc.

Discrimination in education prohibited. Or. Rev. Stat. § 659.850 (West Supp. 2015).

Discrimination prohibited. 740 Ill. Comp. Stat. § 23/5 (2004).

Discrimination prohibited. 34 C.F.R. §100.3 (2015).

Dryer, D. (2016). Appraising translingualism. *College English*, *78*(3), 274–283.

Elliot, N. (2016) A theory of ethics for writing assessment. *The Journal of Writing Assessment*, *9*(1).

Elliot, N., Deess, P., Rudniy, A. & Joshi, K. (2012). Placement of students into first-year writing courses. *Research in the Teaching of English*, *46*(3), 285–313.

Elul, H. (1998). Making the grade, public education reform: The use of standardized testing to retain students and deny diplomas. *Columbia Human Rights Law Review*, *30*, 495–536.

Every Child Succeeds Act, S. 1177 (2015). https://www.gpo.gov/fdsys/pkg/BILLS-114s1177enr/pdf/BILLS-114s1177enr.pdf.

Fassold, M. (2000). Disparate impact analyses of TAAS scores and school quality. *Hispanic Journal of Behavioral Sciences*, *22*(4), 460–480.

Federal authority and financial assistance to programs or activities by way of grant, loan, or contract other than contract of insurance or guaranty; rules and regulations; approval by President; compliance with requirements; reports to Congressional committees; effective date of administrative action. 42 U.S.C. § 2000d-1 (2012).

Gallagher, A., Bridgeman, B. & Cahalan, C. (2002). The effect of computer-based tests on racial-ethnic and gender groups. *Journal of Educational Measurement*, *39*(2), 133–147.

Glau, G. (1996). The "stretch program": Arizona State University's new model of university-level basic writing instruction. *WPA: Writing Program Administration*, *20*(1/2), 79–91.

Good, C., Aronson, J. & Inzlicht, M. (2003). Improving adolescents' standardized test performance: An intervention to reduce the effects of stereotype threat. *Journal of Applied Developmental Psychology*, 24(6), 645–662.

Green III, P. (1996). Can Title VI prevent law schools from adopting admissions practices that discriminate against African-Americans? *Southern University Law Review*, 24(2), 237–261.

Grego, R. & Thompson, N. (1995). The writing studio program: Reconfiguring basic writing/freshman composition. *WPA: Writing Program Administration*, 19(1/2), 66–79.

Grego, R. & Thompson, N. (2007). *Teaching/Writing in thirdspaces: The studio approach*. Southern Illinois University Press.

Griggs v. Duke Power Co., 401 U.S. 424 (1971).

H. R. Misc. Doc. No. 124, 88th Cong., 1st Sess. 3, 12 (1963).

Haertel, E., Moss, P., Pullin, D. & Gee, J. (2008). Introduction. In P. Moss, D. Pullin, J. Gee, E. Haertel & L. Young (Eds.) *Assessment, equity, and opportunity to learn* (pp. 1–16). Cambridge University Press.

Hunter, R. & Shoben, E. (2014). Disparate impact discrimination: American oddity or internationally accepted concept. *Berkeley Journal of Employment & Labor Law*, 19(1), 108–152.

Implementation of the Fair Housing Act's Discriminatory Effects, 78(32) Fed. Reg. 11460–11482 (2013). http://portal.hud.gov/hudportal/documents/huddoc?id=discriminatoryeffectrule.pdf.

Inoue, A. & Poe, M. (2012). Racial formations in two writing assessments: Revisiting White and Thomas' findings on the English Placement Test after 30 Years. In N. Elliot & L. Perelman (Eds.) *Writing assessment in the 21st Century: Essays in honor of Edward M. White* (pp. 343–36). Hampton Press.

Isaacs, E. (2018). *Writing at the State U: Writing instruction and writing program administration at 106 U.S. representative institutions*. Utah State University Press.

Jaeger, R. (1976). A word about the issue. *Journal of Educational Measurement*, 13(1), 1.

Johnson, L. (1965, June 4). To fulfill these rights. [Commencement Address] Howard University, Washington, DC.

Judicial review; administrative procedure provisions. 42 U.S.C § 2000d-2 (2012).

Kane, M. (1982). A sampling model for validity. *Applied Psychological Measurement*, 6(2), 125–160.

Kane, M. (2006). Validation. In R. Brennan (Ed.), *Educational measurement* (4th ed., pp. 17–64). Rowman & Littlefield Publishers.

Kane, M. (2010). Validity and fairness. *Language Testing*, 27(2), 177–182.

Kane, M. (2011). The error of our ways. *Journal of Educational Measurement*, 48(1), 12–30.

Kane, M. (2012). Validity, fairness, and testing. [Presentation] Conference on Conversations on Validity Around the World, New York, NY. https://www.ets.org/c/18486/pdf/19633_ets_tc_validityconference_Kane%202012_03_28.pdf.

Kennedy, J. (1963, June 11). A report to the American people on civil rights. [Radio and television address]. Columbia Broadcasting System.

Kidder, W. & Rosner, J. (2002). How the SAT creates built-in-headwinds: An educational and legal analysis of disparate impact. *Santa Clara Law Review, 43*(1), 131–211.

Kochar, R., Fry, R. & Taylor, P. (2011). *Wealth gaps rise to record highs between Whites, Blacks, Hispanics*. Pew Research Center.

Kunnan, A. J. (2000). Fairness and justice for all. In A. J. Kunnan (Ed.), *Fairness and validation in language assessment* (pp. 1–14). Cambridge University Press.

Ladson-Billings, G. (1994). *The dreamkeepers*. Jossey-Bass.

Langenfeld, T. (1997). Test fairness: Internal and external investigations of gender bias in mathematics testing. *Educational Measurement: Issues and Practice, 16*(1), 20–26.

Lindsay, P. & Crusan, D. (2011). How faculty attitudes and expectations toward student nationality affect writing assessment. *Across the Disciplines, 8*(4). https://doi.org/10.37514/ATD-J.2011.8.4.23.

Linn, R. (1976). In search of fair selection procedures. *Journal of Educational Measurement, 13*(1), 53–58.

Linn, R. (Ed.). (1989). *Intelligence, theory, and public policy*. University of Illinois.

Lioi, A. & Merola, N. (2012). The muse of difference: Race and writing placement at two elite art schools. In A. Inoue & M. Poe (Eds.), *Race and writing assessment* (pp. 155–168). Peter Lang.

Liu, M., Robles, B., Leonder-Wright, B., Brewer, R. & Adamson, R. (2006). *The color of wealth: The story behind the U.S. racial wealth divide*. The Fair Press.

Lopez, I. (1997). *White by law: The legal construction of race*. New York University Press.

Lu, C. & Suen, H. (1995). Assessment approaches and cognitive style. *Journal of Educational Measurement, 32*(1), 1–17.

Marefat, F. & Heydari, M. (2016). Native and Iranian teachers' perceptions and evaluation of Iranian students' English essays. *Assessing Writing, 27*, 24–36.

Messick, S. (1980). Test validity and the ethics of assessment. *American Psychologist, 35*(11), 1012–1027.

Messick. S. (1989a). Validity. In R. L. Linn (Ed.), *Educational measurement* (3rd ed., pp. 13–103). American Council on Education and National Council on Measurement in Education.

Messick, S. (1989b). Meaning and values in test validation: The science and ethics of assessment. *Educational Researcher, 18*(2), 5–11.

Migration Policy Institute. (n.d.). https://tinyurl.com/mrs6yzav.

Mislevy, R. J., Haertel, G., Cheng, B., Ructtinger, L., DeBarger, A., Murray, E., . . . Vendlinski. T. (2013). A "conditional" sense of fairness in assessment. *Educational Research and Evaluation: An International Journal on Theory and Practice, 19*, 121–140.

Moss, P., Pullin, D., Gee, J., Haertl, E. & Young, L. (Eds.). (2008). *Assessment, equity, and opportunity to learn*. Cambridge University Press.

Murray, V. (2008). *The high price of failure in California: How inadequate education costs schools, students, and society*. Pacific Research Institute.

National Center for Educational Statistics. (2012). Improving the measurement of socioeconomic status for the National Assessment of Educational Progress: A theoretical foundation. https://nces.ed.gov/nationsreportcard/pdf/researchcenter/Socioeconomic_Factors.pdf.

Nguyen, H. & Ryan, A. (2008). Does stereotype threat affect test performance of minorities and women? A meta-analysis of experimental evidence. *Journal of Applied Psychology, 93*(6), 1314–1334.

Nieto, S. (2013). *Finding joy in teaching students of diverse backgrounds: Culturally responsive and socially just practices in U.S. classrooms.* Heineman.

Office of Management and Budget. (1995). *Standards for maintaining, collecting, and presenting federal data on race and ethnicity.* Federal Register. https://www.whitehouse.gov/omb/fedreg_race-ethnicity.

Perry, P. (1991). Two faces of disparate impact discrimination. *Fordham Law Review, 59*, 523–595.

Petersen, N. & Novick, M. (1976). An evaluation of some models for culture-fair selection. *Journal of Educational Measurement, 13*(1), 3–29.

Pfeifer, C. & Sedlacek, W. (1971). The validity of academic predictors for black and white students at a predominantly white university. *Journal of Educational Measurement, 8*(4), 253–261.

Phillips, S. & Camara, W. (2006). Legal and ethical issues. In R. Brennan (Ed.), *Educational measurement* (4th ed.) (pp. 733–755). Rowman & Littlefield Publishers.

Poe, M., Elliot, N., Cogan, J. & Nurudeen, T. (2014). The legal and the local: Using disparate impact analysis to understand the consequences of writing assessment. *College Composition and Communication, 65*(4), 588–611.

Pollock, M. (2005). Keeping on keeping on: OCR and complaints of racial discrimination 50 years after Brown. *The Teachers College Record, 107*(9), 2106–2140.

Popham, J. (2012). Assessment bias: How to banish it. *Mastering assessment: A self-service system for educators* (2nd edition). Pearson.

Powe v. Miles, 407 F.2d 73 (1968).

Prohibition against exclusion from participation in, denial of benefits of, and discrimination under federally assisted programs on ground of race, color, or national origin. 42 U.S.C. § 2000d (2012).

Pullin, D. (2008). Assessment, equity, and opportunity to learn. In P. Moss, D. Pullin, J. Gee, E. Haertl & L. Young (Eds.), *Assessment, equity, and opportunity to learn* (pp. 333–351). Cambridge University Press.

Pullin, D. (2013). Legal issues in the use of student test scores and value added models (VAM) to determine educational quality. *Education Policy Analysis Archives, 21*(6), 1–27.

Pullin, D. (2014). *Performance, value, and accountability: Public policy goals and legal implications of the use of performance assessments in the preparation and licensing of educators.* Council of Chief State School Officers and Center for Assessment, Learning and Equality of Stanford University.

Rendell-Baker v. Kohn, 457 U.S. 830 (1982).

Ricci v. DeStephano, 557 U.S. 557 (2009).

Richardson v. Lamar County Board of Education, 729 F. Supp. 806 (1989).

Robinson v. Kansas, 295 F.3d 1183 (10th Cir. 2002).

Rubin, M., Denson, N., Kilpatrick, S., Matthews, K., Stehlik, T. & Zyngier, D. (2014). "I am working-class": Subjective self-definition as a missing measure of social class and socioeconomic status in higher education research. *Educational Researcher, 43*(4), 196–200.

Ryan, J. (2003). Race discrimination in education: A legal perspective. *Teachers College Record, 105*(6), 1087–1118.

Sackett, P., Kuncel, N., Arneson, J., Cooper, S. & Waters, S. (2009). *Socioeconomic status and the relationship between the SAT® and freshman GPA: An analysis of data from 41 colleges and universities.* College Board.

Save Our Valley v. Sound Transit, 335 F.3d 932 (9th Cir. 2003).

Sawyer, R., Cole, N. & Cole, J. (1976). Utilities and the issue of fairness in a decision theoretic model for selection. *Journal of Educational Measurement, 13*(1), 59–76.

Selmi, M. (2006). Was the disparate impact theory a mistake? *UCLA Law Review, 53*(3), 701–782.

Shapiro, T., Meschede, T. & Osoro, S. (2013). The roots of the widening racial wealth gap: Explaining the black-white economic divide. *Research and Policy Brief.* Institute on Assets and Social Policy.

Shermis, M., Lottridge, S. & Mayfield, E. (2015). The impact of anonymization for automated essay scoring. *Journal of Educational Measurement, 52*(4), 419–436.

Shohamy, E. (2011). Assessing multilingual competencies: Adopting construct valid assessment policies. *The Modern Language Journal, 95*(3), 418–429.

Sinharay, S., Dorans, N. & Liang, L. (2011). First language of test takers and fairness assessment procedures. *Educational Measurement: Issues and Practice, 30*(2), 25–35.

Sireci, S. & Green, P. (2005). Legal and psychometric criteria for evaluating teacher certification tests. *Educational Measurement: Issues and Practice, 19*(1), 22–31.

Sireci, S. & Parker, P. (2006). Validity on trial: Psychometric and legal conceptualization of validity. *Educational Measurement: Issues and Practice, 25*(3), 27–34.

Slomp, D. (2016). Ethical considerations and writing assessment. *Journal of Writing Assessment, 9*(1). https://escholarship.org/uc/item/2k14r1zg.

Slomp, D., Corrigan, J. & Sugimoto, T. (2014). A framework for using consequential validity evidence in evaluating Canadian large-scale writing assessments. *Research in the Teaching of English, 48*(3), 276–302.

Smith, L. & Hambleton, R. (1990). Content validity studies of licensing examinations. *Educational Measurement: Issues and Practice, 9*(4), 7–10.

Solano-Flores, G. (2002). Assessing the cultural validity of assessment practices: An introduction. In M. Basterra, E. Trumbull & G. Solano-Flores (Eds.), *Cultural validity in assessment: Addressing linguistic and cultural diversity* (pp. 3–21). Routledge.

Solano-Flores, G. & Nelson-Barber, S. (2001). On the cultural validity of science assessments. *Journal of Research in Science Teaching, 38*(5), 553–573.

Soliday, M. (2002). *The politics of remediation: Institutional and student needs in higher education.* University of Pittsburgh Press.

South Camden Citizens in Action v. New Jersey Department of Environmental Protection, 274 F.3d 771 (3rd Cir. 2001).

Steele, C. & Aronson, J. (1998). Stereotype threat and the test performance of academically successful African Americans. In C. Jencks & M. Phillips (Eds.), *The Black-White test score gap* (pp. 401–427). Brookings Institution.

Sternglass, M. (1997). *Time to know them: A longitudinal study of writing and learning at the college level.* Erlbaum.

Stricker, L. J. (2008). The challenge of stereotype threat for the testing community (ETS RM-08-12). Educational Testing Service.

Stricker, L. J. & Ward, W. C. (2004). Stereotype threat, inquiring about test taker's ethnicity and gender, and standardized test performance. *Journal of Applied Social Psychology, 34,* 665–693.

Teixeira, R., Frey, W. H. & Griffin, R. (2015). *States of change: The demographic evolution of the American electorate, 1974–2060.* Center for American Progress, American Enterprise Institute & Brookings Institution.

Texas Department of Housing and Community Affairs v. Inclusive Communities Project, Inc., 576 U.S., 135 S. Ct. 2507 (2015).

U.S. Const. amend XIV.

Verdun, V. (2005). The big disconnect between segregation and integration. *Negro Educational Review, 56*(1), 67–82.

Walker, M. & Bridgeman, B. (2008). *Stereotype threat spillover and SAT® scores.* Research Report No. 2008–2. College Board.

Walton, G. & Spenser, S. (2009). Latent ability: Grades and test scores systematically underestimate the intellectual ability of negatively stereotyped students. *Psychological Science, 20*(2), 1132–1139.

Washington v. Davis, 426 U.S. 229 (1976).

Watson, S. (1990). Reinvigorating Title VI: Defending health care discrimination—It shouldn't be so easy. *Fordham Law Review, 58*(5), 939–978.

West-Faulcon, K. (2009). The river runs dry: When Title VI trumps state anti-affirmative action laws. *University of Pennsylvania Law Review, 157*(4), 1075–1106.

Willborn, S. (1985). The disparate impact model of discrimination: Theory and limits. *The American University Law Review, 34,* 799–837.

Wilson v. Collins, 517 F.3d 421 (6th Cir. 2008).

Wilson, J., Olinghouse, N., McCoach, D., Santangelo, T. & Andrada, G. (2016). Comparing the accuracy of different scoring methods for identifying sixth graders at risk of failing a state writing assessment. *Assessing Writing, 27,* 11–23.

Worrell, F. (2014). Forty years of Cross' nigrescence theory: From stages to profiles, from African Americans to all Americans. In J. Sullivan & A. Esmail (Eds.), *African American identity: Racial and cultural dimensions of the Black experience* (pp. 3–28). Lexington Books.

Xi, X. (2010). How do we go about investigating test fairness? *Language Testing, 27*(2), 147–170.

Yaeger, D. & Walton, G. (2011). Social-Psychological interventions in education: They're not magic. *Review of Educational Research, 81*(2), 267–301.

Yu, C. H. (2003). Resampling methods: concepts, applications, and justification. *Practical Assessment, Research & Evaluation, 8*(19). http://PAREonline.net/getvn.asp?v=8&n=19.

Zwick, R. & Green, J. (2007). New perspectives on the correlation of SAT scores, high school grades, and socioeconomic factors. *Journal of Educational Measurement, 44*(1), 23–45.

Zwick, R. & Himelfarb, I. (2011). The effect of high school socioeconomic status on the predictive validity of SAT scores and highschool grade-point average. *Journal of Educational Measurement, 48*(2), 101–121.

CHAPTER 16.

# LET THEM IN: INCREASING ACCESS, COMPLETION, AND EQUITY IN ENGLISH PLACEMENT POLICIES AT A TWO-YEAR COLLEGE IN CALIFORNIA

**Leslie Henson**
Butte College

**Katie Hern**
California Acceleration Project

*This essay uses a disparate impact analysis framework to assess the impact of a policy change in writing assessment that roughly doubled the proportion of students placing into college English at Butte College, a two-year college in California. After establishing the disparate impact of placement, we tracked how students performed in college English, subsequent college courses, and overall college completion under the new policy. We found that substantially more students completed college English compared to previous cohorts, with Asian, African American, Latinx, and Native American students' completion of college English doubling or tripling. Upon taking subsequent college courses, students placing into college English under the new policy performed as well as those who had qualified for college English under the more restrictive policy. Overall college completion outcomes, including degree completion and meeting the criteria for transferring to 4-year universities, have generally improved and become more equitable since the 2011 policy change. These findings suggest that broadening access to college English can be a powerful lever for reducing racial and ethnic gaps in the completion of college English and may help to reduce gaps in the attainment of other, longer-term college completion outcomes.*

DOI: https://doi.org/10.37514/PER-B.2024.2326.2.16

## BUTTE COLLEGE AND THE NEED FOR DISPARATE IMPACT ANALYSIS IN WRITING ASSESSMENT

California's Student Success Scorecard shows a stark divide between "college prepared" and "unprepared" students. When incoming community college students are designated prepared for college-level work in English and math, they go on to complete degrees, certificates, and transfer-related outcomes at a rate of 71% within six years. For students designated as unprepared and required to enroll in developmental courses, that figure is just 41% (California Community Colleges' Chancellor's Office, 2017). Unfortunately, most California community college students are assigned to the unprepared group. Statewide, more than 80% of incoming students enroll in one or more developmental courses (Mejia, Rodriguez & Johnson, 2016). These courses, which we also occasionally refer to as "remedial" or "basic writing" courses, do not carry credit toward bachelor's degrees.

These statistics are often seen as the inevitable result of students' academic deficiencies. However, research has shown that the standardized tests community colleges rely on to assess college readiness are a large contributor to the problem. Though these tests are used to determine which students have access to college-level courses, they are simply not very good at predicting students' performance in college. In one study, analysis of data from a statewide community college system revealed that placement test scores in reading/writing explained less than 2% of the variation in students' first college-level English grades (Belfield & Crosta, 2012, p. 23). A study of a large, urban community college system estimated that 61% of incoming students could pass college English with a C or higher if allowed to enroll directly, but only 19% were designated college ready by the placement test (Scott-Clayton, 2012). While these studies are relatively recent, more than 20 years ago the Conference on College Composition and Communication (CCCC) Executive Committee (1995) released a position statement on writing assessment that acknowledged the limited usefulness of standardized multiple choice tests in assessing student writing and making decisions about their learning. The organization emphasized that such tests "misrepresent disproportionately the skills and abilities of students of color" (CCCC Executive Committee, 1995). In a 2016 white paper on placement reform, the Two-Year College English Association (TYCA) makes the point emphatically: "High-stakes testing, which even now dominates placement practices at two-year colleges, is unsound and unfair" (p. 3).

In response to such concerns over standardized tests, the American Educational Research Association, American Psychological Association, and National Council on Measurement in Education (2014) included more emphasis on fairness when codifying their new standards for educational assessment. However, writing assessment experts note that psychometric standards of fairness involve a certain "self-referential solipsism and silence on consequences" (Slomp, 2016) and do not ensure that the constructs being measured–whether via standardized tests or other writing assessments–are themselves fair to the "knowledges, languages, ways, and values" of all students (Cushman, 2016). Special issues of leading journals in writing studies have attempted to fill in these gaps, focusing around issues of ethics (Kelly Riley & Whithaus, 2016), social justice (Poe & Inoue, 2016), and diversity (Poe, 2014). Within this body of work, writing assessment experts show that fairness is "the first virtue of writing assessment," and that statistical attention to disparate impact is key to ensuring that writing assessments will be used ethically (Elliot, 2016).

Borrowed from the legal field, disparate (or differential) impact refers to "the unintended racial differences in outcomes resulting from facially neutral policies or practices that on the surface seem neutral" (Poe, Elliot, Cogan & Nurudeen, 2014, p. 593). Poe and Cogan (2016) emphasize that "differences in test scores alone do not constitute disparate impact; students come to college with different writing proficiencies. Rather, disparate impact occurs when a facially-neutral test places an unfair disadvantage on one group versus another." Disparate impact analyses correct what Behm and Miller (2012), drawing on the work of Bonilla-Silva, identified as the use of color-blind frames

> to explain why students from minority groups perform poorly on placement tests; to rationalize the disproportionate enrollment of minority students in developmental writing courses; or to deflect attention away from how a writing program and its various assessment practices may work unwittingly to maintain white privilege by reducing the opportunities of students of color. (p. 132)

Disparate impact analyses can help writing programs to assess and then remedy the differential effects of writing assessment, allowing programs to meet their goals for student learning without perpetuating disadvantage for various racial and ethnic groups (Poe & Cogan, 2016).

In one example of a disparate impact analysis, Inoue (2015) contended that we should be suspicious of any assessment–including the California State University system's holistically scored Early Placement Test–in which writing by White students was consistently rated as college ready while writing by students of color was disproportionately rated as remedial (pp. 35-42). Rather than assuming that our constructs and measurements are race-neutral and that students of color just aren't up to the job of producing college ready writing, Inoue made it clear that we should question our constructs, as well as the way in which they are being measured, when this measurement results in racially disparate outcomes. Inoue's analysis led to the adoption of a contract grading system in California State University, Fresno's writing program. Similarly, after finding that African American, Latinx, and Native American students placed into basic writing at higher rates and had lower graduation rates than Asian and European American students, faculty at the pseudonymous Brick City University decided to change their overall approach to placement and curriculum. In the new system, all students would begin in college-level English, and the locally developed placement exam would be given at the beginning of the term to identify students who could benefit from additional support services (Poe et al., 2014, p. 603).

Disparate impact analyses are particularly needed at majority European American institutions where faculty members are disproportionately European American. Butte College is one such institution. A rural college at the base of the Sierra Nevada Mountain Range in California, Butte College sits–though without official acknowledgment by the College–on the ancestral homelands of the Maidu-speaking people of the region. A majority of the College's service area is European American (75% in 2017), as are a majority of students at the College (57% in 2017). In 2010–2011, when this study began, 63% of the students at the College were European American, followed by Latinx (15%), Asian (6%), African American (3%), and American Indian or Alaskan Native students (2%). Sixty percent of students used the Board of Governor's fee waiver for low-income students. Along with a majority-European American student body and service area, European American teachers are over-represented in the faculty ranks. In 2010–2011, European Americans represented 87% of all faculty, but just 63% of students. By 2017, the proportion of European American students dropped to 57% of students at the College, but European Americans still comprised 89% of the faculty teaching those students. By proportion, there are now 4 times as many students of color in the student population (43%) as there are teachers of color in the faculty population (11%). Such majority European American demographics, as Coleman, DeLong, DeVore, Gibney, and Kuhne (2016) argued, do not "just happen. They are a result of the cumulative legacies of violent, historical, cumulative, contemporary, and ongoing institutional exclusion and oppression" (p. 368), and they play a role in producing "disproportionate, repeated, and patterned failure for certain students in writing classrooms and programs" (p. 365).

In March of 2011, Butte College began to examine the role of writing assessment in perpetuating the "disproportionate, repeated, and patterned failure" of students of color when the English department replaced the Assessment and Placement Services (APS) English Writing test, a multiple choice test of grammar and sentence editing, with the ACT's COMPASS English Placement Test, another multiple choice test of grammar and sentence editing. To assist faculty in setting cut scores for the new test, Butte College's assessment officer,

Eric Hoiland, examined ACT's recommendations on cut scores, averaged cut scores from over a dozen other community colleges, and conducted a version of the Modified Angov method in which three to four faculty members for each course took the COMPASS and responded to the test questions as if they were a student who was "barely ready" for that course. Hoiland also had a sample of students at each level take the COMPASS assessment, and he compared those scores against students' end-of-semester grades and the other data on cut scores. After faculty set cut scores, the College conducted a consequential validity study during weeks 5 through 7 of the first semester in which students had been placed using the new test. Faculty were asked to rate each student's preparedness for the course into which they had been placed, using a 5-level Likert scale. In the process, Butte College faculty were surprised to see that under the cut score range they had set for scoring into college English (73-99), many more students were being classified as college ready. Instead of 23% of students who took the assessment test having access to the gateway college-level English composition course, 48% of students did. Butte faculty considered lowering the cut scores in order to maintain the prior ratio of college-ready/basic writing, but, conscious of the high rates of attrition and the inequities in developmental course sequences, they decided to let the new cut scores stand and see how students performed.

This article describes what happened–initially and longer term–using a disparate impact analysis framework to assess the department's shifting policies. After establishing the disparate impact of placement, we tracked outcomes in four phases. In the first phase, we considered completion of college English, grades, and success rates for students in college English before and after the assessment change. We found that after the 2011 policy change, substantially more students completed college English across all ethnic groups, with gaps between groups narrowing. Students of color–who had fared the worst under the prior policy–saw the greatest gains for this outcome, with Asian, African American, Latinx, and Native American students' completion of college English doubling or tripling under the new policy. Examining success rates and grade distributions after the 2011 policy change, we found that, among students who previously would have been placed into basic writing coursework, 40% earned As and Bs in the college-level course. In the second phase, we considered whether allowing more students to bypass basic writing could have meant that these students were less prepared for success in downstream coursework. Comparing success rates in downstream coursework for students placing into college English before and after the assessment change, we found that students placing into college English after the policy change succeeded at rates that were virtually identical to those of their counterparts placing into college English under the previous system. In the third phase of our analysis, we considered whether allowing more students to bypass basic writing may have impacted longer-completion outcomes for the incoming student population overall. We found that, across the entire first-time student population, all groups earned degrees at higher rates, with the exception of African Americans, whose degree completion rates remained the same. All groups met the criteria for transferring to four-year universities at higher rates after the assessment change, and the gaps in the rates at which students of different races/ethnicities attained this outcome narrowed. These findings suggest that broadening access to college English can be a powerful lever for reducing racial and ethnic gaps in the completion of college English and may help to reduce gaps in the attainment of other, longer-term outcomes. In the fourth phase, we have speculated on the results of Butte College's new multiple measures placement policies, effective for students beginning in fall 2017, and a new co-requisite English course, expected to become available beginning in fall of 2018. (Prior to students beginning in Fall of 2017, students were placed primarily by their test scores, with high school grades playing a role only for students with scores near the cut-offs.) While these changes promise to further reduce the disparate impact of placement, we argue that the statewide multiple measures placement guidelines the department adopted in fall of 2017 do not go far enough toward creating equitable access to college English, that math policies need to change along with English policies, and that complying with an existing California educational regulation that protects students' right to enroll in courses unless they are "highly unlikely" to succeed would produce more ethical and equitable placement and improved student outcomes at Butte College and in California community colleges system-wide.

## THE DISPARATE IMPACT OF PLACEMENT

College completion outcomes are affected by multiple intersecting factors including race, socio-economic status, gender, sexuality, and other issues. However, in this study, we limited our examination to race/ethnicity because at Butte College, as in community colleges across the US, students of color are disproportionately placed into non-credit-bearing developmental courses. According to 2009 data from the National Center for Education Statistics, 62% of White community college students in the United States took remedial courses, compared to 71% of Black and Latinx students and 68% of Asian students (Witham, Malcom-Piqueux, Dowd & Bensimon, 2015). More striking is the fact that Black and Latinx students were twice as likely to have to take three or more developmental courses than White students were (43% of Black and Latinx students vs. 22% of White students) (Witham, Malcom-Piqueux, Dowd & Bensimon, 2015). A 2010 study showed that in California, more than half of Black and Latinx community college students who are placed into developmental coursework begin three or more classes away from a transferable, college-level math course. Students of color are also disproportionately represented in the lowest levels of English coursework: Compared to White students, 3 times as many Black students begin three or more classes below college English, and twice as many Latinx and Asian students do (White: 8%, Black: 25%, Asian: 19%, Latinx: 17%) (Perry, Bahr, Rosin & Woodward, 2010). In Table 6.1, we see that Butte College follows these larger trends in placement.

A chi-square analysis of these data was conducted to test the chances that the disparities in placement might have been due to random variation. Results of this analysis are included in Appendix A and show that the probability that the disparities between White students and other races/ethnicities occurred by chance was statistically insignificant ($p < .05$) for all groups excepting American Indian students under the old test. (The sample size for this group may have been too small to allow the chi-square analysis to detect disparity beyond what might be expected to occur by random chance.) With these results, we can reasonably conclude that the tests themselves explain the disparities in placement. Also, note these figures exclude students who took the assessment test but did not enroll at the College. They also exclude students taking no-cost or community-based courses. As seen in Table 6.1, under Butte College's more restrictive cut score policy in 2010, 35% of White students were classified as college ready and given access to college English, a rate 2.8 times higher than for Black students. After the assessment change in 2011, all students had greater access to college English, and the gap between groups had narrowed, with White students' access shrinking to just 1.6 times Black students' access. However, students of color were still disproportionately excluded from the college-level course, which is required for students to earn an associate's degree and/or transfer to a four-year university. In comparison, gaps in access between socioeconomic groups have been consistently smaller. For example, in Fall 2016, 47% of Pell recipients had access to college English versus 54% for students not receiving Pell funding, which is not a substantial gap. Pell grant receipt, while not a perfect indication of low income, is a more selective measure than the Board of Governor's fee waiver and is the current measure Butte College uses to track outcomes for low-income students.

Students of color were also still disproportionately represented in Butte College's lowest levels of basic writing. During the time of this study, students who placed below college English were required to take between one and four non-transferable English courses before taking college English, depending on their assessment results. In Fall 2012, Latinx students constituted 24% of the students who started three to four courses below college English but only 16% of the overall student population. Similarly, Asian students represented 15% of the students starting three to four courses below college English but only 5% of the Butte student population (California Community Colleges Chancellor's

Office, Management Information Systems Data Mart, Basic Skills Progress Tracker, n.d.).

Table 6.1. Placement Into College English Before and After the 2011 Assessment Change

| Group | Placed into college English in Fall '10 (before assessment change) | Placed into college English in Fall '12 (after assessment change) |
| --- | --- | --- |
| European American | 35% | 58% |
| Asian | 10% | 32% |
| Latinx | 17% | 39% |
| American Indian | 27% | 44% |
| African American | 12% | 36% |

These disparate placement rates unfairly disadvantage students of color because, for each additional developmental course required, students' completion of college-level English and math courses declines (Bailey, Jeong & Cho, 2008; Hern & Snell, 2010; Perry et al., 2010), and students who don't complete college English and math requirements are ineligible to earn an associates degree or transfer to a four-year university. At Butte College, only 50% of students who began one course below college in writing in Fall 2010 completed college English within two years. For students who began two courses below college in writing, that number dropped to 27%. Among students starting three to four courses below college English, just 18% completed college English within *four* years (timeframe extended because of time required to progress through the basic writing sequence) (California Community Colleges Chancellor's Office, Management Information Systems Data Mart, Basic Skills Progress Tracker, n.d.).

The implications of these statistics for students of color are troubling. In one study, initial placement was estimated to explain as much as 50% to 60% of the racial inequity in college completion outcomes (Stoup, 2015). Thus, while placement policies might seem facially neutral, as noted earlier, they can in fact result in unintended racial differences in outcomes (Poe et al., 2014).

## PHASE 1: COMPLETION OF COLLEGE ENGLISH, GRADES, AND SUCCESS RATES IN COLLEGE ENGLISH

The COMPASS placement test and policy were implemented in Spring 2011, but during the 2011–2012 year, many students enrolling in English courses were placed using the previous APS English writing test. These data therefore exclude the 2011–2012 year and focus on the four years preceding the change and the

Let Them In

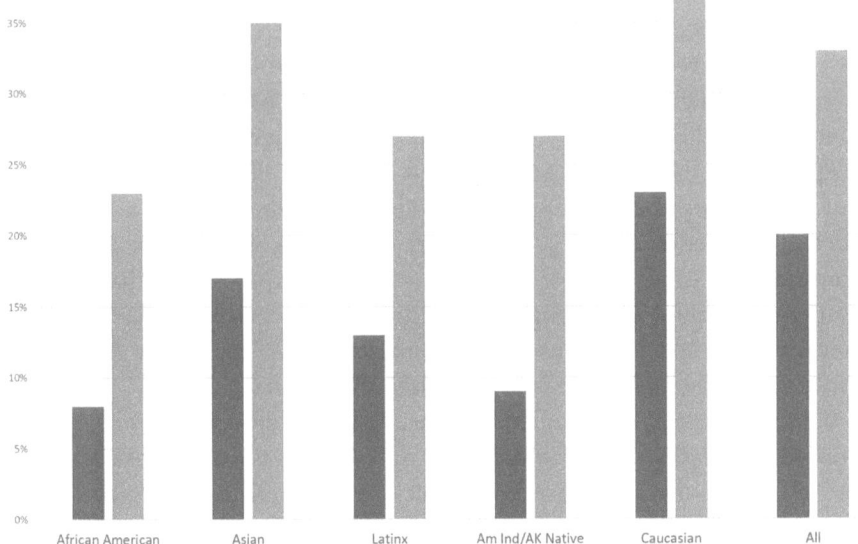

| African American | Asian | Latinx | American Indian/Alaskan Native American | European American | All |
|---|---|---|---|---|---|
| 2.8 times higher in broader access | 2.0 times higher in broader access | 2.2 times higher in broader access | 3.0 times higher in broader access | 1.6 times higher in broader access | 1.7 times higher in broader access |
| n=284 (07–11) | n=485 (07–11) | n=1092 (07–11) | n=195 (07–11) | n=4250 (07–11) | n=6972 (07–11) |
| n=145 (12–14) | n=283 (12–14) | n=746 (12–14) | n=147 (12–14) | n=2014 (12–14) | n=3475 (12–14) |

*Figure 6.1 Butte College First-Time Student Cohorts: Completion of College English Within One Year. Includes all first-time students enrolled in basic writing/basic math and transfer-level credit courses, excepting those with previous concurrent enrollment*

two years after full implementation. We looked at completion of college English across the entire population of incoming students–those placed into basic writing and those placed directly into the college level. Students enrolled in no-cost or community-based courses were excluded from this analysis. As Figure 6.1 makes clear, under the less restrictive policy, substantially more students completed college English within one year across all racial/ethnic groups. Students of color—who had fared the worst under the prior policy—saw the greatest gains: Native

169

American and African American students' completion tripled or nearly tripled, and Latinx and Asian students' completion more than doubled. And, while gaps between groups persisted, they narrowed. European American students' completion of college English was 2.9 times higher than African American students under the more restrictive policy; under the new policy, it was just 1.6 times higher.

Appendix B shows a chi-square analysis of these results. Under both assessment instruments, there were statistically significant differences between White students' completion of college English and that of all other groups, excepting Asian students, at $p < .05$. Because there is a very low probability that the different rates of completing college English could have occurred through random chance, we can conclude there is still disparate impact for Native American, African American, and Latinx students under the new test.

We also examined two-year data for the 2012-2013 group to see whether the increased completion might be driven by the one-year timeframe of the study. After all, under the more restrictive policy, more students were placed into developmental coursework, which delayed their enrollment in college English. Would they catch up if given more time? We found that, while students in both groups made gains in year 2, completion of college English continued to be higher under the new policy (Fall 2012 to Summer 2014: Across every ethnic group, completion was 12 to 13 percentage points higher than under the more restrictive policy).

An additional question we considered was whether other factors could be driving the increase in completion. The change in placement at the college level meant a reduction in the number of students placed into basic writing courses. The biggest change was in the course two courses below college English. In Fall 2010, 33% of incoming students had been placed two courses below college English; in Fall 2012, 17% were (changes in the placement test appear to have shifted many of these students up to one course below college English). It is possible that these students contributed to the overall completion gains because more of them could have progressed through college English within a year under the new policy. Another possible factor is Butte's accelerated developmental course. The accelerated course admits students who would otherwise have had to take a sequence of two basic writing courses, enabling them to progress to college English in just one semester. The course has substantially increased completion of college English among students at this placement level, a finding that is consistent with Hern and Snell's (2010) discussion of how accelerated coursework improves student outcomes by reducing the "exponential attrition" built into the structure of prerequisite developmental sequences.

In the years 2012-2013 and 2013-2014, Butte offered 21 sections of accelerated English, enrolling 478 students. During those years, the College also offered 243 sections of college composition, enrolling 7,007 students. While we were not able to determine the precise degree to which the accelerated course was a factor in the college-wide completion gains, the relatively small scale of these offerings leads us to conclude that much if not most of the improvement was driven by the changes in placement policy.

With so many more incoming students allowed to skip basic writing coursework and enroll directly in college English, the first question most teachers will ask is this: How are they doing in the course? Are they unprepared for the rigor of the college level? Are they failing out at high rates? It is important, then, to look not only at overall completion rates (Figure 6.1) but at students' performance within the college course. It should be noted that online sections were not included in the analysis of success rates. Many of these sections were outliers, and we wanted to leave out issues with course modality and its effect on student success. There were two to four online sections of college English offered each semester of this study.

In 2012-2013, the first year of full implementation, there appeared to be a modest decrease in average success rates across sections (students passing the course with a C or higher). Butte offered 119 sections of first-year composition that year, with a median success rate of 63%. The following year, the median success rate was also 63%. Prior to the policy change, the median success rates had varied from about 67% to 72% annually. So, by this measure, students do appear to be performing slightly less well in college English under the new policy.

However, it is important to note that Butte offered 83 to 119 sections of college English during each year of this study, and there was tremendous variability in success rates across sections. In 2013-2014, for example, success rates ranged from a low of 27% to a high of 97% across sections. Further, prior to the new policy, the median success rates varied by as many as 5 percentage points year to year, so a decline of 4 to 9 percentage points in the median is not a substantial deviation, particularly when considering the difference between sections within any given year.

To further investigate student success rates, we analyzed data from English instructors who had taught sections of college English before and after the policy change to determine whether their own success rates had changed (Fall 2007 to Spring 2014). Of these 21 instructors, eight had higher mean success rates after the placement change, three had no change in their mean success rates, and 10 had lower mean success rates. Among instructors whose success rates had increased or decreased, most saw a change of fewer than 10 percentage points, typical of the variation teachers normally see in their classes. Most interesting: Across all 21 instructors, the mean success rate dropped just 2.8 percentage points under the new policy, and the median less than 1 percentage point.

As an additional test of whether students were less prepared to succeed under the new policy, we looked at course grade distributions for students who placed into college English from different scoring ranges on the new test. The data we analyzed included all students who qualified for college English under the new placement test and enrolled in the course, including repeat enrollers. We were particularly curious about the performance of students who would have been assigned to basic writing under the old system but who were now allowed to begin directly in college English. While it was not possible to identify these students with certainty because the testing instrument had changed, we could estimate this group by considering the ratio of students placed into/out of college English under the old system. In using this method, we assumed that differences between the old and new tests and what they measured were less important than the increased access to college English afforded by the cut scores established for the new test. If Butte faculty had decided to narrow the cut score range and revert to previous placement ratios when they implemented the new test, students scoring between 73 and 88 would likely have been placed into remediation, while those scoring between 89 and 99 would likely have had access to college English. Table 6.2 shows these two groups' grade distributions under the new placement policy.

These data show that students testing into college English in the lower range of scores had slightly lower success rates than their higher-scoring counterparts (41% earned grades of D/F/FW/W compared to 36% of students in the higher-scoring range). They were also less likely to earn As. However, they did not markedly underperform in comparison to the higher-scoring students. We found it noteworthy that the lower scoring group did not receive a disproportionate number of Cs, as might have been expected if they were borderline college ready. In fact, 40% earned As and Bs in a course they would have been excluded from under prior placement ratios.

When considering rates of non-success among lower-scoring students, an important question to ask is whether they would have had better outcomes if required to first enroll in a basic writing course. Among students who began one course below college English in Fall 2010, just 39% completed college English within a year. This makes clear that, while we might be concerned that only 59% of the lower-scoring group succeeded in college English, requiring these students to enroll in a basic writing pre-requisite would not have led to more of them successfully completing the college English course.

It should be acknowledged that this study has not examined evidence of student writing, such as performance on a departmental exam or portfolios of student work; scoring of student writing samples would have added inter-observer reliability to this study. That said, if large numbers of students were unable to produce writing that met their college English instructors' expectations, we would see it in the data on course grades and rates of success. Taken together, course success rates and grades in college English suggest that dramatically increasing

Table 6.2. Grade Distributions in College English Under the Broader Access Policy

| Placement Score Range | A | B | C | D | F/FW | W |
|---|---|---|---|---|---|---|
| Students likely to have placed into college English under the old ratios (Scores: 89–99 on new test) n = 2,481 | 22.69% | 26.56% | 15.03% | 5.88% | 21.36% | 8.46% |
| Students likely to have placed into remediation under the old ratios (Scores: 73–88 on new test) n = 1,927 | 15.46% | 24.65% | 18.53% | 6.90% | 22.78% | 11.68% |

the number of students classified as college ready resulted in little change in students' performance inside college English. While there was a modest decline in the aggregate success rate across sections, we are reluctant to conclude that this is evidence that students were less prepared to succeed. With success rates varying so widely across sections and a smaller drop in course success rates for instructors who taught both before and after the change, it's clear that instructor-level effects–rather than simple student preparation levels–are playing a role in this outcome. In addition, more recent data show a rise in success rates: In Fall 2016, success rates in college English were 72%, equivalent to average success rates in the course before the assessment change. More study is warranted to see if this trend will continue and, if so, whether it reflects normal year-to-year variation and/or other factors, including recent equity-focused professional development efforts at the College. Regardless of variations in rates of success, more students are completing college English since the policy of broader access was implemented. In raw numbers, roughly 200 to 300 more students have completed college English each fall since the policy change (Michels-Ratliff & Henson, 2017).

## PHASE 2: DOWNSTREAM COURSE SUCCESS FOR STUDENTS PLACED INTO COLLEGE ENGLISH BEFORE AND AFTER THE POLICY CHANGE

The data showing that more students were completing college English have been shared widely at the College. However, many faculty–from English and other disciplines—have expressed concern that allowing more students to bypass basic writing may have resulted in students who were less prepared to do the writing required in their other college-level courses. While we were conscious that this concern stemmed from the uninformed belief that students' performance on a single multiple-choice test of sentence editing correlates with their writing abilities overall, we were curious to see if faculty members' apprehensions were borne out by the data.

To get at the question of student preparedness for writing in other college-level courses, Butte College research analyst, Emelia Michels-Ratliff, selected high-enrolled courses that had college English as a pre-requisite or recommended preparation (i.e., "downstream" courses). These included courses in history, communication studies, political science, and English. Of these courses, History 8, History 10, and Communication Studies 2 require 2,500 words of writing, and English 11 requires 6,000 to 8,000 words. If allowing lower-scoring students to take college English had resulted in students who were less prepared for the demands of writing in their other college courses–if college English instructors had lowered their standards and passed unprepared students–we might expect to see lower success rates in downstream courses for the new group of students placing into college English. This is not what these data show. Figure 6.2 shows success rates in downstream courses for students who placed into college English before and after the assessment change. As shown in Figure 6.2, students who were placed into college English after the assessment change were not less successful compared to students who were placed into college English previously. Rather, they succeeded in downstream coursework at rates that were virtually identical to those for students placed into college English previously (Michels-Ratliff & Henson, 2017).

## PHASE 3: LONGER-TERM OUTCOMES FOR ALL FIRST-TIME STUDENTS

Phase 2 analysis was limited to examining downstream outcomes for students who were assessed as college-ready in English. However, we also wanted to see what impact the assessment change might have had on longer-term outcomes for the entire incoming student population, not just those placing into college English. Did the policy change allow more students to complete degrees and transfer to four-year universities? To investigate this question, we examined degree completion and transfer-readiness rates for all first-time students–those assessed as college-ready in English and those assessed as needing basic writing–in the three years before and the two years after the assessment change. Consistent with the rest of this study, students with previous concurrent enrollment or who enrolled only in no-cost or community-based courses were excluded from this analysis. As detailed earlier in this study, after the assessment change, a substantially larger share of students could access college English without having to complete a basic writing course first, and another share had access to accelerated English coursework that

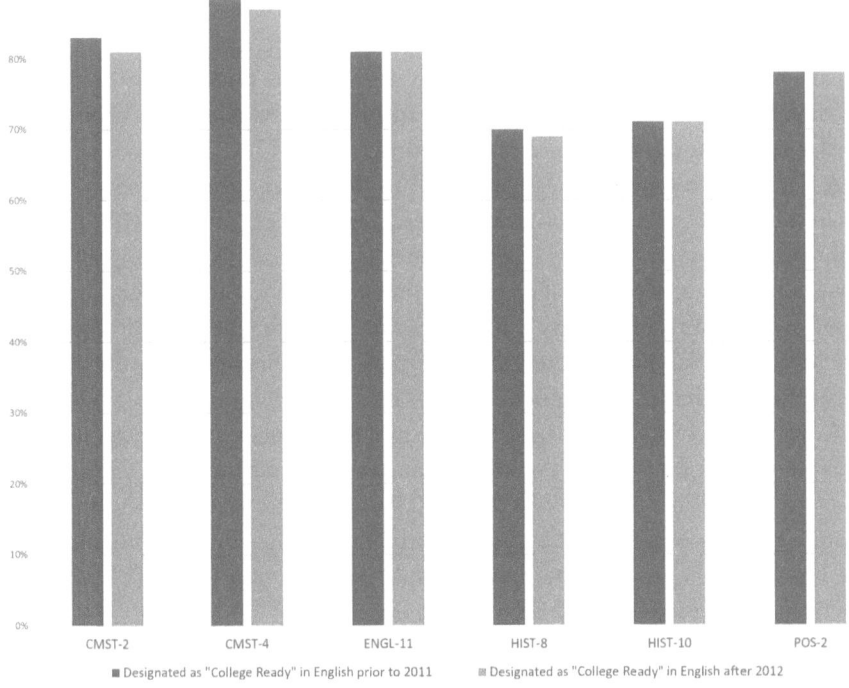

*Figure 6.2 Success Rates in Downstream Courses Before and After Assessment Change. Notes: Cohort 1 (n=1667) Includes new students Fall 2009 through Spring 2011. Cohort 2 (n=3032) includes new students Fall 2012 through Spring 2014. Enrollments by transfer level course varied.*

cut their time in basic writing in half. We were curious to see if removing these barriers early in students' educational careers might have led to differences in longer-term outcomes college-wide. The longer-term completion outcomes were tracked for four years for all students in this phase of our analysis.

Comparing degree completion rates for all first-time students before and after the assessment change, we found that degree completion increased for all groups except African Americans, whose completion rate remained constant. Overall, there was a 25% increase in degree completion college-wide–from 9.86% of first-time students who started between Fall '08 and Fall '10 to 12.28% of first-time students who started between Fall '12 and Fall '13.

We also investigated the rates at which all first-time students became ready to transfer to four-year universities. Students are considered "transfer ready" if they complete at least 60 units of transferable coursework, have a GPA of 2.0 or higher, and have successfully completed both college-level math and college-level English with grades of C or higher. Overall, the College saw a 29% increase in transfer-readiness college-wide—from 14% of first-time students attaining this outcome before the change to 18% after the change. As shown in Figure 6.3, transfer-readiness rates increased for all groups.

A *z*-test of proportions was conducted to determine whether the pre- and post-test rates of transfer readiness differed significantly or fell within what might be expected to occur by chance. The *z*-test showed statistical significance between the pre- and post-change rates of transfer readiness for students overall, as well as for White and Latinx students. Sample sizes for the other groups may have been too small for the *z*-test to pick up on differences beyond what might be expected by chance. See Appendix C for these results.

As with completion of college English, students of color saw the biggest gains in transfer readiness: African American transfer-readiness increased 71%, Latinos 50%, American Indians 43%, Asians 23%, and European Americans 20%. Relative to European American students, attainment gaps for African-American and American Indian students have shrunk, and the gap between European American and Latinx students disappeared entirely.

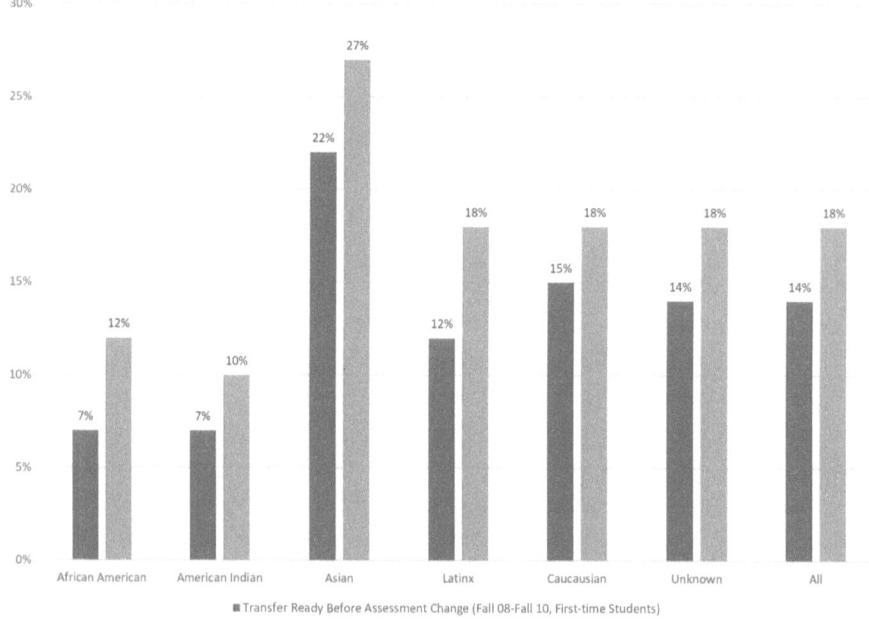

*Figure 6.3. Transfer-Readiness Rates for First-Time Students Before and After the Assessment Change*

## PHASE FOUR: ONGOING CHANGES IN PLACEMENT

In the six years since Butte College began its experiment in placement, the landscape for placement has shifted statewide, and there is more widespread awareness of the problems that stem from using a single score on a placement exam to determine students' educational fates. Directly acknowledging the limitations of the test in predicting college readiness, the manufacturer of COMPASS pulled their product from the market in November of 2016 (Bailey & Jaggars, 2016, p. 2). There is now a growing movement to use high school performance information to place students into college courses. High school performance data—in particular, students' high school GPAs—have been shown to correlate more strongly with students' actual performance in college courses than placement test scores (Bailey et al., 2016; Fagioli, 2016; Hodara & Cox, 2016; Multiple Measures Assessment Project [MMAP], 2016; Scott-Clayton & Stacey, 2015; TYCA Research Committee, 2016).

Following these trends, Butte College's writing program decided to adopt the multiple measures "decision rules" recommended by California's MMAP for placing students. By these rules, students with high school GPAs of 2.6 or higher or a qualifying test score will be eligible for college English, beginning with students enrolled in Fall of 2017 (MMAP Research Team, 2016). While data for students placed under this new policy were not available at the time of this writing, Michels-Ratliff (2016) predicts that, for students who can be placed using high school measures, access to college English will increase from approximately 49% to 71% of incoming students. In addition, while racial and ethnic gaps in access to college English will still exist, they will be smaller. Under the new placement rules, 76% of European American students are predicted to have access to college English, versus 70% of Asian students, 59% of American Indian/Alaskan Native students, 57% of Latinx students, and 55% of African American students (Michels-Ratliff, 2016).

Effective Fall of 2018, the Butte College writing program will also be adding a new co-requisite English course for students from the next lowest placement category. The co-requisite course is classified as a college English course and will meet the same requirements as the College's regular college English course, but it will include more time in class with the instructor in order to help students be successful. Students will qualify for the course based on their test score or an 11th grade high school GPA of 2.3 or above. This course is predicted to increase access to college English for another 17% of recent high school graduates. If the projections are correct, 88% of incoming students will have access to a college English course after the new policies are implemented, and racial and ethnic gaps in access to college-level coursework will shrink even more.

After implementation of the new course and multiple measures placement policies, 92% of European American students are predicted to have access to a college-level course in English, compared to 86% of Asian students, 79% of Native American students, 78% of Latinx students, and 74% of African American students (Michels-Ratliff, 2016).

Previous gains in completion of college English were accomplished by simply reducing the barrier and allowing more–and more diverse—students to enroll. No additional instruction was provided. Now, with the additional instruction time in the co-requisite course, evidence suggests that Butte College will see further reduction in inequality and more students completing college English. Nationally, co-requisite models have been shown to increase completion of college-level courses (Complete College America, 2016), particularly for students who score low on standardized assessments (Office of the Vice Chancellor of Academic Affairs, 2016). Co-requisite models are thought to support the contextual, non-linear way in which literacy develops. As Judith Rodby and Tom Fox (2000) concluded after the CSU, Chico English department replaced non-credit basic writing courses with a co-requisite model that allowed low-scoring students to take credit-bearing, college-level English: "1) One learns to do college writing by being in the context of college writing, not in some other context; and 2) literacy learning does not come in discrete levels" (p. 84). These principles of literacy development may explain why California colleges have seen positive results from co-requisite models and multiple measures placement policies that allow more students to begin in college-level English coursework. For example, when Solano College implemented high school grades in placement and added a co-requisite English course that allowed students from a lower placement category to enroll in college English with extra support, disparate impact in placement almost disappeared, and success rates in college English were unchanged (Henson, Hern & Snell, 2017). These results suggest that the previous use of placement to funnel students into basic writing had underestimated students' capacity for college-level writing in English.

## DISCUSSION

Butte College's experience demonstrates that broadening access to college English can be a powerful lever for reducing racial and ethnic gaps in the completion of college English and may help to reduce gaps in the attainment of other, longer-term outcomes. After increasing students' access to college English in 2011, Butte College saw large, institution-wide increases in completion of the gateway college composition course, a critical early momentum point on the path to degrees and transfer to a four-year university. The data from Butte confirm other studies showing that a substantial number of students assigned to basic writing courses on the basis of standardized placement exams could, in fact, be successful if given access to a college-level course. That this problem went undetected for so many years is consistent with Scott-Clayton's (2012) description of under-placement as "invisible to the naked eye": "When a student is placed into a college-level course and fails there (an over-placement error), the fact that there has been a placement mistake is painfully obvious to all" (p. 35). On the other hand, Scott-Clayton (2012) writes, "Among students who do well in a remedial course, it may be difficult for an instructor (or even the student herself) to know whether they were appropriately placed or might have succeeded in the college-level course as well. In any case, when a student does well in a remedial course, it is unlikely to be perceived as a problem" (pp. 35–36). Butte College faculty's previous lack of attention to the disparate impact of placement surely also played a role.

Some faculty might express concern about the initial modest drop in Butte's aggregate success rates and the fact that, during the first two years of the new placement policy, lower-scoring students–the ones likely to have been placed into remediation in the past–were 5% points more likely to earn grades of W, D, or F in college English than higher-scoring students (41% vs. 36%). But given that 40% of the students in this scoring range earned grades of A or B, it would be hard to justify excluding them from the course. Further, California community college regulations protect students' right to enroll in a course unless they are "highly unlikely" to succeed without a prerequisite (Policies for Prerequisites, Corequisites and Advisories on Recommended Preparation, 2018). Students with a 59% chance of success in college English are not "highly unlikely" to succeed in the course, making it problematic to require these students to take prerequisite coursework before being allowed to enroll in college English. And while we might still be concerned about their 59% success rate, this is a substantial improvement over the number of students who complete college English after starting out in a basic writing course. A return to the more restrictive policy of enforced pre-requisite coursework is clearly not in these students' interest.

On the contrary, Butte's experience reveals that increasing student access to college-level English may be a powerful lever for reducing equity gaps in both short- and longer-term outcomes. While all students saw greater completion of college English after the policy change, students of color saw the greatest gains, narrowing the gap between their completion of college English and White students' completion. This is likely because students of color are much more likely to be classified as "underprepared" and denied access to college English based on placement tests assessing sentence-editing skills in standard English. In short, because students of color were more disadvantaged by the previous policy, they had more to gain from the change. Implementation of co-requisite English and multiple measures placement policies promises to add to these gains and further reduce disparity in completion of college English.

Longer term, students who place into college English do not seem to be less prepared for success since the policy allowing more students direct access to college English was implemented in 2011. Students who qualified for college English after the policy change are performing equally well in downstream courses when compared to students who qualified for college English before the assessment change. This suggests that allowing more students to bypass basic writing has not resulted in inferior preparation for writing in other courses. In fact, rather than harming students, the policy change may have actually allowed more students to complete longer-term outcomes. When measured across the entire first-time student population–those placing into college English and those placing into basic writing–rates of degree completion have increased modestly. Degree completion rates may also have been impacted by other efforts at the college, including first-year experience courses that emphasize the importance of associate's degrees, and a vigorous process for ensuring that students complete the paperwork to receive a degree.

Overall, the College saw a 29% increase in transfer-readiness college-wide–from 14% of first-time students attaining this outcome before the change to 18% after the change. As with completion of college English, students of color saw the biggest gains in transfer readiness: African American transfer-readiness increased 71%, Latinos 50%, American Indians 43%, Asians 23%, and European Americans 20%. Relative to European American students, attainment gaps for African American and American Indian students have shrunk, and the gap between European American and Latinx students has disappeared entirely. These numbers are consistent with Stoup's (2015) finding that initial placement explains a substantial portion of the inequities in completion of long-term outcomes. As Stoup's model predicts, after reducing the inequities in students' initial placement in English, Butte College saw a narrowing of gaps in the rates at which students of different races/ethnicities met longer-term criteria for transferring to four-year universities. While these data do not provide conclusive evidence that the assessment change is the sole or primary cause of increased transfer-readiness and degree completion rates, the assessment change is likely to have played a role in both. These findings suggest that broadening access to college English may have benefited students longer term, particularly students of color, and that the prior policy had strong negative consequences for students' educational progress. These consequences fell disproportionately on students of color because they were excluded from college English and required to take basic writing coursework at higher rates under the more restrictive policy.

However, completion rates at Butte College continue to be low overall. Fewer than one in five first-time students becomes ready to transfer to a four-year university within four years of starting at the College. While there was a 29% increase on this metric after the English assessment change, math placement policies did not change, and these policies are generally the greater barrier to student completion. California's 2017 Student Success Scorecard shows that, of first-time students who started at Butte College in 2014-2015 and completed six units after attempting any math or English in their first year, 56.3% completed a college-level course in English in their first or second year, compared to just 28.6% of the same cohort completing a college-level course in math within that same timeframe (California Community Colleges' Chancellor's Office, 2018). At Butte College and throughout California, access to math courses that count towards a bachelor's degree is still highly restrictive. Even under new multiple measures placement criteria (effective Fall 2017), the majority of Butte College students are still blocked from access to math courses that count towards bachelors' degrees, with disproportionate impact in access for Native American, Latinx, and African American students (Michels-Ratliff, 2016). This is troubling because, similar to findings in English, evidence suggests that a majority of students can be successful in college-level math–particularly, college statistics–when given access and additional support (Logue, Watanabe-Rose & Douglass, 2016; Henson, Hern & Snell, 2017). These findings point to the need for Butte College to consider changing policies concerning math placement and remediation in order to ensure that comprehensive reform efforts underway at the college do not continue the legacy of disparate impact for students of color.

Results for students taking English courses under Butte College's new multiple measures placement policies were not available at the time of this writing. However, the disproportionate exclusion of students of color from college English is predicted to continue under these policies. To correct the issue, Butte College should align its math and English placement policies with California's Title V regulation protecting students' right to enroll in a course unless they are "highly unlikely" to succeed without taking a prerequisite. The current state-recommended MMAP placement rules adopted at Butte College do not align with this standard. Students with 11th grade high school GPAs between 1.9 and 2.6 and grades of C or higher in 11th grade English are predicted to pass college-level English at a rate of 62% (MMAP Research Team, 2016, p. 7). Yet under the current placement rules, students with GPAs below 2.3 will be excluded from a college-level English course (unless their test scores qualify them to enroll). This exclusion is a result of setting placement criteria to maximize course success for the limited number of students granted access, rather than setting placement criteria so as to maximize completion of college-level courses for all students. In developing their recommended placement rules, MMAP researchers were asked to provide placement criteria that would maintain or improve existing success rates within college-level courses, limiting college English access to just those students whose average predicted pass rate is at least 70%, and limiting co-requisite English access to students with a predicted success rate of 65%. These pass rates represent a "highly likely to succeed" standard for determining access, not the "highly unlikely to succeed" standard for barring access specified by the Title V state regulation. As a result, some Butte College students with a 62% chance of passing college English–similar to current pass rates in the course–will be required to take one or more prerequisite English courses, substantially reducing their chances of completing college English and longer-term outcomes. Most troubling, this group will disproportionately consist of students of color (e.g., 8% of European American students required to start below a college-level course vs. 26% of African American students required to start below a college-level course).

The disproportionate exclusion of students of color from college-level courses is highlighted in the Association of American Colleges and Universities' (Witham et al., 2015) publication *America's Unmet Promise: The Imperative for Equity in Higher Education*. Researchers from University of Southern California's Center for Urban Education explain the stakes, writing that disproportionately excluding students from college-level courses "contributes to further disparities . . . in retention and completion rates, graduate school participation rates, and access to opportunities for deep and engaged learning throughout their postsecondary careers" (Witham et al., 2015, p. 17). Placement and remediation policies appear, on their face, to be race neutral, with a veneer of scientific accuracy provided by the processes through which colleges validate cut scores and set placement criteria. But students of color are being disproportionately excluded from college-level courses based on criteria that do not accurately reflect their ability to succeed, and this exclusion has very real and measurable consequences for their educational progress. To correct these issues, colleges should apply California's existing standard for requiring students to take prerequisite courses. That is, students should have access to college-level courses–including ones with co-requisite support–unless a rigorous analysis of prior high school performance and other multiple measures shows that they are "highly unlikely" to succeed without a prerequisite course, particularly when there is disparate impact for underprivileged racial/ethnic groups. This standard meets the criteria for a theory of ethics in writing assessment laid out by David Slomp (2016); in particular, it holds institutions to "actionable standards of ethical practices" and has "an ecological orientation . . . that pays attention to the role assessment plays both within broader systems of education and within society as a whole."

The intent of our policies may not have been exclusionary. But given the evidence that placement into remediation leads to worse outcomes, we need to acknowledge and address the role our assessment policies play in perpetuating stark racial and ethnic disparities in college completion. The authors of *America's Unmet Promise* recognize that, given the complex roots of educational inequity, "No single reform initiative can address all of these challenges" (Witham et al., 2015, p. 3). But they urge practitioners to confront inequities within their sphere of influence. We must, they write, "be willing to disrupt the current systems of higher education and take responsibility for those aspects of inequality that are under our control" (Witham et al., 2015, p. 3).

## POSTSCRIPT

After this article was completed, the California legislature passed a law that aligns with the placement principles we advocate. Among other specifications, AB 705 requires community colleges to follow the "highly unlikely to succeed" standard for barring access to college-level math and English. Further, colleges must ensure that students' initial placement in English and math gives them the best chance of completing transferable, college-level courses. Initial MMAP data show that under AB 705 criteria, all or close to all incoming students will have access to college-level English and college statistics, with or without corequisite support. Colleges must fully adhere to AB 705 by Fall 2019 (California Community Colleges' Chancellor's Office, 2018).

## REFERENCES

American Educational Research Association, American Psychological Association & NCME. (2014). *Standards for educational and psychological testing*. American Educational Research Association.

Bailey, T., Bashford, J., Boatman, A., Squires, J., Weiss, M., Doyle, W., Valentine, J. C., LaSota, R., Polanin, J. R., Spinney, E., Wilson, W., Yeide, M., Young, S. H. (2016). *Strategies for postsecondary students in developmental education—A practice guide for college and university administrators, advisors, and faculty*. Institute of Education Sciences, What Works Clearinghouse.

Bailey, T. & Jaggars, S. (2016). When college students start behind. *The Century Foundation*. 1–15. https://tcf.org/content/report/college-students-start-behind/.

Bailey, T., Jeong, D. W. & Cho, S. W. (2008) Referral, enrollment, and completion in developmental education sequences in community colleges. *CCRC Working Paper No. 15* (Rev. Nov. 2009). Community College Research Center, Teachers College, Columbia University. https://tinyurl.com/yu2n4s5w.

Behm, N. & Miller, K. (2012). Challenging the frameworks of color-blind racism: Why we need a fourth wave of writing assessment scholarship. In A. B. Inoue & M. Poe (Eds.), *Race and writing assessment* (pp. 127-138). Peter Lang.

Belfield, C. & Crosta, P.M. (2012). Predicting success in college: The importance of placement tests and high school transcripts. *CCRC Working Paper No. 42*. Community College Research Center. http://ccrc.tc.columbia.edu/publications/predicting-success-placement-tests-transcripts.html.

California Community Colleges' Chancellor's Office. (2017). *Student Success Scorecard. Statewide.* http://scorecard.cccco.edu/scorecardrates.aspx?CollegeID=000#home.

California Community Colleges' Chancellor's Office. (2018). *What is AB 705?* https://assessment.cccco.edu/ab-705/.

California Community Colleges Chancellor's Office, Management Information Systems Data Mart, Basic Skills Progress Tracker. (n.d.). Butte College. http://datamart.cccco.edu/Outcomes/BasicSkills_Cohort_Tracker.aspx.

Coleman, T. J., DeLong, R., DeVore, K. S., Gibney, S. & Kuhne, M. C. (2016). The risky business of engaging racial equity in writing instruction: A tragedy in five acts. *Teaching English in the Two-Year College, 43*(4), 347–370.

Conference on College Composition & Communication Executive Committee. (1995). *Writing assessment: A position statement.* National Council of Teachers of English. http://www.csun.edu/~krowlands/Content/Academic_Resources/Composition/Responding/Writing%20Assessment%20A%20Position%20Statement.htm.

Complete College America. (2016). *Co-requisite remediation: Spanning the divide—breakthrough results fulfilling the promise of college access for underprepared students.* http://completecollege.org/spanningthedivide/#the-bridge-builders.

Cushman, E. (2016). Decolonizing validity. *The Journal of Writing Assessment, 9*(1). https://escholarship.org/uc/item/0xh7v6fb.

Elliot, N. (2016). A theory of ethics for writing assessment. *The Journal of Writing Assessment, 9*(1). https://escholarship.org/uc/item/36t565mm.

Fagioli, L. (2016). Common assessment regional meeting: MMAP report. https://tinyurl.com/mry9p66p.

Henson, L., Hern, K. & Snell, M. (2017). Up to the challenge: Community colleges expand access to college-level courses. The California Acceleration Project.

Hern, K. & Snell, M. (2010). Exponential attrition and the promise of acceleration in developmental English and math. *Perspectives.* Research and Planning Group. http://www.rpgroup.org/resources/accelerated-developmental-english-and-math.

Hodara, M. & Cox, M. (2016). *Developmental education and college readiness at the University of Alaska* (REL 2016-123). Washington, DC: U.S. Department of Education, Institute of Education Sciences, National Center for Education Evaluation and Regional Assistance, Regional Educational Laboratory Northwest. http://ies.ed.gov/ncee/edlabs.

Inoue, A. (2015). *Antiracist writing assessment ecologies: Teaching and assessing writing for a socially just future.* The WAC Clearinghouse; Parlor Press. https://doi.org/10.37514/PER-B.2015.0698.

Kelly Riley, D. & Whithaus, C. (2016). Introduction to a special issue on a theory of ethics for writing assessment. *Journal of Writing Assessment, 9*(1). https://escholarship.org/uc/item/8nq5w3t0.

Logue, A. W., Watanabe-Rose. M. & Douglas, D. (2016). Should students assessed as needing remedial mathematics take college-level quantitative courses instead? A randomized controlled trial. *Educational Evaluation and Policy Analysis, 38*(3), 578–598. https://doi.org/10.3102/0162373716649056.

Mejia, M. C., Rodriguez, O. & Johnson, H. (2016). *Preparing students for success in California's community colleges*. Public Policy Institute of California. http://www.ppic.org/main/publication.asp?i=1215.

Michels-Ratliff, E. (2016). Understanding multiple measures placement: A retrospective analysis and look to the future [Unpublished PowerPoint]. Butte College.

Michels-Ratliff, E. & Henson, L. (2017). Presentation at Acceleration Across California, the first annual conference of the California Acceleration Project. http://accelerationproject.org/Acceleration-Across-California.

Multiple Measures Assessment Project. (2016). Presentation to the RP Group, April 8, 2016. The Research and Planning Group for California Community Colleges. http://rpgroup.org/Our-Projects/All-Projects/Multiple-Measures/Presentations-and-Webinars.

Multiple Measures Assessment Project Research Team. (2016). English placement models for the Multiple Measures Assessment Project—Phase 2 (Rev. November 2016). http://rpgroup.org/Portals/0/Documents/Projects/MultipleMeasures/DecisionRulesandAnalysisCode/English-Decision-Trees-1_11_2016.pdf.

Office of the Vice Chancellor of Academic Affairs. (2016). Co-requisite remediation full implementation 2015-2016. Tennessee Board of Regents. http://www.aacc.nche.edu/Resources/aaccprograms/pathways/Documents/TNBoardRegents_FullImplementation2015-2016.pdf.

Perry, M., Bahr, P. R., Rosin, M. & Woodward, K. M. (2010). *Course-taking patterns, policies, and practices in developmental education in the California community colleges*. EdSource. http://edsource.org/wp-content/publications/FULL-CC-DevelopmentalCoursetaking.pdf.

Poe, M. (2014). The consequences of writing assessment. *Research in the Teaching of English, 48*(3), 271-275.

Poe, M. & Cogan, J. A., Jr. (2016). Civil rights and writing assessment: Using the disparate impact approach as a fairness methodology to evaluate social impact. *The Journal of Writing Assessment, 9*(1). https://escholarship.org/uc/item/08f1c307.

Poe, M., Elliot, N., Cogan, J. A., Jr. & Nurudeen, T. G., Jr. (2014). The legal and the local: Using disparate-impact analysis to understand the consequences of writing assessment. *College Composition and Communication, 65*(4), 588-611.

Poe, M. & Inoue, A. B. (2016). Toward writing as social justice: An idea whose time has come [Special issue]. *College English, 79*(2), 119-126.

Policies for Prerequisites, Corequisites and Advisories on Recommended Preparation, 5 CA ADC § 55003 (2018).

Rodby, J. & Fox, T. (2000). Basic work and material acts: The ironies, discrepancies, and disjunctures of basic writing and mainstreaming. *Journal of Basic Writing, 19*(1), 84–99.

Scott-Clayton, J. (2012). Do high stakes placement exams predict college success? *CCRC Working Paper No. 41*. Community College Research Center. http://ccrc.tc.columbia.edu/publications/high-stakes-placement-exams-predict.html.

Scott-Clayton, J. & Stacey, G. W. (2015). *Improving the accuracy of remedial placement*. Columbia University, Teachers College, Community College Research Center. http://67.205.94.182/publications/improving-accuracy-remedial-placement.html.

Slomp, D. (2016). Ethical considerations and writing assessment. *Journal of Writing Assessment, 9*(1). https://escholarship.org/uc/item/2k14r1zg.

Stoup, G. (2015). *Using data to identify emergent inequities and the effective practices to address them*. Presentation delivered at Success and Equity: Regional Conference for Collaboration. Modesto Junior College.

Two-Year College English Association Research Committee. (2016). *TYCA white paper on placement reform*. National Council of Teachers of English.

Witham, K., Malcom-Piqueux, L. E., Dowd, A. C. & Bensimon, E. M. (2015). *America's unmet promise: The imperative for equity in higher education*. American Association of Colleges and Universities.

CHAPTER 17.

# NEURODIVERGENCE AND INTERSECTIONALITY IN LABOR-BASED GRADING CONTRACTS

**Kathleen Kryger and Griffin X. Zimmerman**
University of Arizona

*This essay explores how labor-based grading contract (LBGC) systems can be informed by neurodivergence. To date, little research has described how grading contracts impact students of varying neurological abilities. This essay addresses this gap by investigating how neurodivergent students experience LBGC systems. Neurodivergent students face increased academic and emotional labor, thus shifting power and ease of access in such contract-grading classrooms to neurotypical students who may be more adept at "performing" academic labor. First, we articulate the ways in which neurodivergence is defined and made invisible, how it manifests in our writing classrooms, and the ways in which our institutions uphold normative conceptions of neurological ability. Second, we illuminate how grading contracts, by altering the activity systems of schooling and writing classrooms, create barriers to accessibility that heighten neurodivergent students' experiences of schooling- and grade-related anxiety. Finally, they offer an ethnographic exploration of ways to unite the socially just aims of LBGC systems with the intersectional lens inherent in a consideration of the neurodivergent student experience.*

Assessment is directional. As Sara Ahmed (2017) notes, "power works as a mode of directionality, a way of orienting bodies in particular ways, so they are facing a certain way, heading toward a future that is given a face" (p. 43). Conventional writing assessment systems, like other structures of sociocultural power, are presented as meritocracies that orient students toward academic advancement and bright futures. However, composition as a discipline has been grappling for decades with the stark reality that this representation elides a reality in which historically oppressed students are pointed in the opposite direction of their White, socioeconomically advantaged peers.

Grading contracts are one answer to this need to create more egalitarian composition pedagogies, yet power still flows through, to, and around them. As Spidell and Thelin (2006) and Inman and Powell (2018) both explain, alternative assessment systems challenge students to rethink not just composing practices, but also the purposes and functions of schooling and grading. Grading contracts challenge students to negotiate their classroom anxieties, to navigate their emotional and affective investment in grades and teachers, and to (re)orient themselves to a new schooling system. Rethinking can create productive discomfort; rethinking can be generative. But this rethinking is also labor: cognitive, emotional, embodied, intangible. And for some folx, that labor is less visible than others.[1] For some folx, that labor is magnified.

Inman and Powell (2018) write, "To dismiss cultural constructs such as grades, a repeated part of the education system from students' earliest memories of schools, ignores the affective domain of learning" (p. 34). We begin with these thoughts to highlight the systems in place that keep these populations fearful, that keep them/us (re)pressed in powerful ways. As Marylin Frye argues, to be "oppressed" is to be "pressed": "Something pressed is something caught between or among forces and barriers which are so related to each other that jointly they restrain, restrict or prevent the thing's motion or mobility. Mold. Immobilize. Reduce" (as cited in Ahmed, 2017, pp. 49-50). We begin also with this dissonance to demonstrate the power teachers have in e/affecting students, especially those who are neurodivergent, those who are multiply oppressed, those who are marked by their (ab)normality. As feminist scholars who feel called to socially just and fair composition pedagogies and praxes, we are sensitive to the ways these writing assessment practices (and the larger ecologies in which they function) create inequities not only based on race and class, but also based on physical and neurological ability, and the interstices of these and other identities.

The goal of this essay, then, is to articulate the ways in which neurodivergence as a lens can contribute to our field's understanding and application of classroom assessment practices, especially in the context of labor-based grading contracts (LBGCs). As a beloved colleague once told Kathleen, "Good writing is good thinking." While there exists a great deal of scholarship about what constitutes "good" writing, we must also be critically engaged with normative assumptions and expectations that underpin conceptions of "good" thinking. In solidarity with the authors in this special collection, we believe writing assessment must be a site of social justice intervention, and we add our voices to illuminate the challenges of the often invisible marginalized and non-normative populations:

---

[1] Folx: a genderqueer alternative for "folks." When we use this term, we do so to intentionally center the various gender-expansive identities that fall outside of the binary categories of men and women that "folks" has traditionally encompassed.

neurodivergent students, especially for those who experience multiple marginalizations. By focusing on these students, we offer a lens through which we can begin the work of shifting our assessment ecologies from single-axis interventions to sites that acknowledge the complex interconnected nature of a student's intersectional identities.

We explore the intersections of neurodivergence and socially just writing assessment scholarship. First, we articulate the ways in which neurodivergence is defined and made invisible, the ways in which it manifests in writing classrooms, and the ways in which academic institutions uphold normative conceptions of neurological ability. Second, we illuminate how LBGCs, by altering the activity systems of schooling and writing classrooms (Russell, 1997; Spinuzzi, 2008), can create barriers to accessibility that force students to reject their own ways of learning, knowing, being, and languaging. And, finally, we use our experiences as neurodivergent students and teacher-scholars in an ethnographic exploration of the various opportunities to create interventions on our interventions: to unite the socially just aims of LBGCs with the intersectional lens inherent in a consideration of the neurodivergent student experience.

## DEFINING NEURODIVERGENCE

We proceed with the assumption that neurodivergence exists and intersects with the fields of disability studies and rhetoric/writing studies in meaningful ways. Scholars and activists such as Melanie Yergeau (2018), Alison Kafer (2013), Margaret Price (2011), and Eli Clare (2017) have illuminated descriptions of neurodivergence in fuller capacities in their own work. While we will reference and build upon their important scholarship, we will maintain a focus on how LBGCs complicate and illuminate labor considerations for neurodivergent populations in writing assessment ecologies that uphold normative conceptions and frameworks of academic performance and labor.

Typically referred to as "mental disorders" or "mental health issues," neurodivergence can be defined as any biological or trauma-induced condition that manifests in differences in cognitive function, processing, sensory processing, or stimulus response from the cognitively normative (or neurotypical) population (Yergeau, 2018). We assert that neurodivergence is an implicit, value-neutral part of an individual's overall personhood and, as such, is a substantive consideration in a student's overall experience within the classroom. In solidarity with the broader disability studies narrative, we argue neurodivergence is the appropriate terminology (as opposed to the above; there are additional terms used within disability studies that apply to specific populations and are outside the scope of this essay). The term neurodivergence centers the experience of the individuals within these communities and rejects mainstream narratives of deficit and/or cure. In all instances where the phrases "mental disorders" or "mental health issues" are used, we use quotations to denote our rejection of the implications inherent in the terminology.

## POSITIONALITY

As feminist scholars, we are committed to the tradition of critically engaging with our own positionalities and biases as they intersect with and inform our scholarship. We are both White, settler-colonial, first-generation, middle-class folx who were assigned female at birth. Kathleen is a cisgender woman with a history of trauma. Meanwhile, Griffin is a non-binary trans man with intermittently (in)visible chronic illness and physical disability. We both benefit from multiple privileges, among them our socialization into a White, middle-class *habitus* (Inoue, 2015) and our current access to higher education. We acknowledge that we each benefit from our U.S. citizenship status and our White privilege.

In addition to these already complex interlocking identities, we are also both neurodivergent. Griffin is autistic with anxiety, depression, and complex post-traumatic stress disorder, diagnoses that carry with them not only social judgment, but a host of sensory and executive processing issues intimately linked to their personal and professional identities. Kathleen has experienced generalized anxiety disorder and panic disorder since adolescence, the results of which have had multiple physical, cognitive, and emotional effects. Though we are more than our disabilities, these experiences live with us, move us, shape us—discursively, cognitively, physically, and emotionally.

We disclose our positionalities as an acknowledgment of how our identities privilege us and orient our perceptions. We speak from a White perspective, one that certainly cannot represent perspectives crucial to historically oppressed peoples; we recognize and remind our readers that our experiences are not comparable to those who have experienced racial discrimination and/or historical trauma (see Gobodo-Madikizela, 2016). Our current positions as White college educators and doctoral students at a predominately White institution allow us to use academic language and a cerebral approach to the visceral experiences of individuals. While we recognize the limitations of our perspective, we are committed to sharing this language and our experiences, so future teacher-scholar-activists may more easily advocate for neurodivergent-accessible academic spaces. As we move through our argument, we will use our experiences as both teacher-scholars and students to exemplify different challenges for neurodivergent students, as well as offer ethnographic perspectives on opportunities for LBGCs to be leveraged in service to a more intersectional assessment ecology.

## LBGCS' SINGLE-AXIS LENS

Recent scholarship in assessment and higher education has continually pointed out the ways in which the academy has been structured to "limit public access and interaction in such a way as to avoid the chance encounter of diverse populations, creating a series of protected interior and isolated spaces" (Dolmage, 2017, p. 41). Among the solutions created to address the gross inequities built into the culture of higher education, various forms of grading contracts have been designed to address challenges for specific teacher and student populations.

As others in this special edition have historicized/contextualized, grading contracts as an intervention into issues of student agency and social justice in writing classrooms are not new. In his 1973 article "Teaching without Judging," Mandel addressed many of these same issues, and scholars such as Moreno-Lopez (2005), Danielewicz and Elbow (2008), and Shor (2009) have also taken up these critical and liberatory pedagogies. Yet with the publication of his book *Antiracist Writing Assessment Ecologies: Teaching and Assessing Writing for a Socially Just Future*, his Conference on Composition and Communication Chair's Address, and his recent monograph *Labor-Based Grading Contracts: Building Equity and Inclusion in the Compassionate Writing Classroom*, Asao B. Inoue (2015, 2019a, 2019b, respectively) has done substantial work toward making institutional space for antiracist writing assessment praxes. For many, Inoue's LBGC system has provided an invaluable starting place for the practical application of racially just writing assessment. Importantly, grading contracts and other assessment technologies are not apolitical/arhetorical and are thus still subject to critical analysis. As Inoue (2009) explains:

> The problems writing assessments solve refer existentially to— and are constructed by—the socio-cultural forces that define those in and outside the academy and classroom, the ways we define acceptable and unacceptable writers, and the ways in which our assessments construct the naturalness of racial formations, social groups, and other constructs that divide and distinguish people for dominant interests and purposes. Assessment is not a value-free technology because it is more than the methods, machines, and materials we use to make judgements. (p. 101)

We start from this recognition of assessment itself as a technology laden with power because we see our intervention as extending this exact argument: Grading contracts can also "divide and distinguish [students] for dominant interests and purposes," namely for neurological norms of academic performance and labor. While we could provide a simple and easily replicable list of methods and practical applications that would undoubtedly be useful for many well-intentioned teachers and administrators, we would be perpetuating that which we claim to be disrupting. It is not the assessment technology itself that does the social justice work; it is how we implement, explain to stakeholders, critically analyze, and recursively revise the technology that matters. When we overintellectualize these issues and divorce ourselves from the normative expectations naturalized and enforced in our assessment ecologies, we give them power: the power of silence, the power of institutional space, the power of naturality/neutrality. By focusing on neurological ableism in LBGCs, we seek to give language to and begin making institutional space for these concerns.

We begin our argument from a place of acknowledging the unavoidably complex and interwoven contexts in which writing assessment practices are deployed. It is our contention that contract-based assessment systems, while doing important work, are missing a vital intersectional lens and thus continue to privilege certain populations. We move with a "both/and" mindset; we resist the notion that grading contracts are either "good" or "bad." To make such claims, we rely on Kimberlé Crenshaw's (1991) theorization of intersectionality, or the ways in which multiple identities that both marginalize and empower an individual co-construct the social, political/structural, and representational experiences of a person or marginalized group. Crenshaw (1991) explains, "My focus on the intersections of race and gender only highlights the need to account for multiple grounds of identity when considering how the social world is constructed" (p. 1245). Contrary to the ways in which the term intersectionality has been co-opted as a label to simply denote the different/various identities to which a person may belong (May, 2015), our work centers interwoven power dynamics; that is, we advocate research and pedagogical interventions that acknowledge and attempt to disrupt the ways in which various identities interact with power structures. As Ahmed (2017) writes, "Intersectionality is a starting point, the point from which we must proceed if we are to offer an account of how power works" (p. 5). For us, too, intersectionality is our locus.

Thus, while acknowledging the impactful work that Inoue and others (Elliot, 2016; Green, 2016; Poe, 2014) have contributed to forwarding antiracist assessment theories/praxes, we believe this work can further benefit from the scholarship of disability studies, especially that which centers neurodivergence and intersectionality. For example, Sami Schalk (2018) explicates how race and disability are linked:

> Due to the conflicting social norms and stereotypes of various genders and races, certain behaviors and states of mind are

> interpreted in divergent ways when expressed and interpreted by differently situated individuals. In other words, a black woman behaving in one way is likely to be interpreted differently than a white man behaving the same way. (p. 64)

Schalk (2018) explains the ways in which multiple identities combine in experiences of marginalization as well as the ways in which one social identity can actually increase the likeliness of being labeled with or included in another marginalized status. Here, Schalk articulates how Black students are more likely to also be classified as "mentally disabled," or neurodivergent. Given the ableist and discriminatory underpinning of the academy in general (aptly illustrated as "steep steps" articulated by Dolmage, 2017), it becomes incumbent upon us as educators to center neurodivergence in our own labors. In light of our current sociocultural contexts (notably the global pandemic and police brutality against Black Americans), we see this work as more important than ever.

## NEURODIVERGENCE AND THE WRITING CLASSROOM

What has become apparent to us as neurodivergent teacher-scholars is that the deeply naturalized invisibility of neurodivergent students makes them a forgotten population—a heterogeneous group who experience a deficit of scholarship, even while they are often overrepresented in our classrooms, to the point of almost being a non-minority. Additionally, as we will soon explore, this population is an inherently intersectional one, and efforts to meet the needs of neurodivergent students offer the opportunity to "trickle up" in such a way as to meet students at the nexus of the multiple intersections they may hold.

While recent research in rhetoric and composition has begun challenging White supremacy and other social inequities within our assessment systems (see Elliot, 2016; Inoue, 2015; Poe, 2014; Poe & Inoue, 2016), little scholarship has tended to disability's role in assessment theory. Disability scholarship has been intervening in composition studies for a few decades now, with scholars like Dunn (1995), Brueggemann (2001), Brueggemann et al. (2001), Feldmeier White (2002), Lewiecki-Wilson et al. (2008), Browning (2014), and Kerschbaum (2015) leading the way. In addition, Jay Dolmage (2014, 2017, 2018) has published extensive scholarship describing how academic institutions are founded on systems that are deliberately excluding to disabled persons. And Tara Wood (2017) explains how the disabled student experience is heavily impacted by normative constructions of time and temporality. However, none of these scholars have specifically interrogated the ways in which our pedagogies impact neurodivergent student populations.

Neurodivergence is not a thought experiment; neurodivergence is a daily reality for a large portion of the population of the United States of America:

> According to the U.S. Department of Education, in the year 2003–2004, 22 percent of students with disabilities in college reported having "mental illness or depression"; 7 percent reported learning disabilities; and 11 percent reported attention deficit disorder ("Profile" 133). Results published in the *Archives of General Psychiatry* put the numbers even higher: according to analysis of data from 2001–2002 National Epidemiologic Survey on Alcohol and related Conditions, nearly half (46 percent) of college students reported having experienced some psychiatric disorder in the year the survey was conducted. (Price, 2014, p. 7)

These statistics are staggering when framed in terms of the number of students in each classroom who may be silently, invisibly, and/or unknowingly coping with differences in cognitive function and processing. Neurodivergence can affect any population regardless of personal identifier(s). However, neurodivergence is more likely to affect historically marginalized populations, especially in a capacity outside the diagnostic structures of the medical-industrial complex (Dolmage, 2017; Sutter & Perrin, 2016). Such students are statistically less likely to have access to the ongoing care, especially behavioral health care, which is necessary to diagnose and treat various neurological conditions (Davidson, 2017; Dolmage, 2017; Schalk, 2018). Many of us take for granted our access to adequate health care and medical expertise, without which students are unable to access formal accommodations. Although disability studies remains critical of the U.S. medical field and advocates for constant interrogation of its complicity in systems of oppression, access is still a privilege. Diagnoses and medication are privileges. The current international COVID-19 pandemic has heightened awareness of these privileges to otherwise normative populations as folx grapple with tele-medicine appointments, supply chain issues inducing medication shortages, and deprioritized medical treatment. A popular meme in disability spaces summarizes this phenomenon aptly, describing how it feels like the whole world has suddenly awoken to the dissonance, uncertainty, and executive functioning challenges that trauma survivors consider business as usual.

Beyond issues of access, it is critical to acknowledge the core intersectional nature of the concept of disability itself. In their article, "Work in the Intersections: A Black Feminist Disability Framework," Bailey and Mobley (2018) unpack the spaces in which Black feminist studies can integrate with disability studies to foster a deeper understanding of how disability is intertwined with race and gender. The authors explain:

> Black people cannot afford to be disabled when they are required to be phantasmically abled in a white supremacist society. By bringing disability studies and a Black feminist theoretical lens to address this myth, scholars are better able to explain Black people's reluctance to identify as disabled and potentially offer new strategies for dismantling ableism within Black Studies. (p. 4)

What is deeply generative here is the awareness that concepts of neurodivergence are founded in concepts of race; from the psychiatric condition of drapetomania that marked slaves desirous of freedom as mentally aberrant to measures of cranial size as markers of racial inferiority, Blackness has always been conceptualized as disabling. And likewise, the label of neurodivergent or disabled is segregating, separating those labeled from their normative peers. "Race marks Black people as being inherently disabled, fundamentally other. In this way, race and disability are mutually constitutive" (Bailey & Mobley, 2018, p. 6). Thus, when we ask our readers to consider the presence of neurodivergence in their classroom, we are urging a greater awareness of a set of interconnected identifiers and the mutually constructed, mutually magnifying consequences of their existence for students.

As students and teachers, we have both personally experienced how disabilities are often construed as physical, unfortunate, and unnatural. Disability activist, scholar, and crip scholar Eli Clare (2017) notes:

> Strangers offer me Christian prayers or crystals and vitamins, always with the same intent—to touch me, fix me, mend my cerebral palsy, if only I will comply. After five decades of these kinds of interactions, I still don't know how to rebuff their pity, how to tell them the simple truth that I'm not broken. They assume me unnatural, want to make me normal, take for granted the need and desire for cure. (p. 5)

While Clare and other disability scholars have dedicated their careers to countering this narrative of cure, the strength of disability activism as a whole is still strongly focused on disabilities that are visible. Yet the first step toward any change is recognition, or "seeing" the problem. Whether a student enters a classroom with a faltering gate, a missing limb, or a visible assistive device, the disability is immediately apparent and therefore *knowable* to the observer. That which is known can be accommodated: seating changed, aisles widened, captions added, passing periods extended. We contend that neurodivergence is the silent attendee in our classrooms, one that accompanies roughly one quarter to one half of our students, one that consistently intervenes during their efforts of producing academic labor.

At most, signs of neurodivergence are experienced in a kind of sideways, slipping, liminal way through the constant bouncing of leg and knee, the gaze that never quite makes eye contact, the inability to articulate around a specific topic, or the queer phrasing of written passage. None of these examples specifically outs a student as neurodivergent, but they are all possible extensions of the neurodivergent student experience. Neurodivergence certainly shapes how a student will negotiate their classroom experience. Unfortunately, neurodivergent narratives are lacking in disability pedagogies, accommodation recommendations, and conversations around curriculum and assessment. We have witnessed how trying to imagine a neurodivergent student (and, thus, a neurodivergent student's needs) is to try to put a name to an invisible face.

The invisibility of neurodivergence can be both an advantage and a disadvantage: As with any socially constructed group, there are power structures functioning within difference (Crenshaw, 1991; May, 2015). Because some types of neurodivergence are almost always overlooked, they are not marked by the institution and therefore can escape systemic/sociopolitical oppression. For example, Kathleen's generalized anxiety and panic disorders are invisible to most. Yet many of the coping mechanisms she developed are valorized in a neoliberal capitalist system: perfectionism, inability to say no, overworking, etc. These socially rewarded responses to trauma and chronic stress perpetuate systems that work against relationship- and community-building by prioritizing ideologies of individual competitiveness and productivity. So, while Kathleen's ways of coping are often system(at)ically rewarded (at her own expense, of course), other types of neurodivergence are less socially acceptable and are therefore more easily targeted by stigmatization and discrimination. For example, Griffin's autism results in coping behaviors that are less socially acceptable: isolating from sensory or adverse emotional stimulation, various stimming activities, constant apologies to account for perceptions of unmet social expectations, and a rigidity in method or process in an attempt to supply predictable, navigable situations. All of these behaviors out Griffin as "socially inept," "overwhelmed," "emotional," or just plain odd.

We reveal these "within-group differences" to highlight the ways that neurodivergence, as an already unstable categorization mechanism, is still and always functioning within overlapping and interacting systems of oppression (May, 2015, p. 22). Just as some physical disabilities confer privilege in some scenarios, so do some forms of neurodivergence. We understand on a deeply personal level how neurodivergence is not homogeneous. By centering the neurodivergent experience in our exploration of LBGCs below, rather than the perceived behavioral product of these experiences, we work to provide a better understanding of academic labor and its articulation in college composition assessment ecologies.

## "ACADEMIC PERFORMANCE" AND "LABOR"

When we use the phrase "labor-based grading contracts" (LBGCs), we include any grading system that requires students to meet goals of academic performance rather than standards of academic quality. As Inoue (2019b) explains in *Labor-Based Grading Contracts*, the goal with labor-based assessment ecologies is to shift the assessment criteria from that of quality to that of labor so as to provide students with opportunities to better understand their own languaging practices. While this system provides educators with vital opportunities to reflect more critically on their pedagogies and to dialogue with students about how they labor in their writing processes, LBGCs fundamentally shift classroom activity systems. This shift requires students to adapt to the new schooling expectations and modes of production. To better understand how students experience this shift, we make a distinction between labor and academic performance.

For us, this distinction highlights the ways in which assessment technologies shift power. These closely associated terms are two sides of a subject position and power structure: that of the instructor or broader assessment ecology, and that of the student. We define *academic performance* as the observable or quantifiable products of student participation within academic systems. For example, this may include measures of attendance, verbal participation in class, and submitting assignments. Conversely, we define *labor* as the time, energy, and effort that students invest in the production of and adherence to normative conceptions of academic performance. In other words, students perform what is often impalpable labor, including but not limited to their emotional, psychological, temporal, and intellectual investment in the product of academic performance. Academic performance becomes the visible/tangible products assessed and judged by teachers, similar to what Inoue (2019b) calls "labor power" (p. 83). The primary distinction between the Marxist conception of labor power and academic performance is this: We intentionally claim the performative aspect of academic labor. If we know not all labor is equitable in exchange value, then somewhere in the conceptual liminal space is a socially coded "performance." Thus, we can see how a labor-based system of assessment privileges neurotypical students who are more adept at producing labor in codified ways that meet the requirements deemed appropriate academic labor. As Inoue (2019b) notes, these students are often White and middle-class, and these students are typically intersectionally privileged by their various subject positions and are habituated to the White, middle-class *habitus* of academia.

We focus on LBGCs as a site of intervention both to acknowledge their important interruptions into writing assessment ecologies and to highlight the ways it is incumbent on our professional ethics to further problematize their values and applications. We contend that LBGCs create inequity for neurodivergent students in two central areas: (a) they disrupt the dynamics of the classroom activity system, creating what some may call "productive dissonance," and (b) they focus on labor but may not account for the additional time/labor of adjusting to, adhering to, putting trust into, and understanding the new activity system. These seemingly value-positive interventions may actually further marginalize the neurodivergent student population; we must interrogate and uncover the neurological norms inherent in these systems, so we may better center the needs of all our students when constructing and implementing grading contracts.

## CLASSROOM ACTIVITY SYSTEMS AND NEURODIVERGENT LABOR

All alternative assessment practices change the activity systems of a classroom, whether they be an LBGC or another unconventional grading system. As explained by Russell (1997), an activity system is:

> Any ongoing, object-directed, historically conditioned, dialectically structured, tool-mediated human interaction. . . . The activity system is the basic unit of analysis for both groups' and individuals' behavior, in that it analyzes the way concrete tools are used to mediate the motive (direct, trajectory) and the object (the *problem space* or the *focus*) of behavior and changes in it. (p. 510)

Students become accustomed to the rhythm of these activity systems, and this includes internalized understandings of how to labor in ways recognized as academic performance, how that performance is valorized, and how grades are the primary currency exchanged within the broader academic ecology. When we remove these expected systems, we automatically require students to adapt, to (re)orient. The concept of "productive dissonance" is the belief that it is useful, healthy, and even preferential for students to experience the "academic growth" it takes to make connections between the old activity system and the new. Yet cognitive dissonance can only be "productive" if it is transformed or directed into positive action (such as the discomforts of [un]learning systems of oppression); for neurodivergent students, the converse is often true: The dissonance can stymie growth by trapping the student in unfamiliar and unnavigable territory.

Imagine a common classroom activity used to introduce students to cultural diversity: Students are situated at tables to play a card game with simple rules, one of which is no talking. As they begin to play, students are periodically moved to sit at a different table. They attempt to join in the game at the new table, only to quickly become frustrated by the perception that no one is following the rules. They cannot verbally communicate, so they attempt to gesture or otherwise intervene, which only confounds the other students at the table. Some students become so frustrated they bow out altogether, refusing to play at the "rigged" tables. Only at the conclusion of the activity do the students learn that each table received slightly different rules, and that differing expectations created the conflict.

When we introduce grading contracts, especially contracts that remove grades completely, we are asking students to move to a new card table. And even though we explain that the rules are different, we know it will take time for students to remember and apply the new rules. Except that for some neurodivergent students, anxiety prevents them from remembering the new rules, so they freeze, unable to figure out how to proceed. Other neurodivergent students receive their copy of the new rules overwritten on a previous copy, so they are constantly trying to read the new rules, but the old rules obscure their view. Still others understand the new rules but lack the schema to apply them in the new context. In all these examples, we see that while grading contracts may be steps in a more ethical direction, they are also difficult steps for all students to take with us, and for some neurodivergent students, they are steep steps that create greater barriers to access. Further, it is essential we remember the intersectional nature of neurodivergence. For example, while LBGCs are specifically designed to attend to *linguistic* disparities, they may introduce *neurological* disparities by putting students in a position to perform labor under a societal construction that makes them reluctant to admit to neurodivergence and ask for help, if indeed they had access to the medical resources to acknowledge and diagnose their neurological difference to begin with. What we are emphatically stating is that students do not experience our classrooms through only one axis, and by focusing only on dispelling biases in quality of languaging, we run the risk of creating an inclusive classroom for one aspect of their experience while ignoring or worsening others.

In addition to the challenges presented by changing expectations in grading contract classrooms, some neurodivergent students are also disadvantaged by the removal of certain grading structures, checkpoints, and quantitative representations of progress. For instance, in Inoue's (2019b) system, there is no way for students to calculate their grade in numerical terms. As Inman and Powell

(2018) have shown, the lack of grades causes some distress amongst students, who rely on grades as commodities with which they gain cultural and fiscal capital. Inman and Powell (2018) argue the use of course contracts can gloss over the "affective domain of learning":

> Grades, then, serve as more than measures of identity for these students; they are signifiers of how much work remains to be done for the students to meet their goals and thus enact their desired identities. And these students do not have the authorial confidence to determine for themselves how much work remains; rather, they seem to desperately want a marker capable of making that determination for them. (p. 42)

While this research does not specifically address neurodivergent students, the observation is doubly relevant for this population. When combined with the knowledge of the impact of changing activity systems on students who may approach the new expectations with debilitating dissonance, the further removal of conventional grading systems creates deeply problematic and anxiety-producing terrain for students who are already grappling with the need for increased labor to participate in traditional classroom structures. While "grades, and the lack thereof, are linked to fear" (Inman & Powell, 2018, p. 46), for many neurodivergent students, they are also linked to predictability and clarity; they function as recognizable measures of "correct" labor, teacher expectations, and academic performance that, when absent, plunge neurodivergent students into activity systems in which they do not always have the means, time, or ability to decode. Thus, when implementing LBGCs, we must necessarily view the removal of grades as a step toward ethical improvements in our assessment practices while at the same time acknowledging how they create a culture of increased marginalization for neurodivergent students.

## ASSESSMENTS OF LABOR AND TIME

Our distinctions between academic performance and labor allow us to disentangle some of the complicating factors Inoue (2019b) identifies in his treatise on labor. Inoue (2019b) argues that labor ought to be considered three-dimensionally: how students labor (use-value), that students labor (exchange-value), and why students labor (worth), with worth acting as the most "unaccounted for" and the most important dimension (p. 88). These three dimensions are approached as both discrete and interwoven complexities, so students attune themselves to various aspects of their laboring. Some activities in Inoue's system include labor logs (which track time spent laboring, levels of engagement, etc.), labor journals (weekly reflections), labor snippets (brief updates about their work), and multiple reflection essays (long-term labor reflections) that ask students to track, notice, and analyze their own labors. Despite the pedagogical benefits of these activities, these labors and their exchange-value(s) could do more to consider the additional labor that neurodivergent students are often required to complete to perform in these normative ways.

Inoue's (2019b) underlying premise mirrors our own pedagogies, our own lived experiences with learning both within and without academia: "One learns *in the labors* of researching, drafting, and revising—in the doing—and learns best if one pays attention to how one is doing those labors" (p. 108, emphasis in original). We recognize the ways in which asking students to reflect on their labor is beneficial to most students. The premise is simple enough: To learn is to labor, to labor is to do, and this takes time and effort. But what if to labor does not always mean to produce the appropriate academic performance within the normative time frame? What happens when the "labor power" is not reflective of the intangible labor? Our distinction between "performance" and "labor" still comes to bear in inequitable ways: Neurotypical students who are fully enculturated into the dominant White, patriarchal, middle-class *habitus* of our institutions are more likely to be comfortable *performing* the academic work assigned to them; they will repeat the same well-rehearsed behaviors that have carried them to higher education. We cannot neglect these considerations of academic performance, of ease-in-doing, of habituation; Inoue (2019b) recognizes that certain languaging behaviors will be easier for White, middle-class students to enact, but what of neurological differences in expression, activity, reflection, and action? The orientation to particular schooling activity systems, including the navigation of demands of the writing classroom, are also habituations, performances we learn.

By focusing on these aspects of LBGCs, we are hoping to invite a more expansive, intersectional lens to this invaluable work. In a system that exchanges labor for a final course grade (and thereby access, capital, and affective validation), the exchange-value of labor is not any less disadvantaging for neurodivergent students as a conventional grading system is for students out of tune with White middle-class *habitus*. Labor-based assessment hinges on a key assumption: that each assignment, each product, each performance, requires a roughly equitable amount of labor from each student. Inoue (2019b) recognizes how this assumption is still complex, still unresolved:

> What about students who have other demands on their time, intersections of class and economics, intersections that surely played a role in my own background? Aren't there students who

> likely don't have to work and go to school at the same time? Won't they be just as privileged in a purely labor-based grading system where arguably time is the key factor for success as in typical quality-based systems of grading? Aren't those more time-privileged students also more likely to come from more economically well-off families, and aren't those families statistically more likely to be White families? (pp. 69–70)

Here, Inoue (2019b) reveals the key tension in labor-based assessment systems: Besides the benefits of freedom in languaging, these technologies do not fundamentally intervene on other intersectional dynamics of power and privilege. Instead, they sidestep the deeply problematic and subjective quality-based assessment practices and exchange them for a less understood but still marginalizing focus on labor, performance, ability, and time. While there will always be students who have other commitments outside of the classroom, neurodivergent students frequently need to perform vastly different quantities and types of labor to accomplish the same academic performance. For example, anxiety or depression can cause students to struggle to maintain sustained effort on a task; ADHD can require a student to read a passage multiple times to gain the same benefit as a neurotypical student due to difficulties in managing attention; autistic students may need assistance to produce expected levels of linguistic expression on assignments; and dyslexic students may need to access materials through differentiated technologies that require additional time investments. In each of these cases, neurodivergent students often invest more embodied/physical and emotional/affective labor toward completing the cognitive labor than a neurotypical peer but are provided the same reward for these arguably more extensive efforts.

Thus, inequity is created in LBGCs where the question "Did you complete the task?" flattens student production of academic performance to a variable that is more difficult for neurodivergent students to achieve through their labor, even if there are guided instructions. This labor-based model also elides the difference between "major" and "minor" assignments by arguing that all labor (and thus all academic performance) is equitable in the classroom, which in Kathleen's experience has created opportunities for discussions about which kinds of student labor are often neglected. Likewise, Griffin has noticed students struggling with the lack of self-direction and choice this view of labor creates: Since all assignments have the same exchange-value, students can struggle to choose when and where to direct their labor to maintain a balance between course requirements and personal situations. They don't know whether to invest time in reading or time in this smaller writing assignment or that larger writing project if they have limited labor resources. Wood's (2017) exploration of crip time in the writing classroom, defined as "a flexible approach to normative time frames" (p. 264), helps us make sense of our observations:

> This negotiation reflects the crip time that Nishida theorizes, a space in which the limits and potentials of time are flexible, and all members of the space have a voice in constructing the temporal means of participation. . . . Such pedagogical designs should be negotiated with disabled students, not simply for disabled students. Allowing agentive control reduces the risk of imposing normative or compulsory modes of composing onto students in writing classrooms. (pp. 277–278)

Thus, the prioritizing of academic performance in these assessment systems creates an incomplete narrative, one that obscures the very real and visceral labors neurodivergent students must perform just to access a space in which they may manufacture the academic performance required, and one in which students' negotiation of their own participation is prevented by lack of prioritized labor and quantifiable progress.

A grading system that centers student labor requires a way to assess and reflect on these academic performances. In Inoue's (2019b) model, one method is that of tracking or otherwise attending to the labor (and time laboring) students are investing in the course. Inoue asks his students to maintain a "labor log" that tracks their labor by duration, date, description, location, level of engagement, and mood. Inoue (2019b) argues, "The more time one spends laboring, the more one will learn . . . and that labor is best when it is mindfully done and when one's labors are reflected upon in order to understand them and do them better next time" (pp. 150–151). While we agree that reflection on processes is beneficial, writing teachers—and their assessment technologies—should not presume that all students lack and/or would benefit from such sustained metacognitive efforts. Wood (2017) reminds us that neurodivergent students already "often possess a sophisticated metacognitive awareness of how to navigate the strictures they face in the classroom" (p. 272), helping us understand that this labor-tracking activity may produce a deficit model for neurodivergent students who are already deeply aware of how their laboring differs from the normative population. We maintain Wood's (2017) understanding of crip time and temporal means of engagement, and we turn to our own experiences to explore the difficulties with this type of metacognitive activity, which we believe can be deeply problematic for various neurodivergent students.

In our experience, tracking time is a complex activity that requires not only an attention to types of labor and time spent, but also a kind of rigorous consistency that is simply not accessible to all students. For Griffin, for example, any work is usually divided into either intense "flow" states in which time is not a sense that is easily perceived or, in contrast, choppy, highly fragmented states too divided to be easily tracked with any certainty. Additionally, Griffin's neurodivergence often manifests in a lack of self-awareness such that being aware of physical and emotional states can take conscious effort, and maintaining schedules or executive functioning is in and of itself labor that requires conscious, dedicated effort. Thus, time-tracking activities ask questions that are not only difficult to answer, they raise anxiety and consciousness around difference and redirect energy and labor away from actions that directly contribute to other necessary tasks. In other words, while Inoue (2019b) claims that "the most important factor is how much time the student spends on the labors of learning to write, because the student *has the most control* [emphasis added] over these aspects of learning to write" (p. 151), Griffin's experience is that their neurodivergence directly impacts how they perceive, experience, and mediate time, thus making it a highly unreliable and uncontrollable measure of learning.

Kathleen has experienced the tracking of time laboring as a *both/and*, with both benefits and hazards. In one way, this activity has been useful in reducing her anxiety by helping to maintain balance in her various roles as student, teacher, and administrator. Being able to assure herself that an adequate amount of time was spent on certain tasks has helped her to set and maintain personal/professional boundaries that are often nonexistent for academics, especially those who reward and perpetuate overworking. Despite these benefits, as well as the organizational proclivities that enable them, meticulously tracking time can also trigger or worsen anxiety and lead to panic—when certain parameters aren't met, feelings of guilt, shame, and inadequacy quickly replace any notion of productivity and balance.

As demonstrated by these lived experiences, this time-tracking labor directly influences the affective domains of anxiety, emotion, self-efficacy, and self-worth. Similar to conversations around productive dissonance, some may argue that anxiety can be productive to students' maturation and performance; however, as Wood (2017) notes, "What's crucial here is that when anxiety is connected with disability, reducing said anxiety becomes a matter of access, not only a possible goal but an ethical (and sometimes legal) responsibility" (p. 271). Likewise, asking students to report on their level of engagement, mood, and duration of time all carry normative valuations of "appropriate" labor detrimental to neurodivergent access. In our experience, folx with ADHD in particular struggle tremendously with this sustained task. Measuring duration of labor thus creates an implicit expectation of sustained activity that may range from unattainable to undesirable to a neurodivergent student.

We again recognize that often, when LBGCs are employed, the instructional goal behind tracking this information is to assist students with identifying habits as well as conditions that are most conducive to their own laboring. As Inoue (2019b) explains, "Labor time is not the only way engagement, motivation, and learning can be manufactured in a course's assessment ecology, but perhaps it is a good internally relative indicator" (p. 154). Yet neurodivergent students may have to habitually vary their locations to combat attentive fatigue or may have less consistent patterns than their peers. When mood, duration, and engagement are not necessarily connected to the student's labor, the additional details become so much extra "noise" for neurodivergent students to wade through as they seek to demonstrate adequate academic performance. Students with depression, for example, cannot rely on mood as indicative of their academic performance. Therefore, we encourage instructors to consider how their conceptions of labor, and specifically time, offer (de)limiting experiences for our neurodivergent student populations. As Wood (2017) reminds us, "cripping time means tapping into that awareness and harnessing its potential, not only for particular students but also for the greater possibility that it may release our own pedagogical approaches from the limiting constructs of normativity" (p. 273). As scholars further examine grading contracts' effectiveness, we hope these lesser-known neurological norms are centered and challenged.

## CONCLUSION

Despite these challenges, LBGCs still have much to offer, especially if these assessment systems are paired with the continual (un)learning of systems of oppression and critical investigation of language ideologies, composing practices, sociocultural norms, and the production/consumption of academic performance and labor. We must reiterate here that attending to neurodiversity in writing assessment practices is not separate from attending to antiracism, anticolonialism, and feminism. These pursuits cannot be separated, for they cannot be untangled in the lives of those who live at the intersections of these social systems. As Bailey and Mobley (2019) remind us, "Notions of disability inform how theories of race were formed, and theories of racial embodiment and inferiority (racism) formed the ways in which we conceptualize disability" (p. 9).

As we approach our own classrooms, we have both moved away from strict LBGC systems to those that incorporate elements of LBGCs within a broader consciousness of neurodivergence and intersectional student identities. Kathleen's approach, which borrows in part from Linda Nilson's (2015) specs grading, relies heavily on a dialectic between teacher and students to negotiate what academic performance and labor is reasonable and desirous to demonstrate learning, growth, and the goals of our institution. Griffin's classroom incorporates flexible deadlines that are supported by weekly check-ins where students are able to report on their efforts and progress in the manner that is most productive for them, thus bridging the gap between attentiveness to academic labor and student neurological diversity. Importantly, we both see the separation of grades from feedback as fundamental to our approach to writing assessment.

LBGCs have significant value in compassionately (re)orienting our students to an assessment system that does not value and uphold racist/classist linguistic ideologies. Similar to what Inman and Powell (2018) found in their study, our students have shared with us the perceived benefits of the LBGC—many students said they felt freer, less anxious, and more joyful during the actual composing process. In addition to these benefits, neurodivergent populations certainly benefit from the key tenets of Inoue's (2019b) system: open dialogue about what labor means and how it is produced/consumed/exchanged, critical inquiry into linguistic ideologies, a decentering of Whiteness, and (re)centering of student-led ways of learning and knowing.

For us, an intersectional and neurodivergent model of writing assessment recognizes, investigates, and challenges the existence of neurological norms in the design and implementation of assessment systems at classroom, program, and institutional levels. For us, an intersectional model of writing assessment makes institutional space for a few key conversations: (a) cripping time in our grading systems and program policies so that neurodivergent conceptions of time, effort, and presence can be adequately accounted for; (b) flexible pedagogies for various modes and ways of learning and being; and (c) the denaturalization of White supremacy, especially within linguistic ideologies. For us, an intersectional model of writing assessment sees neurodivergence as the locus of socially just writing assessment for a few reasons: When sites of oppression are multiply invisible or unrecognizable, they are inactionable; when we as a field think about cognition, we often mean neurotypical cognition; and despite the current momentum behind disability-accountable pedagogies, a specific focus on neurodivergent student populations is still nascent.

## REFERENCES

Ahmed, S. (2017). *Living a feminist life*. Duke University Press.

Bailey, M. & Mobley, I. (2019). Work in the intersections: A Black feminist disability framework. *Gender & Society, 33*(1), 19–40.

Browning, E. R. (2014). Disability studies in the composition classroom. *Composition Studies, 42*(2), 96–117.

Brueggemann, B. (2001). An enabling pedagogy: Meditations on writing and disability. *JAC, 21*(4), 791–820.

Brueggemann, B., White, L., Dunn, P., Heifferon, B. & Cheu, J. (2001). Becoming visible: Lessons in disability. *College Composition and Communication, 52*(3), 368–398.
Clare, E. (2017). *Brilliant imperfection: Grappling with cure*. Duke University Press.
Crenshaw, K. (1991). Mapping the margins: Intersectionality, identity politics, and violence against women of color. *Stanford Law Review, 43*(6), 1241–1299.
Danielewicz, J. & Elbow, P. (2008) A unilateral grading contract to improve learning and teaching. *College Composition and Communication, 61*(2), 244–268.
Davidson, S. (2017). *Trauma-informed practices for postsecondary education: A guide*. Education Northwest.
Dolmage, J. T. (2014). *Disability rhetoric*. Syracuse University Press.
Dolmage, J. T. (2017). *Academic ableism: Disability and higher education*. University of Michigan Press.
Dolmage, J. T. (2018). *Disabled upon arrival: Eugenics, immigration, and the construction of race and disability*. The Ohio State University Press.
Dunn, P. (1995). *Learning re-abled: The learning disability controversy and composition studies*. Boynton/Cook.
Elliot, N. (2016). A theory of ethics for writing assessment. *The Journal of Writing Assessment, 9*(1).
Feldmeier White, L. (2002). Learning disability, pedagogies, and public discourse. *College Composition and Communication, 53*(4), 705–738.
Gobodo-Madikizela, P. (Ed.). (2016). *Breaking intergenerational cycles of repetition: A global dialogue on historical trauma and memory*. Barbara Budrich Publishers.
Green, D. F., Jr. (2016). Expanding the dialogue on writing assessment at HBCUs: Foundational assessment concepts and legacies of historically black colleges and universities. *College English, 79*(2), 152–173.
Inman, J. O. & Powell, R. A. (2018). In the absence of grades: Dissonance and desire in course-contract classrooms. *College Composition and Communication, 70*(1), 30–56.
Inoue, A. B. (2009). The technology of writing assessment and racial validity. In C. Schreiner (Ed.), *Handbook of research on assessment technologies, methods, and applications in higher education* (pp. 97–120). Information Science Reference.
Inoue, A. B. (2015). *Antiracist writing assessment ecologies: Teaching and assessing writing for a socially just future*. The WAC Clearinghouse; Parlor Press. https://doi.org/10.37514/PER-B.2015.0698.
Inoue, A. B. (2019a). *How do we language so people stop killing each other, or, what do we do about White language supremacy?* [Chair's address]. Conference on College Composition and Communication, Pittsburgh, PA. https://youtu.be/brPGTewcDYY.
Inoue, A. B. (2019b). *Labor-based grading contracts: Building equity and inclusion in the compassionate writing classroom*, 1st ed. The WAC Clearinghouse; Parlor Press. https://doi.org/10.37514/PER-B.2022.1824.
Kafer, A. (2013). *Feminist, queer, crip*. Indiana University Press.
Kerschbaum, S. (2015). Anecdotal relations: On orienting to disability in the composition classroom. *Composition Forum, 32*. https://compositionforum.com/issue/32/anecdotal-relations.php.

Lewiecki-Wilson, C., Dolmage, J., Heilker, P. & Jurecic, A. (2008). Comment & response: Two comments on "neurodiversity." *College English*, *70*(3), 314–325.

Mandel, B. (1973). Teaching without judging. *College English*, *34*(5), 623–633.

May, V. M. (2015). *Pursuing intersectionality, unsettling dominant imaginaries*. Routledge.

Moreno-Lopez, I. (2005). Sharing power with students: The critical language classroom. *Radical Pedagogy*, *7*(2).

Nilson, L. B. (2015). *Specifications grading: Restoring rigor, motivating students, and saving faculty time*. Stylus Publishing.

Poe, M. (2014). The consequences of writing assessment. *Research in the Teaching of English*, *48*(3), 271–275.

Poe, M. & Inoue, A. B. (2016). Toward writing as social justice: An idea whose time has come. *College English*, *79*(2), 119–126.

Price, M. (2011). *Mad at school: Rhetorics of mental disability and academic life*. University of Michigan Press.

Russell, D. R. (1997). Rethinking genre in schools and society: An activity theory analysis. *Written Communication*, *14*(4), 504–554.

Schalk, S. (2018). *Bodyminds reimagined: (Dis)ability, race, and gender in Black women's speculative fiction*. Duke University Press.

Shor, I. (2009). Critical pedagogy is too big to fail. *Journal of Basic Writing*, *28*(2), 6–27.

Spidell, C. & Thelin W. H. (2006). Not ready to let go: A study of resistance to grading contracts. *Composition Studies*, *34*(1), 35–68.

Spinuzzi, C. (2008). *Network: Theorizing knowledge work in telecommunications*. Cambridge University Press.

Sutter, M. & Perrin, P. B. (2016). Discrimination, mental health, and suicidal ideation among LGBTQ people of color. *Journal of Counseling Psychology*, *63*(1), 98–105.

Wood, T. (2017). Cripping time in the composition classroom. *College Composition and Communication*, *69*(2), 260–286.

Yergeau, M. (2018). *Authoring autism: On rhetoric and neurological queerness*. Duke University Press.

# CHAPTER 18.
# ENGAGING IN RESISTANT GENRES AS ANTIRACIST TEACHER RESPONSE

**Shane Wood**
University of Southern Mississippi

*This essay focuses on teacher response through contract grading and explains how rhetorical genre studies (RGS) offers opportunities to investigate teacher response in antiracist writing assessment ecologies. How do grading contracts change how teachers respond to student writing? How can we better understand teacher response as dynamic genres in antiracist writing assessment ecologies?*

The practices of giving letter-grades to language performances and responding to student writing colonize our students just as they engage meaningfully with them. Letter-grades signal who has authority over classroom assessment, and teacher response has been a site for appropriating student writing. Antiracist writing assessment ecologies that use alternate assessment practices and genres (e.g., grading contracts) may democratize, and even attempt to decolonize, the writing classroom, but they too have limitations and constraints. Classroom writing assessment practices, including teacher response, are never neutral. Teacher response to student writing can perpetuate inequalities and inequities just as much as assigning letter-grades on language practices reinforce power and control. Genres of response (e.g., marginal comments, rubrics) help establish meaningful exchanges between teachers and students but can also be a source of harmful communication and interactions, such as privileging habits of White language over other linguistic variations (e.g., Black English). As rhetorical genre studies (RGS) helps us see, genres are "reproducers of culture—in short, ideological" (Bawarshi & Reiff, 2010, p. 27).

So far, we have good work on grading contracts through antiracist frameworks, such as how grading contracts can challenge White discourse (Inoue, 2019), but we don't know how grading contracts change the way teachers respond to student writing and how response functions in antiracist writing assessment ecologies. How do grading contracts change how teachers respond to student writing, and how can we better understand teacher response as dynamic genres in antiracist writing assessment ecologies?

Grading contract research often focuses on contract construction (Danielewicz & Elbow, 2009; Inoue, 2019), how contracts are implemented in classes (Moreno-Lopez, 2005; Shor, 1996), how contracts are a part of a larger ecology (Inoue, 2015), or student perception and consequences for using grading contracts (Inman & Powell, 2018; Medina & Walker, 2018). Most of the literature makes an argument for grading contract use, but there is little written on what it is like to respond to student writing or how teacher response can complement grading contract ecologies. Grading contracts, of course, vary in design and implementation. In short, grading contracts are assessment genres that reflect pedagogical values (e.g., negotiation, compassion) and classroom initiatives (e.g., social justice, antiracism), shape identities (e.g., of student, teacher), and help carry out particular actions and consequences. It would seem likely, then, that grading contracts would change the nature of teacher response because the values, actions, and consequences of contract ecologies are different than traditional assessment practices; for example, traditional assessment ecologies often emphasize a "product" that is frequently connected to writing "quality" which is tied to Standard Edited American English (SEAE).

I focus on teacher response through contract grading by paying special attention to antiracist writing assessment ecological theory and RGS. Both can serve as frameworks for understanding response in the context of contract grading. Antiracist writing assessment theories have reconceived how we might approach assessment through grading contracts. RGS helps establish a more nuanced view of response as dynamic genres which allow us to see how power is situated within response practices/performances and how genre uptake affects communication between teachers and students: "Genres have the power to help or hurt human interaction, to ease communication or to deceive, to enable someone to speak or to discourage someone from saying something different" (Devitt, 2004, p. 1). I propose an analytical and pedagogical framework that can be used to critically examine genres of response. This framework investigates how habits of White language can be embodied in response genres that circulate in classroom ecologies. In short, the framework provides teachers and students an opportunity to study response and to resist White language supremacy.

## COMPLEMENTING GRADING CONTRACT VALUES WITH TEACHER RESPONSE

In *Alternatives to Grading Student Writing*, Stephen Tchudi (1997) describes differences between responding to student writing and assigning grades and reflects on the tension between teacher instincts and institutional pressures. He shares how teachers have an inclination to move away from grades and move toward response practices. Tchudi (1997) writes that response offers the "greatest range of freedom because it is naturalistic, growing directly from readers' reaction to a text" (xii). He sees response as good and preferable because teachers have more agency in responding to student writing, which comes from a lower degree of institutional pressure. Antiracist writing assessment ecological theory explains why institutional pressure is bad: Institutional pressure is a pressure toward a system of White racial habits of language and judgement that tends to ignore the politics that create those very habits as preferable and simultaneously uses those White biases as a way to punish some students and privilege others. The standards for judging language are racist because they privilege a White, middle- to upper-class, monolingual English user.

The institutional pressure to judge language can be minimized by shifting the classroom assessment practice. Teachers can adopt contract grading, for example, which delays the production and distribution of grades, and thus decreases the pressure to judge language. So grading contracts offer different pedagogical affordances and assessment values than traditional assessment ecologies. The assessment values—the priorities and assumptions in an assessment ecology—influence the nature of teacher response. Labor-based grading contracts, for example, value negotiation and compassion (Inoue, 2019). Teachers can use labor-based grading contracts to invite students to participate in negotiating labor standards, tasks, and responsibilities. Teacher response to student writing, subsequently, ought to come alongside labor-based grading contracts to complement its assessment values (e.g., negotiation and compassion). This interconnected relationship between response and assessment values should help support the larger ecology. So far, we don't have much research that talks about the relationship between teacher response and labor-based grading contracts or how an emphasis on labor, negotiation, and compassion informs how teachers construct responses and what effects it has on student writing. Marginal comments in a labor-based assessment ecology might contain a more negotiable tone that asks questions as opposed to directive statements because the ecology seeks to minimize teacher control over student writing. A teacher might ask a student in the margins, "Do you want to explore this idea more, or do you think it gets at your purposes?" This kind of marginal comment embodies a true sense of negotiation. Or maybe the teacher writes an end comment that praises the students' creativity and perseverance in the revision process, thus embodying compassionate practices.

Knowing the assessment values can help restructure the purposes for responding to student writing in an ecology and can provide a way to examine whether response aligns with such values. Understanding teacher response as a genre that circulates in assessment ecologies, interacts with other genres, and impacts people within the ecology seems important. If response genres are reproducers of cultures, how can teachers use response to support contract ecologies that value antiracism? It would seem likely that teacher response in an antiracist writing assessment ecology would actively deconstruct monolingual English ideologies that circulate in traditional writing classrooms. Teachers might choose to use marginal comments to encourage students to use their regional dialects and language habits as a means for meeting or intentionally subverting genre expectations. Classroom assessment practices, including response, would need to align itself with antiracist aims in order to complement the antiracist grading contract ecology.

Asao B. Inoue (2015) identifies seven interconnected elements that help construct antiracist writing assessment practices. Inoue's framework shows the relationships that exist within and beyond classroom writing assessment systems and the power and politics embedded in assessment practices. He invites teachers to think through the nuances of judging language and asks them to construct more "critical, sustainable, and fair" ecologies (Inoue, 2015, p. 119). The seven elements help inform and organize the assessment ecology and can be used to investigate the "fuller conditions under which [students'] writing is judged" (p. 174):

> Power: the ways of disciplining and control, the instruments, techniques, procedures, and tactics that produce docility and control people
>
> Purposes: the explicit reasons for judging and assessing
>
> Places: where and when do things happen, the figurative and material locations that de(con)fine people and their learning, the locations of shock and change
>
> People: agents in the ecology (e.g., student and teacher)
>
> Processes: what and how things are done, labor practices
>
> Parts: codes, constructs, and artifacts (e.g., texts, rubrics, feedback)
>
> Products: learning, results, consequences, and decisions

One reason this ecological framework is important is because it shows how teacher response is one genre in a much broader system. RGS has used the terms "genre systems" (Bazerman, 1994) and "genre ecologies" (Spinuzzi & Zachry, 2000) to describe the nature of genres working within and beyond broader structures. In Inoue's ecological framework, teacher response is considered a "part," an artifact, text, document, or instrument. As RGS helps us see, response can be better understood as dynamic genres that help make visible values, biases, actions and interactions, and power within a genre system or ecology.

Inoue (2019) also focuses on how classroom assessment practices, such as labor-based grading contracts, can challenge power indifferences and standards that privilege Whiteness. His ecological framework (Inoue, 2015) does not account for the intricacies, complexities, and inner workings of teacher response. It does not indicate how response shifts in contract grading ecologies and how genres of response carry uptakes, "complex, often habitualized, socio-cognitive pathways that mediate our interactions with others and the world" (Bawarshi, 2010, p. 199). Together, antiracist writing assessment theory and RGS offer a more nuanced perspective on how to investigate teacher response to student writing in grading contract ecologies. It's possible we risk undermining grading contract ecologies, and contract values, if we don't recognize how ecologies and genres ought to agree.

Jane Danielewicz and Peter Elbow's 2009 article, one of the most cited in grading contract literature, creates an assumption that responding to student writing doesn't change when teachers use grading contracts. Danielewicz and Elbow (2009) describe how they give evaluative feedback and respond to "strengths and weaknesses . . . just as [they] used to do and as most teachers do" (p. 247). They fail to acknowledge how response ought to shift to complement new assessment ecologies and values. This oversight is problematic because it can lead to a fractured classroom and fractured relationships between teachers and students. For example, if a teacher chooses to use contracts to resist monolingual English ideologies and to invite students to use linguistic varieties, then decides to write a marginal comment telling the student to use "formal" language, or consider their "academic" tone when the student chose to use their regional dialect, the teacher's response undermines the assessment ecology and values (e.g., in an antiracist writing assessment ecology). The feedback, which might have been constructed in a traditional assessment ecology that values SEAE, compromises the antiracist grading contract ecology and sends mixed messages to students. This kind of comment counters antiracist beliefs about writing and language. It also positions the teacher in an authoritative role over linguistic patterns, much like traditional assessment ecologies that give power to teachers to judge language.

As teachers, we need to make sure our responses are complementing our assessment ecology and values. As we adopt new and alternative classroom assessment practices (e.g., grading contracts), and as the ecology shifts, genres of response used to carry out actions within those contexts need to evolve. RGS offers genre uptake which can be used to encourage teachers and students to consider the social-historical-material conditions that help construct genres of response in grading contract ecologies.

# GENRE UPTAKE: POSITIONING TEACHER RESPONSE IN ANTIRACIST WRITING ASSESSMENT ECOLOGIES

RGS provides opportunities to know more about genres, what genres do, and how genres interact, thus offering the ability to examine how response practices/performances fit within antiracist writing assessment ecologies that can help complement contract grading. RGS frames genres as dynamic rhetorical forms (Berkenkotter & Huckin, 1995), as social actions (Miller, 1984), and as organizing structures (Yates & Orlikowski, 2002). RGS has explained genre functions and interactions through genre sets (Devitt, 1991), genre systems (Bazerman, 1994), and genre ecologies (Spinuzzi, 2004; Spinuzzi & Zachry, 2000). Charles Bazerman (1997) describes genres as "ways of being . . . frames for social action" (p. 19). Genres help mediate actions and relationships; genres are social, typified, recognizable, and they organize and construct social realities. RGS helps us see how genres of response (e.g., marginal comments, end comments, rubrics) invite different social actions and consequences. This allows us to study how responses are relational and performative, and how genres of response can help or harm communication between us and our students.

These characteristics of genres, of course, are also characteristics of writing assessment ecologies (e.g., relational, fluid, interactive). Inserting genre terminology implicates other ecological elements, like how genres mediate relations of power (Schryer, 2002; Seawright, 2017). RGS can help explain what's happening in assessment ecologies when teacher response occurs. For instance, after reading a teacher's comment and being confused, a student might revisit the writing prompt to see if they misunderstood some aspect of the assignment. This interaction between the student's paper, teacher's response, and writing prompt shows how genres inform one another in a broader system or ecology and how genres can facilitate and coordinate action. The student takes up, reads, and interprets one genre (e.g., teacher response) and then consults another genre (e.g., writing prompt). Understanding teacher response as dynamic genre performances allows us to explore the multiplicity of factors that inform what happens when we respond to student writing. This nuanced view of response helps us investigate genre "uptake" (Freadman, 1994). Anis Bawarshi and Mary Jo Reiff's (2010) comprehensive book on RGS provides a definition that can help us better understand how uptake is beneficial to analyzing response in grading contract ecologies: "Uptake helps us understand how systematic, normalized relations between genres coordinate complex forms of social action" (p. 86). Bawarshi (2016) adds how uptake "challenges us to consider history, materiality, embodiment, improvisations, emotion, and other agentive factors" ("Accounting for Genre Performances").

RGS gives us something that hasn't been offered in grading contract literature and antiracist writing assessment theory yet: A means to explore and identify the complex social-historical-material conditions of response and an opportunity to identify the uptakes that exist through response practices/performances. Danielewicz and Elbow's (2009) understanding of response in grading contract ecologies, for example, doesn't account for the history, materiality, emotion, and other agentive factors at play when teachers respond to student writing or when students take up, interpret, and use response. Teachers and students have complex histories and memories giving and receiving feedback which can affect and inform their attitudes on current response practices and performances.

For example, a first-year writing student gets their paper back and sees a marginal comment that tells them to provide more evidence for a claim. The student has experienced this comment before in a high school English class. So the situation produces a particular kind of uptake. When the student experiences this marginal comment, even in a new assessment ecology with different values, they do the same thing as before—they decide to provide more evidence to support their claim because the marginal comment is connected to the students' history and the actions and consequences that came from their previous experience. Those experiences, often, come from traditional grading ecologies that contain different values and relations of power between teachers and students. These histories and memories have implications for how response is received and taken up in grading contract ecologies.

And these experiences with response have different consequences for different student identities based on the ways in which language was judged. Danielewicz and Elbow (2009) don't consider how traditional writing assessment practices—judging language based on quality—are connected to standards that privilege a specific kind of languaging, and thus a specific student identity (e.g., White, monolingual English user). The A letter-grade, according to their grading contract, is reserved for students who demonstrate an ability to meet quality-based standards that are set or determined by them, as teachers. But really, that standard is centered on social-historical-material conditions that extend well-beyond Danielewicz and Elbow's perception on writing quality. Quality is constructed on linguistic prejudice—implicit or explicit language standards (e.g., SEAE) and biases that privilege White bodies.

So we can't respond in the same ways as we used to through grading contracts because the system, and thus the values, consequences, and power relationships between teacher and student, are different. We need to investigate how responses are constructed and conditioned by traditional assessment values and judgements of language—and how students experience and remember these genre performances in grading contract ecologies. People, places, and languages are interconnected, and systems and structures are racialized (Inoue, 2015). As writing teachers, we work in and through conditions that have established language hierarchies and standards that inform our responses.

The concept of uptake helps us better understand actions and consequences in antiracist writing assessment ecologies and ecological elements (e.g., power, place, people) by calling us to examine specific genres of response (e.g., marginal comments, end comments, rubrics) and how those genres serve as a connection between a person's actions, memory, relationship with others, and within historical, social, cultural, and linguistic moments and contexts (Bawarshi, 2016). Teacher response is "*situated, embedded, enmeshed,* and *imbricated* in social and material contexts" (Dryer, 2016).

## HABITS OF WHITE LANGUAGE

I have argued so far that writing teachers need to change their response practices if they choose to use contract grading because the ecology is made differently, and the elements are different in nature and function. Some of the most common values in grading contract ecologies include emphases on agency, antiracism, intrinsic motivation, labor, effort, participation, compassion, equity, negotiation, and democratizing learning. Genres of response are bearers of meaning from cultural and social ecologies, sites inside and outside the classroom that are ultimately influenced by how systems and structures accept and value language use. It's possible for response genres in antiracist grading contract ecologies to support the deployment of habits of White language even while the class works to resist dominant discourses.

One difficulty teachers encounter are the contexts and conditions in which they've been trained to respond to student writing. We are informed by our linguistic habits and dispositions, "which are not simply linguistic but embodied" (Inoue, 2019, p. 278). Many of us have been conditioned to identify and respond to "strengths and weaknesses," which is how Danielewicz and Elbow (2009) describe their practices in grading contract ecologies. We have been encouraged to evaluate strengths and weaknesses in students' writing, so they can further engage in the writing process. And these kinds of responses become habitual. Part of the problem exists in the conditions and the standards used to determine what is strong and weak. Strengths and weaknesses relative to what set of language habits? Teachers use these terms to rank, sort, and respond to students. Many of us have used traditional assessment practices at one time or another to teach and assess student writing. Many of us have been educated through traditional assessment ecologies where the teacher has had the power to decide what the strengths and weaknesses are. We have histories and memories that inform how we take up and respond to student writing. In short, universities—sites constructed historically for and from *Whiteness*—have influenced our concept of strengths and weaknesses in student writing and our perception on what language habits are strong and which ones are weak.

As teachers, we invite students to perform and play with language all the time. We often ask students to deploy certain habits of language that will help them take up, navigate, and perform writing tasks based on rhetorical situations (e.g., purpose, audience, context). After asking students to write, we respond to the linguistic habits they chose to use. What's problematic is when teachers ask students to perform the same version of language while not acknowledging language differences, dialects, and linguistic varieties; what's problematic is not talking about the historical, social, and political power enmeshed in language and what students are being asked to do; what's problematic is an unseen standard or assumption that privileges one linguistic pattern (e.g., regional, social, cultural), which takes the form of SEAE. As Vershawn Ashanti Young (2010) says, "It's ATTITUDES. It be the way folks with some power perceive other people's language" (p. 110). We are always-already asking students to deploy habits of language. So the question becomes what habits of language are teachers promoting and what attitudes do they have toward language differences, dialects, and linguistic varieties. When teachers respond to strengths and weaknesses in student writing, attitudes and biases exist about how students are choosing to deploy language.

Identifying students' strengths and weaknesses is important in Danielewicz and Elbow's (2009) grading contract, specifically between the A and B grade, because it is attached to traditional ecologies that reward students who can produce or imitate one kind of languaging. Danielewicz and Elbow (2009), therefore, reserve the A letter-grade for students who can meet a specific linguistic standard by acknowledging they respond "just as [they] used to do and as most teachers do," thus indicating a connection to their previous traditional assessment ecologies (p. 247). This is one example of how teachers can adopt grading contract ecologies and use responses (e.g., rubrics) that embody traditional assessment values (e.g., quality), reinforce power indifferences between teachers and students, and privilege the deployment of one version of language, and thus a specific identity. Rubrics, for example, might help teachers respond to student writing and be a marker for labor/participation in grading contract ecologies. Teachers can problem-pose rubrics by examining how many expectations are tied to unseen standards connected to White middle- to upper-class monolingual English users. Examining academic discourse and assessment genres often reveals manifestations of Whiteness which influence how we see and respond to student writing.

Inoue (2019) identifies six traits of Whiteness that can be used to analyze how power is embedded in judgments of language:

an unseen, naturalized, orientation to the world;

hyperindividualism;

a stance of neutrality, objectivity, and apoliticality;

an individualized, rational, controlled self;

a focus on rule-governed, contractual relationships;

a focus on clarity, order, and control. (p. 27)

Standards associated with quality which are closely connected to SEAE benefit middle- to upper-class White students:

> The dominant discourse that informs those judgments are already constructed by racial structures, for instance, a white racial habitus, or a dominant white discourse, which we might for now understand as a set of linguistic codes and textual markers that are often not a part of the discourses of many students of color, working class students, and multilingual students, but is a part of many white, middle-class students' discourses. (Inoue, 2015, p. 17)

The first habit, the unseen, naturalized orientation to the world is often married to others, like clarity, order, and control. This means that when Danielewicz and Elbow (2009) say they still respond to strengths and weaknesses, they are not acknowledging with students where their habits come from, especially when they award an A letter-grade based on "quality." It's easy for students in that ecology to accept the teacher's ideas as universally right. And it's easy for students to be colonized by a discipline and classroom that only make present a dominant White discourse. Inoue (2015) asserts that racism is pervasive in writing classes because "most if not all writing courses . . . promote or value first a local SEAE and a dominant white discourse, even when they make moves to value and honor the discourses of all students" (p. 14). Like Inoue, Laura Greenfield (2011) connects SEAE with White bodies: "It is no coincidence that the languages spoken by racially oppressed people are considered to be inferior in every respect to the languages spoken predominantly by those who wield systemic power: namely, middle and upper-class white people" (p. 36).

Inoue (2015) and Greenfield (2011) see how academic institutions and writing classrooms demand students produce a dominate discourse linked to White bodies and then "judge them on their abilities to approximate it" (Inoue, 2015, p. 31). And they challenge writing teachers to consider the material conditions of the classroom and students' lives. This reminds us, once again, to think about the habits of language we ask students to deploy through writing tasks and consider our attitudes and biases about language difference and linguistic varieties. Through RGS, genre uptake invites us to consider histories, memories, and material conditions, too. What has shaped our understandings and dispositions to language? How have we been conditioned to see and respond to student writing? Whose language or linguistic habits have been historically privileged in academic institutions?

Genres of response can circulate and reinforce White biases without teachers being aware of the impact or power indifferences being created through response practices/performances because of the histories, memories, and material conditions that have shaped our understanding of language and writing. For example, a writing teacher might not comment on students' writing asking them to use SEAE, but those biases might be embodied through marginal comments telling them to "be clearer." When a teacher chooses to respond this way, they are usually referring to meeting a standard of clarity that either conforms to White academic discourse or conforms to their own disposition of language which has been informed, more often than not, through trainings in academic contexts that embody Whiteness. The comment indicates a *deficit*—a students' lack of knowledge and ability to perform to a certain standard (e.g., SEAE). This kind of teacher response privileges a specific type of languaging and thus student identity—middle- to upper-class White students. Inoue (2015) explains how writing teachers "cannot avoid this racializing of language when we judge writing" (p. 33).

So responses are never just about strengths and weaknesses because we know more about how dominant or hegemonic language practices make particular ways with words "strong" and others "weak," and that these understandings are perceptions filtered through White biases inherent in how language must be judged. Genres of responses are racialized and have racialized consequences. Habits of White language can be investigated through uptake which materializes through genres of response interacting between and beyond grading contract ecologies as well as the conditions and communication by which those interactions occur and are remembered. Habits of White language can be traced through the exchanges between assessment genres within the ecology, as well as other genres, and the way those genres are acting and being acted upon by people. This kind of analysis is tied to genre uptake. Even though genre uptake is difficult to pin down and study because "uptake processes are largely non-visible," the writing classroom can still be a site for uncovering histories and memories of genre performances and for asking students to intentionally reflect on their own uptakes (Bastian, 2015).

Writing teachers can start by considering how teacher response is already a product of a racialized structure. White bodies have always been invited to participate within U.S. universities, which means that White bodies have shaped the standards and the judgments of language. They have shaped the responses and patterns for responding to student writing. SEAE has historically been valued as the superior form of language in U.S. university contexts. This is no coincidence. SEAE is associated with habits of White language. SEAE is not better than Black English. SEAE is just tied to White bodies, and White bodies have historically had power in higher education. Thus, response practices can support the deployment of habits of White language which harm students of color even in grading contract ecologies. So we have to think about the patterns we use to respond to student writing and the consequences of those patterns.

## PATTERNS OF RESPONSE

Most teachers establish patterns for response. Danielewicz and Elbow (2009) write how they respond by identifying strengths and weaknesses in student writing. I want to consider Summer Smith's (1997) good work on the genre of the end comment because her research helps provide a more nuanced understanding of the patterns teachers develop through response as well as the actions and consequences of those patterns. Even though Smith doesn't use grading contracts, her research is valuable in its intersection of RGS and teacher response. I'm attempting to tie her work into more recent complex views on genre uptake. She writes:

> The teacher could have written anything, but she chose to script a statement that closely resembles not only her previous end comments, but also the end comments of other composition teachers. Why? Part of the answer, at least, lies in genre. (1997, p. 249)

Smith describes how routinized end comments help generate "expectations for both readers and writers" (p. 250).

Her data lead her to identify and analyze three groups of *primary genres* (informed by Mikhail Bakhtin's speech genres): Judging genres, reader response genres, and coaching genres. These three groups help reveal the "relatively stable" content and structure of end comments, which helps establish what teachers do when they use end comments or how teachers choose to respond given the situation and socially defined context that results in producing end comments. Each primary genre has a list of descriptors that situates the nature of these responses and what knowledge and action is being communicated through the end comment (see Table 8.1 from Smith, 1997).

**Table 8.1. Smith's Frequencies of Primary Genres in Sample Table**

| Primary Genre | Total Number in Sample |
|---|---|
| *Judging Genres* | |
| Evaluation of development | 199 |
| Evaluation of style | 118 |
| Evaluation of the entire paper | 106 |
| Evaluation of focus | 105 |
| Evaluation of effort | 96 |
| Evaluation of organization | 88 |
| Evaluation of rhetorical effectiveness | 82 |
| Evaluation of topic | 63 |
| Evaluation of correctness | 52 |
| Evaluation of audience accommodation | 51 |
| Justification of the grade | 48 |
| *Reader Response Genres* | |
| Reading experience | 67 |
| Identification | 43 |
| *Coaching Genres* | |
| Suggestion for revision of current paper | 155 |
| Suggestion for future papers | 88 |
| Offer of assistance | 37 |

Table 8.1 shows how the majority of end comments teachers produce are judging genres (n = 1,008) compared to reader response genres (n = 110) and coaching genres (n = 208). Judging genres include evaluations of development, style, focus, organization, rhetorical effectiveness, and correctness. These data help us see how genres of response, such as end comments, become routinized by their nature and the actions they ask students to take up. The number of responses considered judging genres is particularly interesting because of the vast difference in quantity compared to the others (e.g., reader response, coaching) and because of how closely the comments feel connected to habits of White language. It feels as though evaluations of development, style, organization, rhetorical effectiveness, and correctness are asking students to conform to a kind of standard language practice, particularly one that privileges White discourse.

It's possible teachers respond in the same ways from student paper to student paper even though the student, and subsequently their writing, is unique because there's a recurring situation in the writing classroom. Teachers develop patterns of response, or routinized responses, because there's an invitation for students to take up a writing prompt and engage in a line of inquiry, and then turn in their written performance to receive feedback. Because of their routinized nature, response genres can embody characteristics that harm interactions (e.g., habits of White language) with students. Writing teachers are being conditioned through the recurring situation and the genres that help form that situation, for instance, the writing prompt and the student's essay. These uptakes and response performances can be influenced by traditional classroom assessment practices and social ecologies, or spaces outside the classroom, that continue to support White discourse. Inoue (2019) writes that White language supremacy is "structured in assessment ecologies in such a way as to function simultaneously as an ideal and as the norm" (p. 28). The patterns we develop and the genres we use to judge language can act as mediators, carriers of knowledge, reproducers of history, artifacts in students' memory, and circulators of biases that continue to oppress students of color. Genres of response can impact different students differently.

Writing teachers can explore genre memory and uptake by having students think about their previous experiences with end comments, for example. In my class, for instance, I would ask students to identify a specific moment receiving an end comment, how the comment made them feel as writers, and what they chose to do with that response or what action they decided to perform, and what benefits or consequences came from that action. For example, maybe a student has a memory of a teacher using an end comment to tell them to go to the writing center to get help with grammar. How was this experience perceived and taken up? How is it still affecting the way the student sees end comments? This kind of investigation of genre uptake and memory with teacher response can reveal a lot of nuances. Prompting students to think about memory can generate productive conversations in the writing classroom about how response genres influence actions in grading contract ecologies.

Did the student take up the call to go to the writing center? Did the student focus on grammar during their revision? Understanding the memory, emotion, action, and consequences of past experiences with response can help classroom ecologies, like my own, talk through uptakes and the dynamic performances of response. I would use this experience to talk about how that previous comment was working to contribute to White language supremacy by molding the students' language to conform to habits of White language, and how that experience might impact how response is felt, perceived, and taken up in our grading contract ecology. It's important for me to label and connect these comments to White language supremacy and habits of White language. In this example, we also see how teacher response is interconnected with other systems and ecologies, like writing centers. In class, we would also talk about how the end comment perpetuates the notion of writing centers as grammar shops or sites for skill-and-drill. The old comment had a very particular set of linguistic standards in mind—it was subtly entrenched with notions of standardized grammar and an expectation for the student to align with habits of White language.

It also indicates an attempt to remove student agency. This end comment isn't seeking negotiation or reaffirming students' rights to their writing, which are often values in antiracist writing assessment ecologies, but instead is working to reprimand the student's language practices. My class would talk about how our grading contract ecology values negotiation, compassion, and students' rights to their own languages. We would spend time acknowledging how our classroom ecology is different in nature than that previous experience, and how we need to investigate ecologies to see how genres are interacting and influencing actions. You see, a quick glance at that old end comment looks and maybe even feels negotiable. It feels like the student can take up different actions. It masks itself in empowerment. But what were the consequences, and what did the student learn through that experience that would affect them in my classroom? In the past, maybe the consequence was a bad grade. The student still draws on this memory and experience as they read, interpret, and use my end comments, which affects what they choose to do when they revise, including the risks they are willing to take. So even though my grading contract ecology values taking risks in writing, the student might choose not to take any given this past experience. That memory, and the actions and consequences tied to that experience, is very real, and very much felt by the student.

The recurrence of teacher response, the fact that response happens by default in specific spaces on the page, like in the margins or at the end, across various institutional writing classrooms, and the reality that response is meant to produce another action (e.g., revision) reveals the complexity of responding to student writing. Uptake gives us the lens to explore these patterns more. It also shows how response should be investigated closely in antiracist classroom writing assessment ecologies because those classrooms don't have the same values and initiatives as traditional ecologies. And as a result, alternative responses are needed to reflect these different values.

## TEACHER RESPONSE AS RESISTANT GENRES: AN ANALYTICAL FRAMEWORK FOR RESISTING HABITS OF WHITE LANGUAGE

I have argued that writing teachers should think more closely about how their responses are complementing their assessment ecologies and values, and how habits of White language can be embodied in response genres that are routinized and circulate in grading contract ecologies. I have also shared how genre uptake can help classes talk about histories, memories, emotions, and attitudes about response, thus revealing how teacher response can affect students differently because comments can be attached to habits of White language that privilege some students over others. Teacher response is a product of racialized structures, that is, a product of institutions, classrooms, and traditional grading practices that have historically privileged Whiteness and habits of White language. Teacher response to student writing is also racialized; racism and habits of White language are reproduced through genre performances of response.

I offer resistant genres as a way to conceptualize how response can be understood and designed to complement antiracist writing assessment ecologies and grading contract values. What does it mean to see teacher response as resistant genres? It means teachers and students, together, can problematize how response practices are threatening agency for students of color and working to reinforce habits of White language. It means teachers and students can investigate internalized linguistic racism and can use response to complement new pedagogies and practices centered on linguistic justice (Baker-Bell, 2020). For decades, teacher-scholars have asked us to reconsider how we understand, evaluate, and talk about language and literacy (Hooks, 1994; Kynard, 2013; Lippi-Green, 1997; Smitherman, 1977). I offer a framework that asks us to carefully analyze how response practices/performances have the potential to benefit the deployment of a specific kind of languaging while dismissing linguistic variations and other language performances. Centering teacher response as resistant genres would intervene (Bawarshi, 2008) and disrupt what genre performances of response typically and traditionally do: Privilege students who can produce habits of White language. Intersecting RGS and antiracism invites conversations on response as a dynamic genre working within antiracist writing assessment ecologies and can help us investigate different ecological elements that might be informing response practices/performances.

For example, teachers and students might investigate the place (e.g., the classroom), the physical and material location where teacher response happens, and how that impacts people (e.g., student and teacher) and their attitudes on response. This means examining genres and participants within their ecologies. Teachers and students might consider how the writing classroom (e.g., place) has historically threatened people of color through notions of standardized English that attempt to establish power over marginalized populations and disadvantage minoritized bodies. Teachers might examine how agency can be developed and circulated in a number of elements in an antiracist writing assessment ecology, like how it is primarily located in the power relations (the first element in the ecological framework) but embodied in the people, enacted in the processes, and understood and felt by everyone in the place. Inoue (2015) describes how seeing the "relationships between elements" can allow teachers and students an opportunity to "consider local consequences" within assessment ecologies (p. 11).

Teachers who use grading contracts don't have the institutional pressure of judging language with a letter-grade, which is a significant barrier to overcome when attempting to challenge traditional cultural beliefs about writing and language and to respond in ways that are more compassionate and inclusive. Using grading contracts often requires more attention and a higher production of feedback because of assessment values on effort, labor, participation, and negotiation. Writing teachers can examine genres of response, and the patterns they use to respond to student writing, with hopes of uncovering White biases. In an antiracist writing assessment ecology that uses grading contracts to complement antiracist aims, I believe this work is necessary for taking a resistant approach to response. Grading contract ecologies afford opportunities to spend more time talking about the politics of language and how genres of response might privilege certain students over others. In a traditional assessment ecology, teacher response is often used to justify a grade on a final draft. In a grading contract ecology, where grades aren't emphasized, classes can devote time and energy to analyzing the social-historical-material conditions of response, what response is doing, and how response brings up memories and emotions that can impact actions.

So how can teachers and students analyze genres of response for the purpose of resisting habits of White language? I offer a four-step heuristic that allows teachers and students the opportunity to engage in critical reading and to problematize response together. This framework can be used to help center discussions on resisting habits of White language and can be used to reflect on genre uptake of response:

> Step 1: Identify the genre of response (e.g., marginal comments, end comments, rubrics) to analyze, and then select comment(s) to examine;
>
> Step 2: Use Smith's (1997) research to pinpoint different purposes for response (e.g., judging genres, reader response genres, or coaching genres) and the nature of the comment (e.g., evaluation of development, reading experience, suggestion for revision of current paper);
>
> Step 3: Use Inoue's (2019) six habits of White language to identify how White discourse is informing the response practice/performance that is circulating in the ecology; and
>
> Step 4: Reflect on genre uptake, including embodiment, emotion, relationship between other genres, memory, and possible actions and consequences tied to the response that can be experienced and/or taken up.

This framework is designed to bring together teacher response with antiracist pedagogies and RGS. Some teachers might use this heuristic to talk with students about their own responses and bring attention to problems that might be embodied in those practices/performances. Some teachers might use this as an out-of-class activity for students to reflect on their histories with previous responses. I think this framework can be used to have conversations about the social and political nature of teacher response in grading contract ecologies. I also think this framework can be used in other spaces, such as in faculty workshops or WAC/WID contexts to help train teachers to examine their own responses.

I use this framework as an in-class activity after my class has had time to become familiar with antiracist writing assessment theories, informed by Inoue's (2015, 2019, respectively) Antiracist Writing Assessment Ecologies and Labor-Based Grading Contracts, and RGS, informed by Bawarshi and Reiff's (2010) Genre: An Introduction to History, Theory, Research, and Pedagogy. Having these foundations is necessary to centering teacher response as resistant genres. I draw on teacher responses in Twelve Readers Reading: Responding to Student Writing (Straub & Lunsford, 1995), a foundational text that theorizes feedback and offers 60 sets of comments from 12 well-recognized teacher-scholars, to engage in the four steps. The first thing I do in class is talk about how Twelve Readers Reading is full of response practices from White teacher-scholars which allows us to problematize the absence of diverse racial identities in the text, and thus investigate the material and social conditions in which these teacher-scholars are responding to student writing (e.g., R1s, predominately White institutions). I address this lack of diversity first.

I find it necessary to talk about the voices we hear in research and the sites in which those voices come from since they often inform what many teachers do in practice, especially in literature like teacher response. Acknowledging absences and needs for expansion (Green, 2016; Jackson et al., 2019) is critical to this antiracist framework for response. Twelve Readers Reading becomes an opportunity to talk about different institutional locations, and then it becomes a starting point for us to observe and investigate response as a dynamic genre in assessment ecologies. This allows us to turn our attention to resisting the promotion of habits of White language in response practices. Using feedback from Twelve Readers Reading (Straub & Lunsford, 1995) shows how teachers can do the normal good response practices, and doing so can still be a way to value habits of White language.

I select a writing prompt and final draft with comments from different teacher-scholars in Twelve Readers Reading before using the framework in class. For example, I choose the same prompt and same draft with responses from Edward White and Donald Stewart. Choosing the same prompt and draft allows us to have conversations about how writing is interpreted differently and how responses can invite different actions and ideas even on the same text (e.g., student writing). Using the same text helps generate conversations about the subjectivity and biases of reading and responding to writing. It's easy for us to see, for example, how teachers, like Edward White and Donald Stewart, can look at the same piece of student writing and have different judgments and comments. We read the prompt and draft as a class, and then focus on the responses. Teacher response is always working within and between other genres (e.g., writing prompt, draft) in an ecology, so this becomes one way to think more intentionally about the different genres and ecological elements (e.g., power) interconnected with response.

Step 1 is to identify the genre of response to analyze and select the comment(s) we are going to examine more closely as a class. I use this first step to complement my grading contract ecological values: Negotiation, compassion, decentering my position of power and authority as the teacher. I ask students what end comments they want to focus on and analyze more closely to further emphasize that students have agency in making decisions in class and in their writing. They select two to three sentences from each end comment:

> White writes, "Parts of this paper are very fine, rich with detail and emotion. But sometimes your language gets very general, as if from a greeting card . . . look closely at the top paragraph on p. 2 for an example of ways to revise, to make your language more clear and detailed" (as cited in Straub & Lunsford, 1995, p. 51).
>
> Stewart writes, "There's not much to say about the organization of the paper . . . I've already commented on aspects of style of this paper. The good details tell us that you are capable of fresh insights, but, for the most part you do not provide them or cloth them in language which is distinctive. I wish you would consistently work up to your potential" (as cited in Straub & Lunsford, 1995, p. 56).

Most students have experienced these types of comments before—responses about their writing development, style, and organization. It takes critical reading and analysis to understand how comments like the ones above can be problematic because honestly, to many of us, they seem fine and can probably lead to some good revisions. The notion "good revisions," itself, is problematic, though. Good determined by who? Based on what standards? We talk more about how we label and associate words with linguistic habits in class. I explain how one of the difficulties we face as teachers and students are the histories and memories that influence what we consider or define as good revisions. So as a class we share our experiences with what has made revisions "good" and where that measurement or its attachment to language comes from: A society that perpetuates White language supremacy. We attempt to replace those older associations and reconstruct newer conceptions of good revisions that align with our resistant practice and our grading contract ecology.

I also make it a point to tell students I've produced comments like the ones above on development, style, and organization, and they might see similar comments from me because how I've been trained to read and respond to student writing, and the patterns I've developed through those experiences. Those comments aren't inherently bad. It's the unseen standard, or what's assumed, or the attitude about language differences or linguistic varieties, and the consequences that standard, driven by response, has on specific student identities that makes them problematic. It's that these responses are often pushing students to a White discourse that reasserts one language practice is more valuable. This problem-posing allows us to analyze how the structure and system for response is always-already problematic, or how power is unevenly distributed through response, or how good intentions might lead to negative uptakes and memories. It's important, too, for the class to talk about how comments similar in nature—on development, style, and organization—can be used for good and can come from good values and beliefs in antiracist writing assessment ecologies. I stress the importance of seeing response as dynamic and complicated.

After students select two to three sentences from each end comment, we move to Step 2 and turn attention to Smith's (1997) article that establishes different groups of response (e.g., judging genres, reader response genres, or coaching genres) and the nature of those comments (e.g., evaluation of development, reading experience, suggestion for revision of current paper). We reread White and Stewarts' end comments (as cited in Straub & Lunsford, 1995) and determine their purposes and natures based on Smith's work. The conversation is lively because it brings attention to how responses are layered and how students perceive and experience comments differently. There's not a unilateral consensus or feeling, which again, allows us to complicate teacher response and the dispositions teachers bring to writing and the histories and experiences students have when reading, interpreting, and producing action after receiving response. Some students, for example, think White's "from a greeting card" comment is funny while others interpret it as sarcastic and downgrading.

Almost organically, these reactions bring up the complicated nature of response. I use this moment to facilitate conversation on how teacher response, much like the end comments from White and Stewart (as cited in Straub & Lunsford, 1995), and the ones we produce as teachers, have multiple purposes and interpretations. Reading response and doing something with it (e.g., revising) can be really hard. It takes some nimbleness to listen, make sense of comments, and produce a plan for action, both for first-year students and teacher-scholars. So we talk about how end comments contain more than one idea or thought or action to be taken up and how students can navigate these different courses of action.

This helps us to see that even two to three sentences in an end comment can draw on all three primary genres: Judging, reader response, and coaching. We try to do the best we can to come to some sort of consensus to classify the end comments we're analyzing. In this instance, the class decides Whites' comments (as cited in Straub & Lunsford, 1995) are judging genres and coaching genres. Students feel like White offers encouragement in his first sentence (e.g., "very fine, rich with detail and emotion") and then suggestions for revision in his second sentence that align with coaching genres. Students also think White offers an evaluation of development and style in his second sentence by telling the writer that their "language gets very general" and " . . . to make your language more clear and detailed." These comments fit under judging genres, they say.

Next, we analyze Stewart's response (as cited in Straub & Lunsford, 1995). Students feel like his comments fall under judging genres and reader response genres because he references "organization" and "style" in his first sentence, and then talks about the students' inability to produce "language" that is "distinctive." Students collectively agree that the purposes of the first two sentences are tied to judging genres, but they aren't necessarily sure how to identify the nature of them. I decide to write all three observations on the board: Evaluation on development, evaluation on style, evaluation on rhetorical effectiveness. The last sentence, according to students, is linked to reader response genres because Stewart is offering his thoughts and/or feelings based on his experience as a reader. He wants the student to do more, to "work up to [their] potential."

Step 3 draws on Inoue's (2019) six habits of White language in Labor-Based Grading Contracts. Like Step 2, this step invites critical reading and often creates energetic conversations that help us understand the politics of language and how response can privilege some identities over others. Even though my class is familiar with conversations on antiracist writing assessment practices, this step takes a lot of prompting because this kind of problem-posing activity is often new to them. Most students don't have experiences in writing classes that center antiracism and teacher response. So, analyzing the nature of teacher response and how comments might contribute to White language supremacy can be difficult. Using Inoue's six habits, I ask questions to help generate conversation: "Let's take a closer look at White's comments. Does he take a position that assumes the student can see the truthfulness of his observation as if they share the same perspective? Does White focus on clarity, order, and control in the students' writing? When we read his comment out loud, does it sound like he positions himself as knowledgeable, rational, and reasonable? How so? Is it because he says what is 'wrong,' and then offers what is 'right'?" Questions like this have been more productive than asking students to look at the six habits and provide an analysis based on those characteristics alone.

It also helps students see how habits of White language can manifest in different ways through an end comment, much like the purposes and natures of response show how genres of response are complicated. Students, for example, will talk about how White (as cited in Straub & Lunsford, 1995) describes the students' language as "very general" and how he suggests the student be "more clear and detailed." This observation is multi-layered because it connects with Inoue's (2019) first habit—"unseen, naturalized, orientation to the world—an orientation (or starting point) of one's body in time and space that makes certain things reachable"—and Inoue's sixth habit—"clarity, order, and control—a focus on reason, order, and control; thinking (versus feeling)" (pp. 278–279). It's possible White assumes the student understands what he's talking about and has the knowledge to obtain this goal, or ultimate good—the ultimate good here is specificity. As a responder, he positions himself as logical and reasonable. He values rigor and clarity. Students talk about these ideas and start seeing how they are connected to a particular kind of languaging. We problematize and ask more questions: "How does White determine what is 'general'? Why is 'clarity' and 'detail' so important? Clarity to what standard? Who determines that standard?"

Students share how it sounds like White (as cited in Straub & Lunsford, 1995) is saying the students' language is not good enough when he says their writing is "general." They even describe how it feels like White is saying the students' language is "weak," and therefore, it needs to be made "stronger." Again, we talk about whether White is possibly drawing on unseen standards that privilege White discourse. We analyze how White seems to be referring to a very specific standard that values depth and clarity—that feels closely connected to what students say they've experienced in other classes that emphasize "academic" or "formal" language use in writing. This leads to more detailed conversations about SEAE and White language supremacy and allows us to talk more about traditional assessment ecologies versus grading contract ecologies. We problematize how quality, which is often connected to SEAE and habits of White language, is being prioritized. Some students use the word "conform" to describe what White is asking the writer to do. So, we problem-pose, "Conform to what? What standard? What language? And whose body is attached to that standard and language habit, or who is being privileged?"

This probing leads to critical reflection of how genres of response can embody habits of White language, even in grading contract ecologies. For instance, we talk about how the same external norms and pressures from society can reproduce the same kind of comments that can circulate in a grading contract ecology. It should be noted that White (as cited in Straub & Lunsford, 1995) doesn't attach a letter-grade to the students' final draft; instead, he asks them to revise. He's not using grading contracts but probably a portfolio system which offers some similar ecological values (e.g., attention to process, deemphasis on grade). After spending time analyzing White's end comment, the class gains more confidence talking about how habits of White language can manifest in teacher response. So whenever we turn our attention to Stewart's end comment (as cited in Straub & Lunsford, 1995), students are more familiar with the questions we ask, what to look for, and how they can talk about habits of White language.

Students explain how Stewart's end comment focuses on organization, style, and language choice, much like White's. They revisit what we wrote down when describing the purposes and nature of Stewart's response based on Step 2. They talk about how his last sentence focuses on his experience as a reader. I ask, "What do you think that means in relationship to the characteristics of White discourse? When we read it out loud, do you feel like that last sentence feels individualistic? Does it come across as a matter of fact—as 'truth'—as something that needs to be said?" When I ask these questions, students point to Inoue's (2019) second habit of White language (hyperindividualism). Students explain how the sentence "I wish you would consistently work up to your potential" feels self-focused in that it doesn't provide much in terms of the students' writing and/or ways to revise their writing. It sounds more like a critical judgement of the student and their ability to write or perform. The class feels like Stewart (as cited in Straub & Lunsford, 1995) holds his own perspective to a higher level and that his interpretation of the students' writing and labor (and potential) is ultimately "right." I try to weave in understandings of uptake to this conversation because it helps us transition to Step 4.

For example, I ask students to talk about what sentences come before this last comment. Students mention that he responds to the students' organization and style and language. As a class, we connect that to the first habit (unseen, naturalized, orientation to the world) and the sixth habit (clarity, order, and control), and we discuss how these comments might inform or tell us something important about Stewart's (as cited in Straub & Lunsford, 1995) last sentence, which feels more hyperindividualist in nature. Doing this invites us to talk about how uptake exists while teachers respond to student writing. Stewart's last sentence, for example, might symbolize how he and the student have already established a partnership. For instance, this might be the second or third writing assignment.

They've had in-class conversations, perhaps one-on-one teacher conferences where they have developed a kind of rapport. That means Stewart has experienced other pieces of writing from that student. He has observed their writing and labor. He has probably seen the student produce work that exceeds what he is currently reading and responding to. I ask students, "Do you think Stewart is drawing on previous experiences and memories with the students' writing that might inform his last comment on the students' 'potential'?"

This question is about uptake, which leads us to Step 4. Step 4 invites us to explore emotion, attitude, memory, action, consequence, and the relationship responses have with other genres with/in and beyond writing assessment ecologies. I have three overarching purposes in this last step: (a) to encourage students to reflect on what other genres are working in an assessment ecology that are interconnected with response that interact and inform actions and consequences; (b) to challenge students to reflect on their histories, memories, and experiences with response; and (c) to invite an honest reflection on how we, as a class, can resist the production and circulation of habits of White language in our responses (both mine and when students respond to their peers). I want us to be actively antiracist. I want us to be aware of how White language supremacy creeps into seemingly mundane practices and experiences like teacher response to student writing.

We talk about the long-term social consequences of genre performances of response; we focus on social-historical-material conditions of response and how we can better pay attention to how power and agency are connected to response. Step 4 is about critical reflection. I want us to think about the "interlocking systems and forces at play in performances of genres" (Bawarshi, 2016, p. 52). I want students to think about our grading contract, my responses, our assessment values, their memories with response in other classroom ecologies, and emotions they've experienced receiving feedback from others. I want students to reflect on actions they've produced based on previous experiences with teacher response.

My hope is these reflections lead us toward intervention and resistance. As a teacher, I want to construct responses that resist White language supremacy. I also want us to come together as a class to talk about why this kind of intervention is important. I challenge students to reflect on how power is positioned in response and how teacher response can privilege some identities over others. I ask students to write down a memory or experience they have had with teacher response that embodied some of these habits of White language. I ask them to reread White and Stewart's (as cited in Straub & Lunsford, 1995) end comments and reflect on similar experiences they've had receiving this kind of feedback, and I ask them to jot down what actions they produced based on those responses. I share an example of how this happens: "Have any of you read an end comment that asks you to go to the Writing Center for help? Or has a teacher asked you to come to office hours so you can talk more about your ideas? Or has a teacher ever made a comment about your grammar or spelling? What did you do? Did you listen and take up their advice? How did that comment make you feel? How have you taken that memory and experience with you to this class?" These questions prompt students to think about uptake and the actions and consequences that can come from genres of response.

Some of these reflections are personal for students, so I don't ask them to disclose or share them with the class or turn them in. My only goal here is to have students think about these experiences with response and how responding to writing can be harmful. How response has made them feel. How response has resulted in action and consequences. I want us to consider uptake, so we can really start pushing against and resisting response that reproduces and circulates habits of White language in our grading contract ecology. I want students to be able to identify it as soon as they see it—and I want them to feel comfortable holding me accountable for my own response practices.

The goal of this analytical framework is for teachers and students to intervene, problematize, and resist habits of White language embodied in genre performances/practices of response. The framework helps illuminate how responses, such as end comments, can support habits of White language, thus creating an unfair, unjust classroom that counters grading contract assessment values in antiracist writing assessment ecologies.

## CONCLUSION

The four-step analytical and pedagogical framework I suggest provides one way to investigate genre performances of response in grading contract ecologies. RGS offers us a way to problematize teachers' responses and students' readings of those responses in order to cultivate antiracist agendas or antiracist writing assessment ecologies. Teachers can do the normal good response practices, and doing so can easily be a way to reproduce White language supremacy. Good intentions can still have violent consequences. Using antiracist writing assessment theories with RGS opens new conversations in teacher response. This kind of critical reading and attention to response takes a lot of time, on top of the time and energy it already takes to respond to student writing, so we might need to rethink curricula and simplify the amount of labor and assignments we assign students, so we can truly center our classes on teacher response as resistant genres. One primary aim of teacher response should be antiracism. We should always work towards being antiracist responders to student writing. In my class, I frame teacher response as an antiracist practice and attempt to resist monolingual English biases and habits of White language. Critically investigating response, and addressing inequalities and inequities, and changing how we give feedback is just one more way to uproot White language supremacy.

## REFERENCES

Baker-Bell, A. (2020). *Linguistic justice: Black language, literacy, identity, and pedagogy* Routledge.

Bastian, H. (2015). Capturing individual uptake: Toward a disruptive research methodology *Composition Forum, 31*. http://compositionforum.com/issue/31/individual-uptake.php.

Bawarshi, A. (2008). Genres as forms of in(ter)vention. In M. Vicinus & C. Eisner (Eds.) *Originality, imitation, and plagiarism* (pp. 79–89). University of Michigan Press.

Bawarshi, A. (2010). Taking up multiple discursive resources in U.S. college composition. In B. Horner, Lu, M.-Z. & Matsuda, P. K. (Eds.), *Cross-language relations in composition* (pp. 196–203). Southern Illinois University Press.

Bawarshi, A. (2016). Accounting for genre performances: Why uptake matters. In N. Artemeva & A. Freedman (Eds.), *Genre studies around the globe: Beyond the three traditions* (pp. 186–206). Trafford Publishing.

Bawarshi, A. & Reiff, M. J. (2010). *Genre: An introduction to history, theory, research, and pedagogy.* Parlor Press; The WAC Clearinghouse. https://wac.colostate.edu/books/referenceguides/bawarshi-reiff/.

Bazerman, C. (1994). Systems of genres and the enactment of social institutions. In A. Freedman & P. Medway (Eds.), *Genre and new rhetoric* (pp. 79–101). Taylor.

Bazerman, C. (1997). The life of genre, the life in the classroom. In W. Bishop & H. Ostrom (Eds.), Genre and writing: Issues, arguments, and alternatives (pp. 19–26). Boynton/Cook-Heinemann.

Berkenkotter, C. & Huckin, T. (1995). *Genre knowledge in disciplinary communication*. Erlbaum.

Danielewicz, J. & Elbow, P. (2009). A unilateral grading contract to improve learning and teaching. *College Composition and Communication, 61*(2), 244–68.

Devitt, A. J. (1991). Intertextuality in tax accounting: Generic, referential, and functional. In C. Bazerman & J. Paradis (Eds.), *Textual dynamics of the professions: Historical and contemporary studies of writing in professional* (pp. 336–357). University of Wisconsin Press.

Devitt, A. J. (2004). *Writing genres*. Southern Illinois University Press.

Dryer, D. (2016). Disambiguating uptake: Toward a tactical research agenda on citizens' writing. In M. J. Reiff & A. Bawarshi (Eds.), *Genre and the performance of publics* (pp. 60–79). Utah State University Press.

Freadman, A. (1994). Anyone for tennis? In A. Freedman & P. Medway (Eds.), *Genre and the new rhetoric* (pp. 43–66). Taylor & Francis.

Green , D. F., Jr. (2016). Expanding the dialogue on writing assessment at HBCUs: Foundational assessment concepts and legacies of historically Black colleges and universities. *College English, 79*(2), 152–173.

Greenfield, L. (2011). The "standard English" fairy tale: A rhetorical analysis of racist pedagogies and commonplace assumptions about language diversity. In L. Greenfield & K. Rowan (Eds.), *Writing centers and the new racism: A call for sustainable dialogue and change* (pp. 33–60). Utah State University Press.

Hooks, B. (1994). *Teaching to transgress: Education as the practice of freedom.* Routledge.

Inman, J. O. & Powell, R. A. (2018). In the absence of grades: Dissonance and desire in course contract classrooms. *College Composition and Communication, 70*(1), 30–56.

Inoue, A. B. (2015). *Antiracist writing assessment ecologies: Teaching and assessing for a socially just future.* The WAC Clearinghouse; Parlor Press. https://doi.org/10.37514/PER-B.2015.0698.

Inoue, A. B. (2019). *Labor-based grading contracts: Building equity and inclusion in the compassionate writing classroom.*, 1st ed. The WAC Clearinghouse; Parlor Press. https://doi.org/10.37514/PER-B.2022.1824.

Jackson, K. K., Jackson, H. & D. N. Hicks Tafari. (2019). We belong in the discussion: Including HBCUs in conversations about race and writing. *College Composition and Communication, 71*(2), 184–214.

Kynard, C. (2013). *Vernacular insurrections: Race, black protest, and the new century in composition-literacies studies.* State University of New York Press.

Lippi-Green, R. (1997). *English with an accent: Language, ideology, and discrimination in the United States.* Routledge.

Medina, C. & Walker, K. (2018). Validating the consequences of a social justice pedagogy: Explicit values in course-based grading contracts. In A. M. Hass & M. F. Eble (Eds.), *Key theoretical frameworks: Teaching technical communication in the twenty-first century* (pp. 46–67). Utah State University Press.

Miller, C. (1984). Genre as social action. *Quarterly Journal of Speech, 70(2)*, 151–167.

Moreno-Lopez, I. (2005). Sharing power with students: The critical language classroom. *Radical Pedagogy, 7*(2).

Schryer, C. (2002). Genre and power: A chronotopic analysis. In R. Coe, L. Lingard & T. Teslenko (Eds.), *The rhetoric and ideology of genre: Strategies for stability and change* (pp. 73–102). Hampton.

Seawright, L. (2017). *Genre of power: Police report writers and readers in the justice system.* Conference on College Composition and Communication Studies in Writing and Rhetoric.

Shor, I. (1996). *When students have power: Negotiating authority in a critical pedagogy.* University of Chicago Press.

Smith, S. (1997). The genre of the end comment: Conventions in teacher responses to student writing. *College of Composition and Communication, 48*(2), 249–268.

Smitherman, G. (1977). *Talkin and testifyin: The language of Black America.* Houghton-Mifflin.

Spinuzzi, C. (2004). Describing assemblages: Genre sets, systems, repertoires, and ecology. *Digital Writing & Research Lab.* http://www.dwrl.utexas.edu/old/content/describingassemblages.

Spinuzzi, C. & Zachry, M. (2000). Genre ecologies: An open-system approach to understanding and constructing documentation. *ACM Journal of Computer Documentation, 24*(3), 169–181.

Straub, R. & Lunsford, R. F. (1995). *Twelve readers reading: Responding to college student writing.* Hampton Press.

Tchudi, S. (Ed.). (1997). *Alternatives to grading student writing.* National Council of Teachers of English.

Yates, J. & Orlikowski, W. (2002). Genre systems: Structuring interaction through communicative norms. *International Journal of Business Communication, 39*(1), 13–35.

Young, V. A. (2010). Should writers use they own English? *Iowa Journal of Cultural Studies, 12*(1), 110–118.

# CODA

**Victor Villanueva**
Washington State University

I had never been a member of the writing assessment discourse community, really, despite some WPA positions. Writing assessment was more a subset for which I turn to those more expert than me, many (most?) of whom are here in *Considering Students, Teachers and Writing Assessment*. So as I read, a concern would come to mind, and then the concern would be addressed. Still, I find myself thinking about the word *fairness*. It is, of course, the right word, what we all want. But I can't help but see it as some American Platonic ideal, part of the trinity of philosophical liberalism: neutrality, equality, fairness. These are the terms that drive so much of what I read in *Considering Students, Teachers and Writing Assessment*—objective testing and guaranties of equity pursued in the search for fairness in an acknowledged not quite fair system (thinking of "system" in the broadest sense). Ideals are good. It's why we teach: seeking the ideal, working toward it, motivated by it. But I worry nevertheless in terms of racism and other forms of often subtle exclusion (the more blatant forms easily exposed and readily given to attempts at countering the overt bigotry). I worry because even the most academic resistance to Critical Race Theory has argued that CRT seeks to destroy the liberal ideals, argues that there is no neutrality, no equity, no fairness (see, for example, Pyle, 1999). The arguments are not quite false. Critical Legal Studies, the precursor to CRT, really was just that cynical, but CRT has been less so, still believes in the possibility of the ideal but seeks to be pragmatic along the way.

Now, I'm not suggesting that any of the articles in this collection would challenge the perceived tenets of CRT. But it seems to me monodirectional in the way these attempts at fairness are described (and I do mean "seems," since, as I said, my understanding is limited to the pages of this collection). So to get at my really rather simple critique and consideration of *fairness* as almost assessment jargon, I think it's important to refresh our memories of what CRT is, especially given the current attacks on the term (the term more than the theory) as I write this. I can imagine some unfortunate teacher along the line being the subject of some 21st century Scopes Monkey Trial (maybe a Signifying Monkey Trial (thinking of Gates, 1988, with tongue in cheek).

As I write this, CRT has become a catch phrase for representations of racism, as well as other forms of exclusion: gender, gender identity, sexuality, class. But I focus on racism because, even as I realize the real differences among these other

Otherings and recognize that racism extends beyond Black and Latinx, I still find Mike Davis's assertion compelling, in general, that

> no matter how important feminist consciousness must be . . . , racism remains the divisive issue within class and gender [and sexual orientation]. . . . [T]he real weak link in the domestic base of American imperialism is a Black and Hispanic working class, fifty million strong. This is the nation within a nation, society within a society, that alone possesses the numerical and positional strength to undermine the American empire from within. (cited in Villanueva, 1999)

In the words of Peruvian sociologist and decolonial theorist Aníbal Quijano:

> The idea of "race" is surely the most efficient instrument of social domination produced in the last 500 years. Dating from the very beginning of the formation of the Americas and of capitalism (at the turn of the 16th century), in the ensuing centuries it was imposed on the population of the whole planet as an aspect of European colonial domination. (2007, p. 45)

In so saying, Quijano is echoing two of the basic tenets of CRT: (1) that race is a creation, a social construction, as we have become accustomed to saying (and that includes "colorism" the degree to which folks of the same "race" or ethnicity (a troubling word, since it's a euphemism for racism) will frown upon the darker of "their own kind"); and (2)—especially (2)—that it is pervasive, that one cannot escape race or its manifestations as racism. None of us can escape racism; none of us can truly rise above. There is the ideal of neutrality but not its true realization. That's part of what bothers folks like Pyle, above.

Another assertion that arises from CRT is the concept on "interest conversion." In the article by Derrick Bell (1980) that introduced the concept, he argued that racial "progress" tends to be in the interest of power, particularly America's image globally. Now, that is truly cynical. It was an argument that was dismissed in its time. And now, in some sense, the argument is even less important, since if Quijano is right, no country is free from its own forms of bigotry. But I would argue that in America interest conversion is a necessary aspect of maintaining the overall status quo. Or maybe, to say it better, interest conversion allows for the belief in "progress," rhetorician Richard Weaver's "god term" (1985, p.212). We can argue that we are post-racial because we have elected a Black president, a Black vice president, have greater numbers of middle class of color, etc. There has been progress. Yet we know that Obama and Harris have had to contend with racism, that a successful person of color knows that there will be those who believe the person is a token, a product of "reverse racism," some version of the tired affirmative-action argument that continues to plague higher education admissions. The system works, say the anti-CRT. The progress is clear. And each case of a George Floyd or the shooting of an Asian shop, or gatherings of white supremacist groups are anomalies. The system works so well, that introducing something called "CRT" in schools, introducing explicit references to racism and other forms of bigotry are divisive, introduce the bigotries—as if textbooks have anything to do with how children come to know of racism and other Otherings.

So, you say, I'm preaching to the choir; we all know that racism still pervades, sometimes as microaggressions, those unintentional slips (like the compliment I received long ago that the speaker didn't see me as a person of color) that reflect a bias, or the macroaggressions like the current anti-"CRT" movement, which is itself overtly racist, since it's founded on nothing more theoretical than The Three Wise Monkeys who see no evil, hear no evil, and speak no evil. The present indication of the "real" CRT that has gained substantial presence in rhetoric and composition is "the voice of color" and "legal storytelling" wonderfully introduced by Aja Martinez (2020) in *Counterstory: The Rhetoric and Writing of Critical Race Theory*. But there's a tenet at play here, the voice of color, that I missed in the discussions of writing assessment in this collection, in terms of fairness. It's a consideration for the future, I would say.

## BY WAY OF AN EXPLANATION.

I was for a time the director of the university writing program at Washington State University, whose portfolio system has received some attention in *Considering Students, Teachers and Writing Assessment*. Among the readers, the evaluators, were bilingual teachers, not just Spanish-English but Mexican Spanish to English and Puerto Rican Spanish to English, a true polyglot (Greek, Bulgarian, Italian, Russian, English), Asian Americans, an Iranian American, and first-generation graduate students, among others—all of whom were current teachers who included writing in their teaching, though they came from across the disciplines (Foreign Languages, Sociology, Ethnic Studies, Women's Studies, Political Science, Architecture, etc.). Imagine the conversations, the discussions about the students' writings, based not only on theory but on experience—the evaluators' experiences, discussions that would include editing/grammatical matters, no doubt, though also including, for example, how Slavic languages do not use the article (with the exception of Macedonia and Bulgaria, the polyglot would note); that not using the article is not unique to the Asians. Or imagine the discussions of rhetorical effectiveness rather than some monolithic perception of "logic." These are conversations I've heard among the readers. Now, this is a system that had been put in place long before I took over, so though I'm boasting, it's an institutional more than a personal boast. Nor can I claim that the demographics of the reviewers/readers were unique to the WSU program. In fact, I have to assume that many of the designers, psychometricians, evaluators, and the like discussed in the previous pages also came from a broad spectrum of America and the world. But it's only an optimistic assumption. Nothing was said along those lines that I recall in reading the manuscript. That would be a move forward, I'd say.

You see, one of the arguments of Critical Legal Studies that carried over to Critical Race Theory (though softened somewhat) is that political liberalism had a basic flaw, and that is that the neutrality in neutrality, equity, and fairness necessarily operates from a kind of color blindness, a false objectivity (even as we know there is no such thing as "objective language use") that all are created equal, that at bottom we're all the same—which is true biologically, the "race" writ large—so that injustices must be truly visible, like the shooting of George Floyd, the separation of families at the U.S. southern border, and the like. But if racism is woven into the pattern of society like Quijano or the Critical Race Theorists argue, then there are inherent differences, even if socially constructed. The power of counterstory is making the unknown visible to those who cannot know, though that too often puts the burden on the less powerful to teach the more powerful. In terms of writing assessment, the aim tends to be a universal even while recognizing differences. But who is creating these instruments? What is the basis of their knowledge of those not having been treated fairly, equitably, the ones subject to neutrality in an inherently biased set of situations? There are inherent and surely unrecognized biases at play if the designers do not include those who have done any walking in the Othered's shoes.

At the very least, we need to know more about the designers, the good people seeking greater fairness. Who are they? What do they know of the Others and how do they know? Moving forward, I'd make the case for a dialectic of fairness, not just for the students but from the evaluators.

## REFERENCES

Bell, D. A., Jr. (1980). Brown vs. Board of Education and the interest-convergence dilemma." *Harvard Law Review, 93*(3), 518–533.

Gates, H. L., Jr. (1988). *The signifying monkey: A theory of Afro-American literary criticism.* Oxford University Press.

Martinez, A. Y. (2020). *Counterstory: The rhetoric and writing of Critical Race Theory.* NCTE.

Pyle, J. J. (1999). Race, equality, and the rule of law: Critical Race Theory's attack on the promises of liberalism. *Boston College Law Review, 40*(3), 787–827.

Quijano, A. (2007). Questioning 'Race'. *Socialism and Democracy, 21*(1), 45–53.

Villanueva, V. (1999). On the rhetoric and precedents of racism. *College Composition and Communication, 50*(4), 645–661.

Weaver, R. M. (1985). *The ethics of rhetoric.* Hermagoras Press.

# EDITORS AND RETROSPECTIVE CONTRIBUTORS

**Diane Kelly-Riley** is Professor of English and Vice Provost for Faculty at the University of Idaho. She studies writing assessment theory and practice, validity theory, race and writing assessment, public humanities and multimodal composition. She was editor of the *Journal of Writing Assessment* from 2011–2022. She published *Improving Outcomes: Disciplinary Writing, Local Assessment and the Aim of Fairness* with Norbert Elliot (MLA, 2021).

**Ti Macklin** is the Director of First-Year Writing at Boise State University where she teaches courses in composition and rhetoric. Her research interests lie largely in First-Year Writing and writing assessment with a particular focus on assessment at the individual, classroom, and programmatic levels. Her most recent work examines the experiences of graduate and undergraduate students in first-year writing. She was on the editorial staff of the *Journal of Writing Assessment* for nine years.

**Mya Poe** is Associate Professor of English at Northeastern University. For more than 20 years, she has been an advocate for justice-oriented writing assessment practices. Her co-authored and co-edited books include *Race and Writing Assessment*; *Writing Assessment, Social Justice, and the Advancement of Opportunity*; and *Writing Placement in Two-Year Colleges* Her teaching and service have been recognized with the Northeastern University Teaching Excellence Award and the MIT Infinite Mile Award for Continued Outstanding Service and Innovative Teaching. She is the co-editor of *Written Communication*.

**Victor Villanueva** is Regents Professor Emeritus, a former director of comp, director of a university-wide writing program, director of an American Studies program, English department chair (twice!), former editor of the Studies in Writing and Rhetoric monograph series of the Conference on College Composition and communication, former head of that organization, its Exemplar, Rhetorician of the Year, among other honors—especially the honor of having worked with so many undergraduate and graduate students. His work always concerns the rhetorics of racism.

**Carl Whithaus** is Professor of Writing and Rhetoric at the University of California, Davis. He studies the impact of information technology on literacy practices, writing assessment, and writing in the sciences and engineering. His books include *Multimodal Literacies and Emerging* Genres (University of Pittsburgh Press, 2013), *Writing Across Distances and Disciplines: Research and Pedagogy in Distributed Learning* (Routledge, 2008) and *Teaching and Evaluating Writing in the Age of Computers and High-Stakes Testing* (Erlbaum, 2005).

www.ingramcontent.com/pod-product-compliance
Lightning Source LLC
Chambersburg PA
CBHW060557080526
44585CB00013B/596